UNNATURAL EM

UNNATURAL EMOTIONS

Everyday Sentiments on a Micronesian Atoll

&

Their Challenge to Western Theory

CATHERINE A. LUTZ

The University of Chicago Press

Chicago and London

Catherine A. Lutz is assistant professor of anthropology,
State University of New York at Binghamton.

The University of Chicago Press, Chicago 60637
The University of Chicago Press, Ltd., London
©1988 by The University of Chicago
All rights reserved. Published 1988
Printed in the United States of America

97 96 95 94 93 92 91 90 89 88   5 4 3 2 1

Library of Congress Cataloging-in-Publication Data
Lutz, Catherine.
    Unnatural emotions : everyday sentiments on a Micronesian atoll
and their challenge to western theory / Catherine A. Lutz.
        p.   cm.
    Bibliography: p.
    Includes index.
    ISBN 0-226-49721-6.   ISBN 0-226-49722-4 (pbk.)
    1. Ethnopsychology—Micronesia (Federated States)—Ifalik Atoll.
2. Emotions.   3. Micronesians—Psychology.   I. Title.
GN671.C3L87 1988
155.8'0996'5—dc19   88-329
                                                     CIP

For my parents,
and for Yangitelig

It is like a garland we make together . . .
Traditional Ifaluk song

Contents

Contents

Chapter Four

The Ethnopsychological Contexts of Emotion: Ifaluk Beliefs about the Person   81

PART 3
Need, Violation, and Danger: Three Emotions in Everyday Life

Chapter Five

Need, Nurturance, and the Precariousness of Life on a Coral Atoll:
The Emotion of *Fago* (Compassion/Love/Sadness)   119

Chapter Six

Morality, Domination, and the Emotion of "Justifiable Anger"   155

Chapter Seven

The Cultural Construction of Danger   183

Contents

Acknowledgments

The ideas in this book emerged from my encounter with the Ifaluk people during my stay with them in 1977 and 1978. In one very important sense, the Ifaluk *gave* me the ideas about emotion that are presented here, sometimes as my own. They helped me fulfill one of the promises of fieldwork and of cross-cultural encounter more generally—to see the world, including ourselves, in a new way and to remodel our own concepts in ways that make them less a reflection of local and narrow concerns. My respect for the people of Ifaluk and the way they have chosen to live their lives is large. Their nurturance, gentleness, and moral judgment are a model I feel privileged to have been able to see, experience, and learn from. I thank Ilesatil and the other chiefs of Ifaluk for the permission they granted me to live on Ifaluk; Pakalemar and Ilesepemal for taking me into their home, feeding me, and patiently tutoring me in both the morality and pragmatics of island living; Letachiepou for her friendship, her constancy, and her extraordinary ability to translate between our worlds; Tachibelimel and Hachiemai for their help with language and census taking; Yarofemai for his gifts of papaya and concern; Ilemangisep, Lafaulipo, Lefagochang, Letalagupo, and Leyaneouf for being authentic mothers and sisters to me; the people of Saumat, Falulu, Gawong, and Faligiliau households and of Iyefang and Iyieur villages for including me in their feasts and their losses.* *Gaami gai sa gashigshig remawesh.*

There are many other people who have contributed to the formation of the ideas in this book. John Whiting, Beatrice Whiting, Robert LeVine, Jerome Kagan, Steven Fjellman, and Cathy Widom helped me develop the questions with which I went to the field. Beatrice Whiting's NIMH training grant in cross-cultural child development generously funded this research and a Dean's Research Semester from the State University of New York at Binghamton provided the luxury of time to complete several chapters of the manuscript. Margaret Roe graciously typed part of the manuscript. Conversations over the past several years with Geoffrey White, John Kirkpatrick, Donald Rubinstein, Lila Abu-Lughod, Peter Black, Karen Ito, Jane Collins, Margaret Conkey, Fitz Poole, Jane Fajans, and Sara Harkness have helped immensely in the development of my interpretations, as have the comments on drafts of one or more of the chapters by Peter Black, Jane Fajans, Byron Good, John Kirkpatrick, Arthur Kleinman, Susan Montague, Renato Rosaldo, and Geoff White, and the very helpful reviewers for the University of Chicago Press. Michael and Jonathan Schechter have made life outside anthropology very full and very good.

Finally, I thank the family—Carol, George, Mary, Tom, Betsy, Barbara Karina, and Anne—with whom I first learned to reflect on emotion and to see its links to value.

*Other than in these acknowledgments, pseudonyms are used for all persons and villages described.

PART 1
Introduction

CHAPTER ONE

The Cultural Construction
of Emotions

At first blush, nothing might appear more natural and hence less cultural than emotions, nothing more private and hence less amenable to public scrutiny, nothing more inchoate and less compatible with the logos of social science. These views can be treated, however, as items in a cultural discourse whose traditional assumptions about human nature and whose dualisms—body and mind, public and private, essence and appearance, and irrationality and thought—constitute what we take to be the self-evident nature of emotion. This book uncovers some of the cultural assumptions found in Western thinking about the emotions and contrasts them with those I encountered during fieldwork on the one-half-square-mile atoll of Ifaluk in the southwest Pacific. I have two aims. The first is to deconstruct emotion, to show that the use of the term in both our everyday and social-scientific conversation rests on a network of often implicit associations that give force to statements that use it. The second is to describe my understanding of everyday life on Ifaluk, whose people speak about emotions in ways that reflect their values, their power struggles, and their unique atoll environment.

The concept of emotion plays a central role in the Western view of the world. While words like "envy," "love," and "fear" are invoked by anyone who would speak about the self, about the private, about the intensely meaningful, or about the ineffable, they are also used to talk about devalued aspects of the world—the irrational, the uncontrollable, the vulnerable, and the female. Both sides of what can be seen as an ambivalent Western view of emotion are predicated, however, on the belief that emotion is in essence a psychobiological structure and an aspect of the individual. The role of culture in the experience of emotion is seen as secondary, even minimal, from that perspective. Culture or society can do little more than highlight or darken particular areas of the given psychobiological structure of emotions by, for example, repressing the expression of anger in women, calling for smiles to mask natural feelings of fear in certain situations, or emphasizing shame in one society and guilt in another. And while emotions are often seen as *evoked in* communal life, they are rarely presented as an *index of* social relationship rather than a sign of a personal state.

Although the value of emotion as symbol is not dependent on some objective relationship to the body, my aim is not to cut the body out of emotions or simply to civilize them. It is to deconstruct an overly naturalized and rigidly bounded concept of emotion, to treat emotion as an ideological practice rather than as a thing to be discovered or an essence to be distilled. Michelle Rosaldo has suggested the felicitous notion that emotions be seen as "embodied thoughts" (1984:143); Scheper-Hughes and Lock (1987) talk of the "mindful body"—each suggesting possible routes around the difficulties presented by the dualisms of our traditional ways of thinking about issues of mind and body, of nature and culture, of thought and emotion. Those dualisms create our compulsion to ask for a strict accounting of what is biological in the emotions and what is cultural and to seek the essence of a psychobiological process behind the stage front of cultural and linguistic forms. Discourse about emotion constitutes it as a social object, however, and it is with conventions and uses of the term "emotion" that we have to start. With no privileged route to some underlying and unmediated psychophysical emotional reality, we might be not resigned to but intrigued by the task of elucidating our understandings of what we and others mean, intend, feel, and do when we traffic in "emotion."

After deconstruction, the word remains. By making emotion the focus of this study, I both deconstruct and reconstruct the term, both undermine its foundations and elevate it to a more central analytic place. Revealing some of the cultural foundations and conceptual machinery behind the smooth, commonsense surface of the language of emotion does not mean that the term "emotion" can or should be jettisoned by those who study human behavior. My alternative view of emotion contests, but must of necessity maintain some dialogue with, an unreconstructed view of emotion. And so the reader will find a text that is not hermetically sealed but that to some degree simultaneously takes and undermines a position. After deconstruction, emotion retains value as a way of talking about the intensely meaningful as that is culturally defined, socially enacted, and personally articulated. It retains value also as a category more open than others to use as a link between the mental and the physical (Scheper-Hughes and Lock 1987) and between the ideal or desired world and the actual world. As the undervalued member of the dualism it participates in with "thought," emotion is also less likely to be taken, at least in its traditional forms, as the only important human capacity, and so might better provide a route by which these two capacities are reunited. And it retains value as a way of orienting us toward things that matter rather than things that simply make sense.

Although we may experience emotion as something that rises and falls within the boundaries of our bodies, the decidedly social origins of our understandings of the self, the other, the world, and experience draw our attention to the interpersonal processes by which something called emotion or some things like joy, anger, or fear come to be ascribed to and experienced by us. I will demonstrate that the use of emotion concepts, as elements of local ideological practice, involves negotiation over the meaning of events, over rights and morality, over control of resources—in short, involves struggles over the entire range of issues that concern human groups. As Clifford has noted of culture itself, emotion is "contested, temporal, and emergent" (1986:19). Once de-essentialized, emotion can be viewed as a cultural and interpersonal process of naming, justifying, and persuading by people in relationship to each other. Emotional meaning is then a social rather than an individual achievement—an emergent product of social life.

This book attempts to demonstrate how emotional meaning is fundamentally structured by particular cultural systems and particular social and material environments. The claim is made that emotional experience is not precultural but pre*eminently* cultural. The prevalent assumption that the emotions are invariant across cultures is replaced here with the question of how one cultural discourse on emotion may be translated into another. As I listened to people speak the language of emotion in everyday encounters with each other on Ifaluk atoll, it became clear to me that the concepts of emotion can more profitably be viewed as serving complex communicative, moral, and cultural purposes rather than simply as labels for internal states whose nature or essence is presumed to be universal. The pragmatic and

5

associative networks of meaning in which each emotion word is embedded are extremely rich ones. The complex meaning of each emotion word is the result of the important role those words play in articulating the full range of a people's cultural values, social relations, and economic circumstances. Talk about emotions is simultaneously talk about society—about power and politics, about kinship and marriage, about normality and deviance—as several anthropologists have begun to document (Abu-Lughod 1986; Fajans 1985; Myers 1979; Rosaldo 1980).

The present work draws on a number of the new approaches to emotions that have developed over the past ten to fifteen years. It benefits, most of all, from the seminal work of Briggs, Levy, and Rosaldo, whose ethnographies of the Utku Eskimos, Tahitians, and Ilongot of the Philippines, respectively, were the first to ask how emotions are understood indigenously (see also H. Geertz 1959, C. Geertz 1973). Each of these scholars takes emotions to be structured in part by the meanings locally attached to them, and in so doing helped found the field of ethnopsychology. Each also gives an at least partially reflexive analysis in which we see the emotional life of the ethnographer and his or her society reflected as an exotic phenomenon in the eyes of the people encountered.

While Levy and Briggs to some degree are committed to linking the cultural meaning of emotions to a more universal psychobiological conception of emotional functioning that derives ultimately from Freud, I am concerned with questioning the embedded Western assumptions that the psychodynamic view of emotions brings with it. Both Briggs and Levy, however, give valuable examples of the depth and richness of the understandings of self and emotion that exist in other societies. From the very different tradition of symbolic anthropology, Rosaldo sees emotions as forms of symbolic action whose articulation with other aspects of cultural meaning and social structure is primary (see also Myers 1979; Shore 1982). More than her predecessors, she explores the importance of emotions for a theory of culture and social action.

Another important influence on the view of emotions I present here is the work of the philosopher Solomon (1976), who has developed an eloquent critique of the "myth" that emotions are hydraulic in operation and beyond the control of individuals. He substitutes a scheme in which emotions are subjective judgments which both reflect and constitute our individual views of the world, and notes that feelings then can be seen not as the essence but the "ornament" (1976:158) of emotion. His views can be adapted to account for the

6

variations that exist cross-culturally in emotional meaning if we note that the construction of cultural (as well as personal) subjectivities is a matter of the learning of emotions. His critique of the hydraulic model of emotions can also be extended from an intellectual to a cultural and deconstructive one.

Solomon's more rational conception of emotions is consistent with recent moves made in psychology and anthropology to reconsider the links between cognition and emotion. The cognitive theories of emotion, such as those of Arnold (1960), Lazarus (1977), and Beck (1967), were developed out of a sense of the inadequacy both of an overly instinctual view of emotion and of the too mechanical view of the human as information processor introduced by the cognitive revolution of the 1960s and '70s. The approach to Ifaluk ethnography taken here draws on the cognitive tradition in asking how understanding and reasoning about emotion among the Ifaluk are evident in the language they use to talk about it (Holland and Quinn 1987; Quinn 1982). I am concerned, however, with viewing that process of understanding as a social or interpersonally negotiated one (Black 1985) and with situating it more fully than have many cognitive anthropologists in the social structures and social behaviors that drive it.

Finally, social-constructionist and critical theory have been drawn on to frame my more basic understandings of the goals and limitations of ethnographic research on emotions. Gergen (1973, 1985), Sabini and Silver (1982), and Averill (1980, 1982, 1985) have developed furthest the argument for viewing psychological phenomena such as emotions as a form of discourse rather than as things to be discovered beneath the skin or under the hat. Averill, in particular, has developed the constructivist theory of emotions and has written extensive and erudite treatments of several emotions, including anger and love. Another strain of critical theory, one that comes from marxist and feminist sources, has also informed my attempt to link the cultural forms of emotional meaning with much broader political and economic structures and to question the "dispassionate" and value-neutral self-image of theorizing on self and emotion (e.g., Foucault 1980; Hochschild 1983; Scheper-Hughes 1985). These analyses add power as a crucial factor in the constitution of subjectivity, something which constructivist analysis tends to ignore in favor of a focus on language per se and the metaphor of speech as "game." Like Foucault, I am interested in how the emotions—like other aspects of a culturally postulated psyche—are "the place in which the most minute and local social practices are linked up with the large scale organization of power" (Dreyfus and Rabinow 1983:xxvi).

7

The process of coming to understand the emotional lives of people in different cultures can be seen first and foremost as a problem of translation. What must be translated are the meanings of the emotion words spoken in everyday conversation, of the emotionally imbued events of everyday life, of tears and other gestures, and of audience reaction to emotional performance. The interpretive task, then, is not primarily to fathom somehow "what they are feeling" inside (Geertz 1976) but rather to translate emotional communications from one idiom, context, language, or sociohistorical mode of understanding into another.

If it is assumed that emotion is simply a biopsychological event and that each emotion is universal and linked neatly to a facial expression (of which even careful and intentional masking leaves unmistakable clues), the process of emotional understanding across cultural boundaries becomes a simple one of reading faces or looking for "leaks" from the inner pool of emotional experience; one looks for the occurrence or nonoccurrence of particular emotions whose meaning is considered unproblematic. If, however, emotion is seen as woven in complex ways into cultural meaning systems and social interaction, and if emotion is used to talk about what is culturally defined and experienced as "intensely meaningful," then the problem becomes one of translating between two different cultural views and enactments of that which is real and good and proper.

It has commonly been observed that the process of translation involves much more than the one-to-one linking of concepts in one language with concepts in another. Rather, the process ideally involves providing the context of use of the words in each of the two languages between which translation is attempted. The shift from a concern with language as semantics to an emphasis on language as social action was heralded early on in the history of anthropology by Malinowski but has only recently been taken up widely.

Michelle Rosaldo first raised the issue of the translation of emotional lives across cultures in part by questioning the traditional anthropological assumption that the "symbolic" realms of ritual and art require translation, whereas the everyday words of commonsense and mundane conversation do not. This leads us, she pointed out, to "fail to see that common discourse as well as the more spectacular feats of poets and religious men requires an interpretive account" (1980:23). Rosaldo situated emotion talk within the language games that Wittgenstein and Ryle before her outlined, and demonstrated that the sense of emotion words for those who use them is as much to be found in how they work in social life as in any necessary resonance with a preverbal emotional experience.

This latter, pragmatic view of emotional and other language has had to struggle for acceptance against the implicit assumption, widespread in Western thinking, that words have labeling or reference as their primary function. (For comments on the Western view of language, see Crapanzano 1981 and Good and Good 1982.) The referential view of language goes hand in hand, in the West, with a tendency toward reification, or the confusion of words with the objects about which they are used to talk. This confusion has been identified in marxist thought as a concomitant of social relations under capitalism. These two aspects of the Western approach to language—as something which primarily *refers to* or even *is* a series of things—act together to predispose us toward a particular view of the words used to talk about emotion, such as "anger," "fear," "happiness," or "emotion" itself. At best, these words are seen as labels for emotion "things"; at worst, the words *become* the things themselves rather than human, cultural, and historical inventions for viewing self and relations with others.

The problem of the referential and reified view of language is found in even more extreme form in the domain of emotion words than it is elsewhere in language. This is so because the Western approach to language reinforces the already existing view of emotions as primarily physical things. "Anger," "fear," and "happiness" are treated, through the process of reification, not as concepts used to do certain kinds of things in the world but as labels for concretized psychophysical states or objectivized internal "event-things." When emotion words are confused with things, the tendency is to look at the emotion terminologies of other cultures as being either "accurate" or "inaccurate" labels for the presumably universal underlying things, which is to say, to look at the emotions as objective natural events (e.g., Needham 1981).

The critique of reification in thinking about the emotions and the emphasis on translation are not meant to imply that we need only look at words (or the ideational) in order to understand any experience construed as emotional. The concept of emotion arose in part in response to the fact that the human body has the potential for being "moved," and it has been used in part to talk about the force of events seen as "intensely meaningful." The relationships among the physical, the mental, and the emotional are some of the thorniest tangles in our conceptual forest; those relationships will be treated in the first

9

two chapters as a problem that is historically and culturally specific (though not necessarily unique) to the West.

The model used for discussing emotion words in this book differs in two fundamental ways from that which has predominated in social science. First, it is ethnopsychological, or concerned with indigenous models (also termed cultural models or folk models) used to understand and explain the person. Symbolic and psychodynamic as well as cognitive and linguistic concerns have driven the surge of interest in ethnopsychology (Briggs 1970; Geertz 1973; Heelas and Lock 1981; Holland and Quinn 1987; Kirkpatrick 1983; Levy 1973; Rosaldo 1980; Shore 1982; Shweder and Bourne 1982; White and Kirkpatrick 1985), but most researchers share an interest in the socio-cultural processes by which such understandings are formed. Emotion words are treated here as coalescences of complex ethnotheoretical ideas about the nature of self and social interaction. Each emotion word evokes in the listener of shared cultural background some variant of an elaborate "scenario" or scene (Fillmore 1977; Quinn 1982; Lakoff and Kövecses 1987). To understand the meaning of an emotion word is to be able to envisage (and perhaps to find oneself able to participate in) a complicated scene with actors, actions, interpersonal relationships in a particular state of repair, moral points of view, facial expressions, personal and social goals, and sequences of events.

The translation of emotion concepts between languages, then, involves the comparison of these ethnotheoretical ideas and the scenes they are encoded in, in each of two cultures. While the Ifaluk term *song* may be translated as "anger," because the scenarios that both *song* and "anger" evoke and the uses to which the terms are put in social interaction show some broad similarities, the scenes each call forth are at variance in important ways. In particular, the term *song* evokes in the Ifaluk listener a much more vivid and unambiguous scene of moral transgression on the part of one person and of moral condemnation of that violation by the person who is *song*.

Second, emotion words are treated not only as clusters of ethnotheoretical ideas but also as actions or ideological practices. In other words, the postulation of ethnopsychological structures is balanced with the observation that ideas and words are used, manipulated, misunderstood, reconstrued, and played with. In particular cultures and contexts, emotion words may be used to theorize about events, to moralize about or to judge them, and to advance one's interests by defining the situation in a particular way. Thus, the calling up of a scenario by the speaker of emotion words is done in particular contexts for particular ends, to negotiate aspects of social reality and to create that reality.

Emotion words have force, then, both for the speaker who attributes emotion to him- or herself and for the listener who may be compelled to come to terms with the theory of events posited by the use of the word and the threat or promise of action embedded in the particular emotion term. To speak of one's feelings of "compassion," for example, is to attempt to portray an event as having an actor who is suffering rather than comfortable, and perhaps to suggest that actions ought to be taken to alleviate that condition. It is to attempt to characterize and to move events, not merely or even mainly to map them.

One of the classic problems in ethnographic description concerns the degree to which we paint the members of another society as either "just like us" or as "not at all like us." The former strategy tends to be associated with an anthropologist's assumption of a basically universal human nature, while a more exotic rendering of others is often correlated with a more relativistic or culturological stance. The dilemma in cultural description is how to balance the competing demands of these two tendencies such that these other people can be portrayed as recognizably human without "human-ness" being reduced to the terms of a Western and hence culturally provincial definition.

In the translation of emotions across cultures, this problem presents itself as that of how to understand cultural others as living emotional lives that are "sensible" without introducing unexamined and untenable assumptions about the universal nature of emotional experience or of the self. The challenge is to avoid portraying the lives of others as so emotionally different as to be incomprehensible and bizarre or as so emotionally unremarkable as to be indistinguishable in their motivational underpinnings from those of our Western contemporaries. To translate in a way that is both humanizing and valid has seemed to require a particular stance toward fieldwork. This stance, which has been taken by a few anthropologists, requires one to make explicit the ways in which the cultural encounters of fieldwork involve both the shock and fascination of the emotionally new and the comfort and unsurprising nature of the emotionally familiar, ignoring neither aspect in favor of the other (e.g. Briggs 1970; Crapanzano 1980; Riesman 1977).

Briggs was the first anthropologist to demonstrate that learning about the emotional worlds of other societies involves more than the simple one-to-one matching of emotion vocabularies between language groups. Rather, the Utku Eskimo emotion terms that she encountered were an opening into an immense and elaborate ethnopsychological belief system that characterized both human nature and everyday interactions. She also demonstrated that coming to understand another emotional world is an often painful process of *self-discovery* as well. As she struggled to bring her own world, however truncated, into an Utku igloo—as she brought her typewriter and her ways of viewing anger into the system of a local family, she found not only an exotic Utku emotional world, in which anger was anathema but an exotic emotional self as well, a self which she recognizes (but does not explore) as American, middle class, and Protestant. Briggs's description of her reactions to the igloo ceiling's dripping onto her typewriter keys, and to the expectation that the resident child's "imperious" demands for her own carefully hoarded raisins be met, introduces a novel view of fieldwork. It is one that at least implies that the emotional worldview of the anthropologist merits as much attention as that of the culture we ostensibly go to "observe." For it is clearly to this emotional self that we implicitly compare the emotional lives of others. How, we necessarily ask as human observers, are they emotionally like me, and how different? The process of translating emotional worlds involves then an explication of the theories of self and emotion in two cultures (such as the American and the Ifaluk) and an examination of the use to which emotion terms are put in concrete settings in each society.

This book presents a view of the emotional, moral, and social world of the Ifaluk. In the process, I will weave back and forth between that world and necessarily brief sketches of some related and contrasting middle-class American ideas about emotion. Chapter 2 considers the historical context within which this research project was conceived. This includes the American social context that helped create normative and feminist responses to the problem of emotions, a history of indigenous and colonial paths to and from Ifaluk, and a description of the conditions under which my fieldwork was conducted there. Chapters 3 and 4 set the broader context of cultural knowledge within which understandings of each individual emotion are set. I look first at the concept of emotion as an element in Western cultural discourse and then at some Ifaluk theories about the nature of the person and about the origins of behavior and consciousness. A third and major section of the book examines the relationship between the creation and organization of events in everyday life and several Ifaluk emotion concepts, including *fago* (compassion/love/sadness) in chapter 5, *song* (justifiable anger) in chapter 6, and *metagu* (fear/anxiety) and *rus* (panic/fright/surprise) in chapter 7. Each of the latter three chapters draws comparisons between Ifaluk and American discourses on these emotions. In concluding, I present the three senses in which emotion is constructed as a social object and an experience (chapter 8). In the process, the concept of emotion is reconstructed to integrate the emotional more closely with what we term the cultural, as well as with the cognitive, the moral, and the socially emergent dimensions of personhood.

CHAPTER TWO
Paths to Ifaluk

The road that leads to any anthropological fieldwork is both a personally and an historically and culturally determined one. Descriptions of that journey can be seen as a necessary and integral part of ethnography rather than an adjunct to it. The field experience has become, for many anthropologists, the centerpiece for interpretation rather than the unspoken and unproblematic source of ethnographic description. This approach can be distinguished from positivist accounts of field methodology, which focus on the way a particular research question is "operationalized" without acknowledging the cultural foundations of the question and its terms themselves. Moreover, many ethnographers who examine the anthropological field encounter more explicitly and critically fall short of producing a fully cultural account. They describe the nature of the field experience as the outcome, almost exclusively, of the individual characteristics of the field-worker or of the cultural features of the host society which constrain "their" view of, or reaction to, the anthropologist (e.g., Berreman 1962; Briggs 1970; Golde 1970).

The present account of everyday life among the Ifaluk is written in the belief that a more fully cultural description of the "natural" history of any particular anthropological field project is both possible and necessary. A truly cultural description of the ethnographic encounter examines the interaction of both of the two cultural meaning systems involved (those of ethnographer and host), as well as the

14

nature of, and shifts in, the power relations between the two parties, as is done, for example, by Rabinow (1977), Dumont (1978), and Dwyer (1982). The emotional lives of the Ifaluk people I met were certainly not experienced in precisely the way that I present them here, nor would any Ifaluk rendition of that experience "capture" it either. My account is rather the result of the culturally constructed questions that I brought to the field, questions that were altered as everyday conversations overheard between the islanders hinted at other, more locally relevant questions that people asked implicitly or explicitly of each other. Although my personal constructions of reality are relevant to an understanding of the fieldwork process, I choose to view them here, not as the constructions of a unique individual, but as those of an American female at a particular point in historical time. The questions and concepts used and the behavior exhibited in the field are examined as the outcomes of both American and Ifaluk cultural processes and of the sociopolitical context within which I was operating.[1] Fieldwork is treated, in other words, as a cultural exercise which must be chronicled, however much that chronicle— being written, in the end, by an American—is itself culturally constrained in its vision.

Before going on to describe the place of emotion in Ifaluk thought and everyday life, I first present a description of how I was motivated and enabled to conduct the fieldwork on which this account of Ifaluk is based. I examine that process in several ways. My description of the Ifaluk has its roots (1) in the Western historical and cultural milieu in which my project was generated, (2) in the more general context of the history of contact and exchange between the Ifaluk and people of other cultural backgrounds, (3) in the crucible of the day-to-day interaction between myself as a female guest and Ifaluk individuals, and (4) in the kinds of ethnographic and language-based methods I used in the study.

The Genesis of the Project

This research project on the relationship between emotion and culture was first conceived in the atmosphere of the social and ideological changes that occurred in the American gender system in the 1970s, changes that were catalyzed and catalogued by the women's movement. As women entered the paid labor force in greater and greater numbers over the previous several decades, academic thought and American gender ideologies more generally underwent some important transformations. Both men and women have been forced to

15

reevaluate their assessments of women's capabilities as their social and economic circumstances have changed. These changes, including the increased numbers of women in academia, meant that the dominant ideological views of women, men, and social life have been challenged. For example, Gilligan (1982), whose work we will examine in the next chapter, has reformulated psychological theory about moral development on the basis of an empirical consideration and a more positive evaluation of the forms of moral thought often characteristic of women. Other studies of moral development (e.g., Kohlberg 1976) have used the mode of moral thinking prevalent in adult men as the implicit standard by which all human morality is judged. In a parallel fashion, a reassessment of the value of emotion in human functioning seemed called for, and I was eventually led to a questioning of the concept of emotion itself.

I began to notice that the study of emotion by American academics reflected the more general cultural association between women, emotion, and the less worthwhile. Gender ideologies in any society reflect the power relations between women and men, and they do this by associating the less powerful gender with culturally devalued characteristics. In the American case, women are that gender and emotion is such a characteristic. Emotion has often been treated as a "mental health" problem or as an animal or mammalian trait rather than as a particularly human, intelligent, and social adaptation. The linking of emotion with the female in American culture (including in social science), and its devaluation relative to rational thought, appeared to me to be a culturally specific idea, advanced within the context of a particular set of gender relations in our society.

I therefore felt it necessary to look for a field research site in which gender relations were more egalitarian than in American society. The underlying schema, however naive, with which I was working was one in which the relationship between women and men was primary in determining the cultural evaluation of emotion, especially in those cases in which emotion or emotionality was particularly associated with one of the sexes. In the absence of detailed information about gender roles and relations in some of the existing ethnographies, I took matrilocal residence, the use of matrilineal principles in reckoning descent and inheritance, and a substantial female role in food production as indicative of relative gender egalitarianism. In order to study emotion, I had also decided to look for evidence in the ethnographies that emotion was something people spoke about relatively freely. Although it is possible for emotional experience to be culturally constructed in such a way as to minimize the use of emotional idioms (Abu-Lughod 1986), I was interested in the opportunity of hearing people discuss with each other—independent of my questions—the emotional meaning of everyday events. I also expected to explore the possibility that emotion would be conceptualized (as well as evaluated) differently in another society. I did not anticipate, however, the extent to which the concept of emotion I was working with was culturally specific or even reified.

By also deciding that I wanted to work in the island Pacific, I followed a long line of outsiders, from Paul Gauguin to the Heyerdahls to Margaret Mead, attracted by the often beautiful images in which the region has been painted in the West. In making this choice, I was aware that I was seeking more than simply an appropriate research site for examining the problem of the relationship between emotion and culture. I was also looking for a people who had devised a cultural and social solution that was not only different from but also somehow *better* than our own. I was interested in seeing if and how it is possible for people to organize their lives in such a way as to avoid the problems that seemed to me to diminish American culture, in particular its pervasive inequality of both gender and class and its violence. It was perhaps by choosing to live and work among a people whose values I felt in advance I shared that I partially avoided what some other anthropologists cannot or do not avoid, which is a fundamental and pervasive clash between one's own deep and central commitments (including the anthropological commitment to at least a minimal cultural relativism) and those of the people who are one's hosts.[2]

The values that I sought in Ifaluk society—particularly gender and resource egalitarianism and interpersonal nonviolence—were ones which, as we will see, did in fact exist there. But I also discovered, as have many anthropologists before me, that prefieldwork images of the place one will work are as much the product of hope, fantasy, and existing cultural images of the other as they are of a reading of the ethnographic record (e.g., Weidman 1970:240).[3] My images of a peaceful society as devoid of anger, for example, were challenged by a constant stream of declarations of anger in everyday life on the island; and the egalitarian gender relations that I imagined must follow from the female role in production, descent, and residence collided with the male view of women as "needy," or subordinate, and the requirement that women walk bent over from the waist when passing a group of seated men.

17

In reviewing the ethnographic literature on the Pacific in the process of this search, I found reports of the 1947 field trip of Spiro and Burrows to Ifaluk atoll (Burrows 1963; Burrows and Spiro 1953; Spiro 1950, 1951, 1952). Although gender roles were not reported in any detail, the island's matrilineality, matrilocal postmarital residence pattern, and women's ownership and management of the horticultural system seemed to augur well for the kind of system I was interested in observing. Most important in determining the choice of Ifaluk as a field site, however, was the frequent emotional idiom evident in the "song-poems" recorded by Burrows during his stay and published as *Flower in My Ear: Arts and Ethos of Ifaluk Atoll* (1963).* These songs speak of their composers' pains and pleasures and reflect the island's emotional tone of interpersonal gentleness and the deeply felt importance of ties to others. In the following four excerpts from longer song-poems, a woman first sings of her son who has died, and another of her secret love; one mother laments her daughter who has left with a new husband for another island, and another sings of her intense pride in her son.

> Dearly I love my son,
> I will never forget him;
> The thought of him lives within me,
> Like a part of my vitals;
> It tears at me inside.
> It is enough to drive me mad;
> I think I have lost my mind!
> (Burrows 1963:313)

> Not everybody can see
> How deep is our love.
> We keep the secret in our hearts,
> How I cherish him within me.
> It is like a garland we make together;
> Neither is happy apart from the other.
> (242–43)

> She is going to sail away with her husband.
> The daughter I nurtured well.
> I want to go aboard and help her.
> "No, you stay ashore!"
> The captain is eager to be gone.

*Permission to reprint brief sections of *Flower in My Ear: Art and Ethos of Ifaluk Atoll,* by Edwin Burrows (1963) is granted by the University of Washington Press.

I want to cry;
I love my daughter dearly . . .
I will go to find her;
My daughter is my very eyes to me . . .
I dream of her
Where she sleeps in the canoe shelter.
I want to put her on my arm;
To lie down beside her,
Hold her close.
Laresh is my perfume,
The waves splash over her,
The salt dries on her face,
At the corners of her mouth.
I miss my daughter so! . . .
My daughter is the flower I wear on my head.
I am worn with grief . . .
Flower in my ear
Fragrant flower of the *warung*
My precious ointment.

(298–300)

Flower I wear in my ear . . .
My son is like a garland for my head;
Like turmeric growing in the taro pool,
That I gather in the morning for a necklace . . .
I am proud to call myself his mother.
I rejoice in his being both shipwright and captain,
And love to hear all the people talking about him;
Their praise delights my ears.

(84–86)

It was with a romantic image of a romantic people that I set out to follow the path to the Pacific already well worn by previous Westerners lured by accounts—perhaps one could say parables—of a world more peaceful and bountiful than many others.

Historical Routes to Ifaluk

Let me begin to describe that path by tracing the routes that history has etched between Ifaluk and the rest of the world, routes which have linked the people of that atoll with their clan brothers and sisters on islands up to 500 miles distant, the chiefly villages of Yap, the Spanish royal court of the 1600s, American and English seaports of the 1800s, Japanese phosphate company towns in Belau and on Fais,

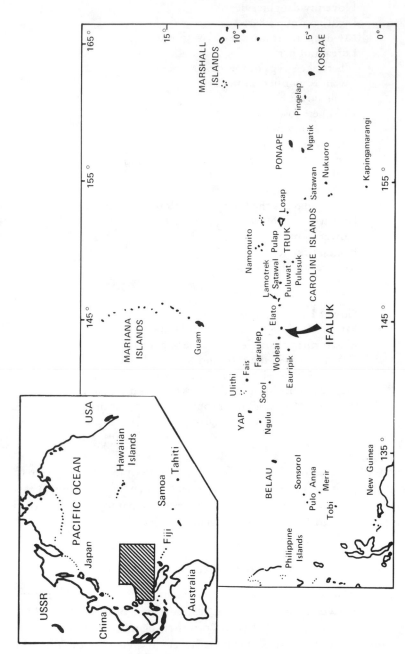

Map 1. The Caroline Islands

and American middle-class neighborhoods of the 1960s and 1970s. People, ideologies, goods, and diseases have traveled these routes, often to the detriment of the health and well-being of the Ifaluk. These realities also provided the context for the way I was received and perceived by the Ifaluk and the way they are portrayed here. That context in fact made it possible for the fieldwork experience to occur at all and to progress as it did, and it provides much of the framework for the emotional positions taken by the anthropologist and the island residents.

Coming from the East to a New Island

The West Caroline Islands may well have been one of the last habitable expanses of the earth to have been populated by humans. While Yap was settled from Indonesia by perhaps 3500 B.C. according to current estimates (Howells 1973), the string of low coral atolls in which Ifaluk is found was settled from the east, presumably as the outcome of migration from Polynesia that eventually reached Truk and, from there, Ifaluk. There is disagreement, however, over when settlement first occurred in this area; Alkire's assessment (1978:21) is for a period just before A.D. 1300, while Rubinstein (1979:22–23) estimates that it occurred in the earliest centuries of the first millennium. The scant archaeological record for the region includes pottery from the nearby atoll of Lamotrek which has been dated to about A.D. 1320 (Shutler 1978).

Ifaluk is not only isolated from the large land masses and population centers of the globe but, being a low coral atoll, is also a precarious human environment.[4] The first settlers in this area may have found abundant fish both within and without Ifaluk's mile-square lagoon, but after landing on the lagoon beach, they would find that their journey inland would take them only fifteen feet above sea level before they descended to the ocean side of the atoll; it would also take them under an hour to circle the two largest islets around the coral ring which, together with two other small uninhabited islets, barely exceed one-half square mile in total area.

As they moved through the interior, they would find both dense vegetation and swampy central areas. These areas would be laboriously developed, in the years to come, into the taro gardens which now provide the Ifaluk's staple crop. They would also plant coconut, breadfruit, banana, and papaya, as well as limited amounts of sweet potato and sugarcane. The coconut tree would also be used for house-

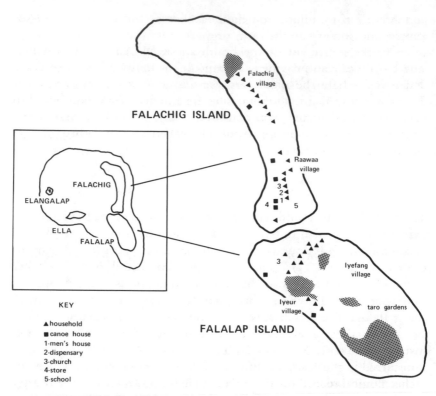

Map 2. Ifaluk Atoll

building materials, and the banana plant would provide the fibers from which they wove their clothing.

Even at the point at which these food resources were sufficient to sustain the reproduction of the colonizing population, the aboriginal Ifaluk people would soon encounter the typhoons that plague the area. It is these typhoons, as much as any other single environmental factor on Ifaluk, that have helped to produce the contemporary social organization and emotional configuration of the island, as we will see. A severe typhoon can result in the near total devastation of the food supply; winds of up to 140 miles per hour can fell the island's massive breadfruit trees as well as coconut trees and buildings. Rising seas can cover the atoll, washing over the taro gardens and killing the plants.[5] It has been estimated that six to ten years may be required after such a typhoon inundation before the island vegetation returns to full flower (Alkire 1978:14). Waves from a typhoon also smash the living coral communities on the reef, thereby cutting back severely on the number of fish they can support.

Since the war, severe typhoons have struck Ifaluk twice, in 1958 and 1975, with minor storms occurring virtually every year.[6] When I visited the Ifaluk several years after the 1975 storm, they still frequently reviewed among themselves the events of the typhoon—their retreat to the concrete, "typhoon-proof" school building located near the high point of the island, where they sat on the desks around whose legs ocean water lapped; the death of a newborn; their feelings about the very real possibility of death for everyone; the fishing that they had to do after the waters receded, leaving a giant pool complete with a shark in the depression of the taro gardens; and their worries about the long-term effects of the typhoon on their food supply.

Paths of Kinship, Paths of Trade, and Paths of Yapese Empire

The past and present inhabitants of Ifaluk responded to the threat that typhoons present to their existence by maintaining close ties with other atolls in the area, including particularly Woleai, Faraulep, Elato, Satawal, Lamotrek, and Eauripik. People have made use of the networks of kinship ties to other islands in order to escape the food shortages that can follow even a relatively minor typhoon. Several Ifaluk families had moved to clan lands on Sorol soon after the typhoon of 1975, and others made long visits with relatives on the food-rich atoll of Elato.[7]

These ties include those of shared clanship. Although some small clans are found on only one island, others are represented on nearly every island from Sorol to Truk. As the clan is seen as the owner of the lands on which households are founded, shared clan membership constitutes a powerful claim to hospitality by visitors from other islands. Marriage or shared parenthood also ties the Ifaluk to other islands. In 1978, of seventy-nine currently viable marriages to the Ifaluk-born, twenty-one had occurred across island boundaries. These included unions between Ifaluk women and men from Woleai, Elato, Lamotrek, Satawal, Sonsorol, and Pulo Anna, and unions between Ifaluk men and women of Woleai, Eauripik, Lamotrek, Ulithi, and Hawaii. The interisland ties that these marriages create are further reinforced by the frequent practice of adoption by the father's mother, which can move children to other islands.

The road between Ifaluk and the other neighboring atolls is worn deeper by the exchange of goods, some of which are manufactured or widely available only on certain islands. Eauripik produces the turtle-shell belts worn by women (and earlier by men), Satawal produces carved coral-rock taro pounders, and Lamotrek and Fais are able to grow tobacco in some abundance.

The people of Ifaluk have ties not only with their atoll neighbors but also with the high volcanic island of Yap. A system of tributary and other ties once linked the coral islands of the Carolines to the Yapese. Islands as far away as Namonuito, 800 miles to the east of Yap, were involved and were internally ranked among themselves (see Lessa 1966; Alkire 1965; and Lingenfelter 1975:147–55). Each of the outer islands sent yearly tribute, consisting of woven cloths, coir, mats, and shells, to Gatchepar village of Gagil district on Yap. In return, the Yapese often provided food, turmeric, flint stones, and other resources, many of which are not found on the outer islands. Alkire suggests that this and other interisland arrangements serve as an "insurance policy" for small atolls at the mercy of typhoons and population vagaries (1978:50–52). Woven skirts are still sent to Yap, and the Ifaluk otherwise acknowledge the dominance of the high islanders by adherence to taboos, such as that against wearing colored cloth when they visit Yap. Although the Yapese empire is today smaller than it once was, its status in the colonial system set up by the United States—as the district center and political majority of an area which runs from Yap to Satawal—has given it new powers.

Carolinean navigators possess a formidable reputation for their long-distance sailing skills. In 1947, Burrows and Spiro (1953) collected sailing directions to Yap, Truk (each approximately 500 miles distant), and Guam (approximately 450 miles north) from Ifaluk navigators. The frequency with which interisland travel occurred in the past is attested to by the number of Carolinean canoes that arrived in the Philippines in the seventeenth century, documented there by Spanish colonists; in 1664 alone, thirty canoes from the Carolines were reported to have arrived in the Philippines (Hezel 1983:40).[8]

Trading voyages between the Mariana Islands and the Carolines by the Ifaluk and their neighbors seem to have predated the first Spanish contact with the area, when Magellan reached Guam in 1521. The Carolineans ceased their northern voyages, most likely at some point after 1668, when they learned that the Spanish had begun to take increasingly repressive measures to gain compliance with their rule and customs from Guam's native Chamorro people.[9] In 1787 and again in 1788, the Lamotrekan navigator, Luito, reopened the path between the Carolines and the Marianas. While there, the Carolineans told the Spanish vice-governor that they "had always been trading with the inhabitants of this island [Guam], and only left off when the white people settled here, whose cruelty they themselves had witnessed" (Kotzebue 1821:207, quoted in Lewis 1972:35).

Regular trading voyages between the Marianas and the Carolines began again in 1805. From that time, yearly visits were made in which the Carolineans traded canoes, shells, and woven hats and mats for iron, tobacco, beads, glass, cloth, and locally produced alcohol (Bates and Abbott 1958:177; Marshall and Marshall 1975:448–49). Marshall and Marshall find strong historical evidence that the technique of manufacturing fermented coconut toddy, and alcohol consumption more generally, reached Ifaluk and neighboring atolls by the path that the Carolineans had forged to the Marianas.[10] This most likely first occurred at some point around the turn of the nineteenth century. Some of the other material and cultural goods that made their way to Ifaluk in this period are indexed by the Spanish words that remain in their vocabulary, including *kalebus* (jail), *gatu* (cat), *korosonai* (heart), *karebau* (beef), and *atios* (goodbye).

The Ifaluk and their neighbors made special use of this rediscovered route to the Marianas in response to two devastating typhoons that hit the area in 1815 and 1865; hundreds of refugees made their way north and were settled in villages by the Spanish. Although there is record of a severe typhoon in 1845 as well (Krämer 1937:3, in Alkire 1965:26), no increase in the normal traffic from the Carolines was noted at that time. That even these paths between the Carolines and the Marianas did not altogether prevent suffering on the islands at the hands of the weather is indicated by several cases in which ships' logs of visits to the Woleai area in the nineteenth century mention the islanders' hunger. A Russian scientific expedition in 1828 found people from Ifaluk and Woleai to Lamotrek asking for food when they arrived. The Lamotrekans ate the wormy biscuits they were offered, and the Ifaluk were ready to exchange even their canoes for food (Lütke 1836, in Hezel 1979:18). On Faraulep in 1839, one ship's log notes, the islanders were "apparently very poor" (Ward 1967:348). These descriptions no doubt represent what was a temporary problem, as they stand in sharp contrast to many other reports of visits to the region. Those reports characterize the Carolineans as interested mainly in trading for iron or tobacco and occasionally mention that the islanders traded local food for European goods.

The Road from Europe and America

More direct experience of European material and social life by the Ifaluk and their neighbors on their home atolls occurred in the period up through the nineteenth century. In forging a route between Europe and China, a number of exploring and trading ships passed through the Carolines. Recorded foreign voyages through the islands which today constitute Yap State (see map 1) include ten ships before 1750, the great majority of which were Spanish, and twelve more in the second half of the eighteenth century, the bulk of which were British (Hezel 1979). Only four ships whose purpose was specifically missionary were recorded as having passed through the Yap region at any time before 1885.

Of the twenty five ships that came through in the period to 1802, only one—the *Duff,* commanded by the British missionary James Wilson—passed close to Ifaluk; this sighting, in 1797, is considered to be the European "discovery" of the island. It is also Wilson who gives one of the first recorded descriptions of any of Ifaluk's nearby atoll neighbors, in this case, the Woleai. As in many of the portraits of cultural strangers produced both by the Ifaluk and by the Europeans who visited them, emotional characterizations play a prominent role. Said Wilson of the Woleaians, they "go from island to island apparently without fear" (Wilson [1799] 1966:304). He also speculated that the infrequency with which women appeared in the canoes that sailed out to greet his ship in this island group signaled that the men might be "more jealous than their eastern neighbors," whom he had just visited (Wilson [1799] 1966:301). The Russian scientist Lütke described the Ifaluk as being of "boisterous spirit" when he visited in 1828. Ulithians—the Ifaluk's fellow Carolinians— were frequently characterized as pleasant by such nineteenth-century Spanish observers as Cantova, who termed them "peaceful, tame, docile, and very affectionate" (quoted in Hezel 1983:57), and Egui, who called them "cheerful and of a fine temperment" (in Hezel 1983:45–46) but who later shot and killed three islanders in his attempt to kidnap one of them for navigation assistance.

Early as well as recent European and American observers have also noted, usually with disapproval, emotional changes they infer are the result of the Carolinians' contact with the cultures of the West. Of the Carolinians he met on Guam in the early nineteenth century, Lütke complained that

> They wear red shirts and straw hats; they say "adios" and "si senor." But with this "civilization," they are to their free countrymen [those on their home atolls, whom he had observed earlier] as a caged parrot is to the magnificent flocks that enchant the traveller in the forest. . . . There is not even the shadow of that uninhibited cheerfulness that they

had before. There is a certain trace of sadness in their forced smile."
(Lütke 1835v2:123–24, in Hezel 1983:107).

Oddly enough, at least one observer noted "fearlessness" as an emotional quality that is apparently lost with the Micronesians' "civilizing." European visitors appeared to prefer the Carolinians, who were "free, naked, agile, and fearless," to the Chamorros who, with their longer experience of European culture, were characterized as the "timid children of Agaña" (Jurien de la Gravière 1854vl:204–5, in Hezel 1983:107). As we will see, this contrasts with the way the Ifaluk have characterized the more recent effects of culture contact. Children learn in school, many people told me, to lose their fear of strangers, as do any people who become used to the presence of numerous and strange others.

Micronesia became a more direct destination in the nineteenth century, when the American whaling industry began fishing in its waters to provide oil for the lamps of North America. The whaling fleet, which numbered 675 ships and 16,000 men in 1844, brought American sailors to shore in great numbers, looking for wood, food, water, and women. The havoc which these men (and their alcohol, firearms, and venereal diseases) brought to the area was generally confined, in its most serious forms, to the larger islands and to the eastern Carolines, particularly Kosrae and Ponape. Although the actual number of whaling-ship contacts was no doubt larger, only eleven whaler visits to islands in what is now Yap State were recorded in the nineteenth century.

More important, however, were the trading ventures that began to bring significant numbers of European and North American ships to the Yap region. Forty recorded trading-ship contacts occurred from 1800 to 1885, the bulk of which were English. These ships were in search of copra, as well as the Chinese trade goods of bêche-de-mer (a food delicacy), turtle shell, and other shells. In return, the European traders brought primarily iron, tobacco, and cloth with them to the islands.

The Road of Colonialism

Although the Spanish had nominal control over the Marshall and Caroline Islands for three centuries, we have seen that it was primarily the Ifaluk who went to the Spanish colonies in the Marianas, rather than the reverse. A more significant path was beaten to Ifaluk's shore in the period after 1885 by the Germans, Japanese, and Americans, who would come in succession to take control of the islands of Ifaluk and of Micronesia more generally. Although Ifaluk's scant one-half square mile of rough coral ground would appear to offer little for outsiders to exploit, copra, labor, and then strategic position would be the prizes for which the imperial powers came to Ifaluk.

A number of European warships, particularly of German and English origins, began to appear in the Western Carolines in the nineteenth century. The visits of ten such vessels were recorded for Yap district in that period, their purpose being both to enforce trading prerogatives in the islands and to police their resident nationals. Some simply surveyed the islands. Although some of these warships ultimately served to protect islanders from the more brutal of the Europeans residing in or passing through the area, others had less benign effects. The crew of a Spanish warship that stopped at Woleai, Ifaluk's nearest island neighbor, in 1874, for example, felled many coconut and breadfruit trees, apparently "leaving the people starving afterwards" (Hezel 1979:22).

The roads to and from Ifaluk narrowed, however, in 1898, when Germany purchased the Caroline Islands from Spain and proceeded to exploit their commercial and agricultural potential more thoroughly. The Germans ordered the consolidation of homesteads on Ifaluk into a row along the lagoon shore and the clearing of underbrush from the village areas (Bates and Abbott 1958:182). The sight of a ship in Ifaluk's lagoon became more frequent in this period. While some of these ships came to trade copra, others brought the misery of "blackbirding," a form of labor recruitment commonly practiced in the Pacific in the nineteenth century that often amounted to slavery (see Hezel 1983). Although the extent to which blackbirding occurred before the German colonial period is unknown, it is clear that the Ifaluk were subjected to this practice, as evidenced by the song-poem collected by Burrows and Spiro in 1947:

> They come to the men's house
> Where the people are assembled,
> And seize the men to take them away.
>
> They came in the afternoon
> And hunted men by night.
> Nobody could sleep for fear of them.
>
> In front of the men's house
> The Germans line up the Caroline men.
> They are pleased to see so many—

Paths to Ifaluk

They have captured ten,
Strong men all.
(Burrows and Spiro 1953:202)

The Germans took Ifaluk's men to toil in the phosphate mines of Angaur and Fais, as did the Japanese who gained control of the islands and the mines in 1914. While the Japanese were also coercive in their labor-recruitment efforts (Burrows and Spiro 1953:204), they appeared usually to offer some compensation to the laborers. It is this compensation and the trade goods it could buy, rather than the coercion, that many older Ifaluk men now remember in discussing the past. The colonists also sent Ifaluk boys to Japanese-language schools on Yap, and many were educated there over the course of several years. I was told that when a boy was born in the Japanese period, people would ask, "Is he a pencil or a shovel?" referring to the two paths—to school or to the mines—he might take. The heavy out-migration of males during the Japanese period is reflected in the marital histories of Ifaluk's older women, many of whom took new husbands when their previous spouses left the island.

The Japanese claimed ownership of Ifaluk's Falalap and Ella islets (see map 2) and left an agriculturalist on the atoll to organize copra production. Forced relocation of Falalap villagers to Falachig followed, as did coerced road construction and land clearing on Falalap. World War II halted these activities and brought with it the bombs, airplanes, and machine guns, whose Japanese labels then entered the Ifaluk language. Several Ifaluk men who were on Yap at the time were conscripted to build an airstrip. They included Gatachimang, a man who, now in his fifties, still vividly relives—in frequent narrative and recurrent nightmares—the American bombing of Yap in 1944 and the hunger and Japanese cruelty that followed.

After the war, American control of the islands was recognized by the United Nations, which assigned most of Micronesia the status of a strategic trust territory with the United States as trustee. The American road into and out of Ifaluk was controlled by the U.S. military through the 1950s and was traveled by few other than its own vessels, a fact evoked by the Ifaluk label for that period—"Navy times."[11] A rudimentary school was established in that period, run primarily by a few island men who had been sent away for teacher training. In the early 1960s, however, American colonial policy changed from a protectionist stance toward a more aggressive one. Given the contemporary, worldwide condemnation of colonialism as well as the

U.S. wish to retain the islands indefinitely, plans were made to create economic dependency in Micronesia, with the hopes of thereby determining the outcome of a future local plebiscite on the islands' political status.[12]

The resultant parade of Americans who began to visit Ifaluk from the inception of these policies in the mid-1960s included, particularly, middle-class men in their early twenties who, as Peace Corps volunteers, were assigned to the island grammar school. The American road mimicked the Japanese road in respects other than education, resulting in an exodus of young men from the island for schooling and training in the language of the colonialists. Teenage males have since gone to Ulithi for high school; in some instances, young men have gone from high school to Ponape or Belau for specialized occupational training and, in three cases, to Hawaii or Oregon for some college training.[13] Japanese traders were replaced by American and Yapese merchants. The trade in copra continued only in those periods in which the food supply had reestablished itself adequately from the effects of the latest typhoon. Copra was, moreover, soon supplanted by the wages of the island's government employees (the teachers, nurses, and political functionaries) as the main medium of exchange for trade goods.

This pattern on Ifaluk reflects the overall nature of the Micronesian political economy. The Micronesians have purchased their iron and tobacco, and, increasingly on many islands, their food supplies with government wages which are subsidized by the United States. In 1977, Trust Territory exports (consisting primarily of copra, tourism, and fish) totaled $7.61 million, while imports (including food and fuel) totalled $40.2 million.[14] Currently, 90% of Micronesia government operating expenses come from U.S. appropriations. That money—$149.1 million in 1978—has gone primarily toward building an economy oriented around consumption rather than production. Grants were targeted primarily at the establishment of a huge government bureaucracy, and for social services rather than for the development of income-producing enterprises or the encouragement of farming and fishing for local consumption. Although Ifaluk has avoided much of this more general Micronesian dependency and has continued to be self-sufficient in food, these latest colonial policies have affected their emotional lives in ways we will explore in a moment.

With this skeletal description of the paths to and from Ifaluk, we can go on to follow the particular road that I took to the island.

One Anthropological Road

There is nothing more central to the process of cultural understanding than the interpersonal relationships that are established between the anthropologist and those she visits. The relationships between myself and people on Ifaluk began to take shape even as I first wrote to the Trust Territory government for permission to conduct research on the island. While welcoming me to work in Micronesia, the territorial government passed my letter down the chain of political hierarchy, with the Yap District government passing it to the representative from the atoll of Ulithi, and from there to the chiefs of Ifaluk for their consideration. The path the letter traced thus reflects both the traditional roads into Ifaluk via Yap and the modern political hierarchy of the region.

Traveling from the west coast of the United States to Ifaluk took me along a trail marked with the progressively decreasing but never absent signs of American economic and military penetration. Descending into Honolulu five hours out of San Francisco, the plane passed over the extensive military installations at Pearl Harbor. On the ground, the two-room homes of Hawaiians and other local residents can be seen perched next to high-rise tourist hotels in sections of Waikiki. Flying eight hours on to Guam, an American territory since 1898, I stepped off the plane to find a McDonald's restaurant, one-third of the island's area in U.S. military hands and closed to casual visitors, and a local newspaper whose banner reads "Guam—Where America's Day Begins."

The biweekly jet flight from Guam to Yap carries an assortment of passengers. A typical flight might include several American experts in areas such as education, agriculture, and anthropology, a few Yapese government employees and elected officials returning from conferences on Saipan or visits to Washington, a Peace Corps volunteer returning from vacation leave in the Philippines, a Yapese student returning from college in the United States, a pair of adventurous Japanese tourists, a Korean construction company official, and a U.S. Navy officer in uniform. Arriving from the airport at the aptly named capital town of Colonia reveals the effects of more than thirty years of planned dependence under U.S. rule. The center of town is marked by the intersection of two dirt roads; it is approached occasionally by a late-model Japanese truck whose destination in the capital can only be the several government office buildings or stores, a gas station, a restaurant, one of two bars or two small hotels, the arts-and-crafts

31

outlet, or the hospital. A farmer's market draws a mere handful of participants, and there are no dockside fishing fleets, no fish- or copra-processing plants, no factories. At the nearby dock, two ships are in port, one bringing imports from Guam and the other carrying imported goods and people to and from the outer islands, including Ifaluk.

I soon learned that Tamalekar, one of the traditional clan leaders of Ifaluk, was on Yap at the time. After being introduced to him and his family, I was invited to come and live in their household when I arrived on their atoll. Although the highest-ranking chief at the time of my stay was Ilesotil, an elderly woman and head of Kovalu clan, Tamalekar occupied the post of "chief for the foreigners" (*tamolni-pusash*) and as such would have had primary responsibility for dealing with me in any case. [15]

One of the first things I recorded in my field notes after this and the other initial encounters I had with outer islanders was the tremendous solicitousness I felt extended to me, with people constantly offering food, reminding me to pull my foot back into the shifting shade, teaching me words, patting my arm, and sitting with me through an illness. My surprise at the treatment I was accorded was one important index of the cultural difference I was noting. Although the attention would of course fade with time and habituation to me, the island ethic of nurturance was to prove pervasive in everyday life and make my stay and work easier than it would have otherwise been and my respect for people on Ifaluk grow daily.

What I would also soon learn was that I was, by various criteria, a "needy" person and was thereby defined as requiring special nurturance. As a female, as someone with no kin and no taro gardens, and as someone relatively young and without children, I was to be "pitied" and cared for. The right and responsibility to nurture is reserved on Ifaluk by those higher in the social hierarchy and exercised toward those below. Although my being a national of the present colonial power no doubt played an important role in allowing me to live on the island in the first place and in structuring my relations with the Ifaluk, my place on the island was constructed more by my being an outsider and a solitary female.

Profoundly embedded in most analyses of the field experiences of American anthropologists has been the assumption of the centrality and independence of the individual fieldworker's *decisions* about how to proceed in the field. Although acceptance of the field-worker's presence and questions and the initial roles assigned (such as "guest" or "spy" or "atheist") are recognized as areas under indigenous control, it is often considered that the way fieldwork will be conducted is decided primarily by the anthropologist (with, of course, the proper personal and ethical controls in place). This assumption arises out of what can be termed an American ethnopsychology, that is, American cultural ideas about the nature of the person and his or her relations with others. In particular, it appears related to the Western individualistic notion of the person as, in Geertz's terms, "a bounded, unique, more or less integrated motivational and cognitive universe, a dynamic center of awareness, emotion, *judgment* and *action* organized into a distinctive whole and set contrastively both against other such wholes and against its social and natural background" (1976:225; emphasis added). Such central and often out-of-awareness cultural ideas have the most important bearing on the way American ethnography is written.

My initial assumption was that I would *allow* myself to be socialized by the Ifaluk to their code of conduct—as anthropological literature and lore suggest one must in order to learn what is involved in another cultural experience. I anticipated that that socialization would be freely chosen and that it would have practical utility as much as, or more than, moral force. My fieldwork experience, however, was profoundly affected by what the Ifaluk expected of me. In this case, the accommodation all field-workers are expected to make to local conditions and mores went, I believe, much further than usual. It gradually was communicated to me that I was to behave, as far as I was able, as a young Ifaluk woman should, and so I was to ask permission of the elders in my household before traveling into the village or giving gifts to others; I grated hundreds of coconuts and assisted the family's relatives in taro gardening; moved quickly with my "mother" to the interior end of the house when male guests came to consult with Tamalekar on chiefly matters; learned that I could and should ask for a "take-home" portion of food for my absent relatives when attending certain feasts; and accompanied my family to sleep at other households when the sickness of kin or other conditions called for a move.

I certainly pressed for, and they accepted, limits to my conformity, limits which they allowed and understood in terms of their own values, including the value of work and the value of obedience to and respect for authority. Thus, I did not have the normal work load of a young, unmarried woman because they considered that my note writing and interviews were a form of "work," somewhat like taro gardening or canoe building, and hence a sign of diligence; and they imagined my thesis advisor (with my self-interested help) as an older male who had sent me to do this work and who would be "justifiably angry" (*song*) if I did not complete it. But, overall, the primary way I was led to think of my position in their society was that I was a guest first, an anthropologist second. Although these conditions were often frustrating, they were also welcomed as a form of acceptance into the community and as a source of both valid (if not always broad) and noncoercively obtained insights.

Learning what was entailed in being a good guest and a good "daughter" was both a painful and a pleasurable process. It was also a process that will be detailed in order to set the stage for the interpretation of emotional experience as it was observed from the vantage point of a female guest.

The Needy Female

The first few days of field notes that I took on the island of Elato, where I stayed for five weeks before going on to Ifaluk, are dotted with speculations about the place I would occupy in the local gender system, references that would appear, in retrospect, very naive. What those notes make clear is that I had expected to be accorded the so-called honorary male status of which other female anthropologists had written, and hence to be able to move in both the world of women and the world of men. It soon became clear that this was not to be and, moreover, that any attempt to commandeer a genderless or nonconformist gender role for myself would be both a moral affront and an emotional threat to others.

The worlds of men and women are sharply separate on Ifaluk. Although some husbands and wives may spend much time together during the day in labor and conversation, men and women generally work and relax in separate locations. Men can be found at sea or more typically at their local canoe house making rope, carving canoes, repairing fishing gear, napping, or supervising toddlers. These canoe houses are taboo to all females over the age of about five or six. Women can be found working in their taro gardens in the interior of the atoll or at their homes, weaving their clothing on back-strap looms, preparing food, or tending to an infant. They might also be found preparing food with relatives, either at the homes of the latter or at the special birth houses where women retire to have their children. The birth houses are taboo to men and older boys.

This pragmatic and moral separation of the sexes is enforced by both gossip and taboos which cause men and women to distance themselves from each other in public. A woman who sees a man approaching her will swerve off the path, and this avoidance is particularly marked if the man is classified as her brother. One of the few times I ever saw an adult hurry or run on Ifaluk was when a woman bobbing in the lagoon saw her clan brother nearing the beach.[16] Although it is considered acceptable and normal for unmarried men and women to have sexual and romantic rendezvous out in the bush after everyone else has gone to sleep, the utmost discretion and avoidance are required during the daytime. A woman and man who are foolish enough to be observed chatting alone together would be assumed to be arranging a night meeting. Perhaps the greatest culture shock reported to me by Gasugulibung, a young man who had been to Hawaii, was seeing American young people walking hand in hand in the daylight. On first sighting this phenomenon, he said, "I thought to myself that they must be [literally] crazy."

Respect (*siro*) is enjoined at all times in Ifaluk social interaction, but certain kinds of respect behavior are required from women in the presence of men. Women must walk bent over from the waist when approaching or walking past a group of seated men, although men also bend over to some degree when walking among a tightly clustered group of people. Women must also bend forward when passing the island's one large men's house, Katelu. This respect behavior takes its most dramatic form between brothers and sisters. A woman who wishes to move past her seated brother in close quarters (such as within the confines of the house) will crawl on her hands and knees to prevent her head from rising higher than her brother's.[17]

Despite these injunctions to avoidance and respect, women enjoy relatively high status in many domains on Ifaluk. Matrilineality in the tracing of descent and in the inheritance both of household land and buildings and of taro gardens gives women important control of the means of production and of their children. Men distribute the fish that they catch, and women govern the distribution of their garden produce. Matrilocal postmarital residence places a woman in the enviable position of remaining within the alliance and support system of mother, sisters, and others that has developed and will grow through her lifetime. Men come to a marriage with only their fishing gear and their claims to particular coconut trees. Although they play an important role in the lives of their sisters and sisters' children, and although they will receive some of the fruits of their sisters' gardens, men are clearly dependent upon the women of both their natal and their marital households for the bulk of their food and their shelter.

The strength of women's hand in the economy and within the household structure is not mirrored, however, in the ideological realm. Although women's economic contribution to the household is explicitly recognized as fundamental by males, men (and occasionally women) speak of the female as the "needy" gender. To be "needy" (*gafago*) is to require the help of other more powerful or resource-laden persons; to be needy is also to be expected to defer to or obey the commands of those who are less needy (see chap. 4). Women are seen by men as in need of protection, both from some physical dangers (men, for example, will sometimes carry women through the shallow water from canoes to the shore) and from the possible physical aggression of others. Men are seen as having the prerogative of making decisions about their sisters' interisland travel. Some men will also express the opinion that women engage in more "bad talk," or gossip, than men and that they are less knowledgeable about a variety of matters they see as crucial, such as the "things of school."

This ideological portrait of women seems to have come into being partially in response to the influence of Japanese and American colonial practices and cultural influences (see Etienne and Leacock 1980 for an analysis of this pattern in other colonial situations). Under both colonial systems, men were treated as more significant actors than women. They were exclusively selected for schooling under the Japanese, as well as for paid labor under both regimes. The influence of American patriarchal culture on Ifaluk patterns is indexed by the recent actions of the young man mentioned above, Gasugulibung, who had been to Hawaii. Traditionally, each person on Ifaluk has a single primary name unique from any other name of the remembered dead and of the living (see chap. 4). Upon the birth of his first child, however, Gasugulibung assigned his name to both the infant and his wife as a surname. Thirty years ago, Burrows and Spiro (1953) asked a group of men whether men or women "were higher" in rank, status or importance. The men's initial responses were that women were higher because "they have babies." Although women's child-bearing ability continues to be held in very high regard, their position, in ideological terms, appears to have worsened as a result of these historical factors.

It was within the terms of this kind of gender environment that I worked on Ifaluk. Local gender realities were, then, at some odds with my prefieldwork expectations about how I might construct my own gender identity. This was brought home during my initial days on Ifaluk. On the first evening, Tamalekar and my "mother," Ilefagomar, gave me a first elementary primer on what I should and should not do; I should say *siro* (respect, or excuse me) when passing a group of seated people; I should use the tag *mawesh* (sweetheart) when addressing someone; I should crouch down rather than remain standing if others were sitting; and, Tamalekar emphasized, I should not go into the island store if there were more than two men inside. I was to consider myself their daughter, they said, and Tamalekar would from then on refer to me before others as his daughter (*lai sari shoabut*). A week later, a *toi,* or "mass meeting," of the island's men was called; on hearing this, I said that I would like to see it and was brought over to the meeting site by a middle-aged man from the village. Tamalekar was already there. Seeing me, he anxiously asked, "Where are you going?" and looked both uncomfortable and displeased when he heard I was interested in observing the meeting. As direct requests are rarely refused, he did not respond but waved me to sit off to the side by his relatives. With this and subsequent encounters, such all-male occasions soon lost their interest for me, and I spent the great majority of my time with women (particularly those classified as my relatives) in cook huts, gardens, and birth houses.

An index of the extent to which the Ifaluk gender roles I lived with were inconsistent with the freedom with which the anthropological field role is typically portrayed is also found in the events surrounding some liquor that came to the island. While in the field, I had twice been mailed a bottle of liquor by well-meaning friends. The first—a bottle of wine—I shared with the two women who had become my closest friends, but greatly regretted doing so the next day. As women do not drink except in secret and when given the local coconut toddy by one of the men who manufacture it daily, and as we had the misfortune to be observed, Tamalekar and the brothers of the two women were justifiably angry (*song*). When a bottle of whiskey arrived for me many months later, I decided that the best course of action would be to give the bottle to Tamalekar. As he drank from it that evening and became progressively more intoxicated, he repeatedly and it seems pointedly made reference to the fact that his daughter had given him a bottle of liquor.

Although I believe he was relieved that I had done the right thing in the situation (i.e., I had treated my belongings as family belongings and had also avoided a repeat of the conflict and social embarrassment caused by my decision in the previous instance), and although he may have been expressing affection by bringing our kinship to the fore, the affective meaning of that event was and remains fundamentally ambiguous. While cultural traditions provide the conceptual tools with which people can create emotional meaning in each new encounter, the whiskey presented an unusual dilemma for both Tamalekar and myself. That dilemma consisted, it appears, in my having created a novel situation about which neither of us was sure how to feel. The meaning of that event for both Tamalekar and me was profoundly ambiguous, as neither of us could use our previous experiences with gender as reliable guides for behavior in that instance. We were each, no doubt, also deeply ambivalent about the situation, as we both were struggling to avoid a violation of the local, expected gender roles, and yet we wanted to continue our relationship for the rewards that it brought us, as tentative friends and as purveyors of both material and less tangible resources. The most fundamental contradiction that this episode brought to the fore, however, was that between the local definition of me as a needy person by virtue of my femaleness, and my obvious ability to gain access to the outer world and its resources.

The Needy Guest

More than gender structured the methods by which I learned about the Ifaluk. A separate but linked factor in that learning was the way the islanders cope with or manage outsiders who come to visit or to stay on their island. Over at least the past hundred years, the Ifaluk have had to develop techniques and ideas for dealing with not only the German copra trader, Japanese plantation manager, Yapese government representatives, and American Peace Corps volunteers, anthropologists, and occasional travelers but also Carolineans of distant clan affiliations who come to the island for refuge from sea or storm or for marriage. Part of the Ifaluk solution, at least under the less physically coercive conditions of their most recent colonial relationship, has been to make insiders of outsiders as much as possible. While we have already seen how these attitudes toward the outsider were expressed in my case and with regard to gender, male Peace Corps volunteers also have been encouraged to dress and eat in the local style and to observe taboos and other local behavior codes. I was told that at least some islands of Ulithi and Woleai atolls and Fais island require that anyone coming on the islands, including the crew of the interisland ship, wear the local dress of lavalava, or loincloth.[18] This cultural solution contrasts with another possibility, which is to protect one's value system by cordoning off the other into the liminal category of the "foreigner." Under this rubric, a visitor might be seen as one whose unusual behavior is simply different, rather than wrong, and who is seen as situationally acceptable rather than a threat to the system.

Beyond the expectation that outsiders will conform to local custom to a great degree, other Ifaluk notions about the visitor affected my relations in the field. The visitor is seen as someone in need of special "protection." On my first days on Elato, the "chief for foreigners" told me several times, "I am responsible for you" and "I and the one who can help you here." On a visit to Lamotrek from Elato, the man who had taken me there with his family explained to me, immediately on our arrival, that "if anyone asks you to go with them to eat or for anything, you should ask me first because I am responsible for you while you are here and I don't want anything to happen to you." These themes would be repeated again and again throughout my stay on Ifaluk—that an individual or family was responsible for my welfare and that moving freely through the island posed some, often unspecified, danger for me. Several people mentioned, however, the possibility of my hearing "bad talk" (gossip, idle talk) as one of those possible threats. The dangers of physical harm from falling coconuts, stepping into wells or coconut-crab holes, or from the sea may have also been on their minds. And finally, it is likely that my host family also wanted to avoid the social obligations they would incur if I were to accept hospitality widely through the island.

These attitudes toward me were not held simply because I was a female or because I was a non-Carolinean. Similar treatment was accorded another island guest, a young man from the culturally related island of Sonsorol who had returned from high school on Ulithi to stay with an Ifaluk friend and his family. Although he was both male and Carolinean, his friend talked about him as I had been spoken of— as someone who was in need of protection. Several months after his arrival, this friend told me, "I worry about him. I don't like him to go off with other people. I am responsible for him on this island, and so I like him to stay at my house."

Atoll living, as we will see, presents special social and emotional problems for permanent and temporary residents alike. Four hundred and thirty people live on less than one-half square mile of land and in households with an average of thirteen persons in each (and up to twenty one in a single-room dwelling). These close quarters may call for special arrangements for the treatment of diversity and of interpersonal relations of authority and independence. In the absence of the means to escape effectively or easily from interpersonal conflicts, centralized chiefly authority and a clear ranking system with agreed upon implications for dominance and obedience have been extensively developed. It may also be that the Ifaluk and other Carolineans have developed these attitudes toward outsiders in partial response to 100 years of intermitteant colonial contact. Rather than reacting passively to foreign intrusion, the islanders have engaged in both conscious and unconscious strategies of countercontrol. It is this as much as anything else that appears to have created the necessity for incorporating outsiders clearly within the bounds and terms of local authority and local understandings.

What I describe here, then, are the emotions of family life, and particularly of one extended family with whom I lived and ate. They are the emotional lives, often, of groups of women as they planted taro, prepared food, and dealt with infant illness. Often the emotions spoken between young adult women, they are only occasionally, peripherally, or not at all the emotions of men relating to each other as on the open ocean or of lovers in the bush at night. A female guest takes a frequently subordinate position vis-à-vis others, and so this account of the Ifaluk may emphasize more than others would the emotions as seen from below in a system of ranked persons. They are, I hope, the emotions that would appear to me in the context of relationships that—however limited by gender, lack of permanence, and our often different goals—had depth and goodness and led to some understanding and not a little love, a little *fago*.

An Approach to the Cross-Cultural Study of Emotion

The methods chosen by American academics to investigate emotion clearly show the imprint of prevailing cultural assumptions about its nature and about the nature of the person more generally. In the first instance, at least four aspects of Western cultural belief tend to push many researchers away from the topic altogether. Two components of the cultural paradigm surrounding emotion (see chap. 3) create an image of emotion as "antimethod," or as something which is not intrinsically amenable to scientific or social-scientific study. On the one hand, the emotions are seen as irrational, or relatively sense-less. Given this "fact," the prospect of attempting to *make* intellectual sense of them cannot be very attractive. On the other hand, passion is sometimes seen as sacred and as therefore having the ineffability of the sacred. Emotion, as another mode of knowing, does not, or should not, translate into the mundane terms of social-scientific or natural-scientific thought. To "dissect" the emotions through analysis—rather than to elevate them through poetic synthesis—might be seen, therefore, as bordering on the blasphemous. Third, emotion is often viewed as something ultimately and utterly private and as potentially immature, primitive, or even pathological. It therefore may be seen as embarrassing and to be avoided on these grounds as well. And, finally, as Hochschild has pointed out, "through the prism of our technological and rationalistic culture," emotions are an "irrelevancy or impediment to getting things done" (1975:281); they are therefore often left by the wayside when research areas are chosen.

The belief that emotions are at base biological or physical events has led to a concern with laboratory measurements of physiological change, such as in pulse rate, galvanic skin response, and facial musculature (e.g., Ekman, Friesen, and Ellsworth 1972).[19] Although other, more psychological factors, including the experienced feeling state, are correlated with the physical measurements, the latter are seen as unequivocally indexing the presence or absence of an emotion. Evolutionary and adaptationist perspectives and methods have been seen as particularly applicable to the problem of an emotion defined both as physical event and as a primitive survival, and so are especially heavily represented in its study (e.g., Eibl-Eibesfeldt 1980; Izard 1977; Plutchik 1980; Chance 1980). Given the assumption that emotions are physical "things," research has attempted to "isolate" emotions within the person's psychophysiological makeup and, sometimes, to locate them in areas of the brain (e.g., Panksepp 1982).

Western cultural ideas about emotion have also predisposed academic efforts toward focusing on the "psychological" paradigm and on clinical methods. Because emotion is seen as a component of individuals rather than of social situations or relationships, the discipline and methods of psychology have been taken as most appropriate for its study. Clinical methods become especially apropos when much negative emotion is seen, as it often is, as an outcome of unrealistic or irrational worldviews or as a symptom of conflicts and traumas in the individual's past. The connotations of "privacy" with which the concept of emotion is imbued also seem to call for the use of the more "intimate" atmosphere of the clinical method. Emotion, as a phenomenon which happens "inside" the person and as something which is sometimes a "symptom," requires the internal probing of psychological methods and the quasimedical model and methods of the clinician.

Social science has tended to see the study of emotions as somehow more problematic than the study of other social phenomena. This view of the emotions is derived from the Western ethnopsychological framework in which emotions are private, psychological, hidden, interior, and ineffable events. While its signs may show on the face, the emotion event occurs primarily inside the person. Unlike kinship relations or food sharing or religious belief, which are or can be public, the emotions, it has been emphasized, are private. Some analysts have been led by this to speak of two kinds of affect, public sentiment and private emotion, and to restrict their analyses to the former. If this stress on the private, unknowable aspects of emotion is recognized, however, as the reflection of a Western cultural emphasis, the translation of emotion worlds can proceed much like the translation of any other aspect of cultural experience. The point is not to ignore the private but to avoid privileging it or dichotomizing it in relation to the public. Abu-Lughod, whose discussion of Bedouin emotional life is an example of how such an analysis ideally proceeds, discusses the apparent disjuncture between the emotions privately expressed in poetry and those articulated in more public contexts. She rejects the idea that the latter emotions are "structured masks, worn for social approval, while . . . the poetic discourse of weakness [is] a simple reflection of personal experience, of real feelings" (1985:253). Rather, she notes, each of the two discourses takes some conventional form and comments on the other in various ways. Through poetic declarations of weakness, for example, "individuals impress upon others that their conformity to the code [of honor] and attainment of the cultural ideals of personhood are neither shallow, nor easy. . . . [Their] poetry may actually increase the value of the strength and independence individuals do display" (1985:258).

The radical separation of the individual and the social in Western thought and the association of emotion with the former has also meant that the more naturalistic and observational methods of sociology and anthropology have not, until recently, been thought appropriate to the study of emotion. While there has been, ever since Darwin (1872), a tradition of interest in the communicative functions of emotion (e.g., Ekman 1977; Eibl-Eibesfeldt 1980), focus has remained on facial expressions, and their value as signals to others of the organism's physiological changes and behavioral potentials (e.g., for fight or flight).

Where anthropological study of emotion has occurred, the cultural assumption that emotions are universal, natural, and precultural has often led to a reliance on empathy as a method and on the unquestioned use of American-English emotion concepts in descriptions of other cultures' emotional patterns (e.g., Spiro 1952). The usual anthropological concern with the problem of translation, of fundamental importance since Malinowski, is often dropped, and it is dropped out of this belief in emotion's "naturalness."

Anthropological method can also militate against an understanding of the nature of emotion, particularly to the extent that the model of scientific observation of the natural world is used in the field. Both the legacy of positivism and the fact that the anthropologist always remains, to an important extent, an outsider in the field have encouraged the ethnographer to take the role of *detached* observer. Bourdieu has pointed out that the anthropologist's understanding of particular aspects of daily life in another society is profoundly affected by his or her social positioning in the field. The anthropologist's outsider status leads him or her to an "exaltation of the virtues of the distance secured by externality [which] simply transmutes into an epistemological choice the anthropologist's objective situation, that of the 'impartial spectator' . . . condemned to see all practice as spectacle" (1977:1). Renato Rosaldo has linked the detached social position induced by the anthropological paradigm and method with the tendency to view the other's emotional experience as reducible to, or only as important as, its ritual expression (as in funerals). "Thus, in most anthropological studies of death, analysts simply eliminate the emotions by assuming the position of a most detached observer" (R. Rosaldo 1984:189) rather than, for example, taking the position of a mourner. What results, he says, is "the general rule . . . that one should tidy things up as much as possible by wiping away the tears and ignoring the tantrums" (1984:189).

In trying to understand emotional life among the Ifaluk, I was concerned with balancing these past methodological approaches with two other, different emphases. I wanted, first, to focus on naturalistic observations of emotions as they occur in everyday life, and, second, to privilege (in several senses of the term) indigenous conceptualizations of the emotions.[20] The social processes by which particular emotional meanings are negotiated, agreed upon, and used by people in day-to-day encounters were the primary object of study. My field notes were heavily oriented toward recording instances of the use of emotional language or of behaviors locally recognized as signaling emotion and details on the context in which each instance of emotion ascription arose. I was concerned with noting and separating my ascriptions of emotion from ascriptions explicitly made by the Ifaluk. More specifically, the method used was comparative and language based, with emphasis on the pragmatic aspects of emotion language. A brief examination of each feature will help to clarify how the emotional structure of everyday life was examined.

All ethnography is comparative, involving either the implicit or the explicit comparison of the culture of the observer with that of the observed. This shibboleth of anthropological method, however, rarely leads to the simultaneous examination of *both* meaning systems. In this ethnography of emotion, such dual explication involved a consideration of the theories of person, situation, morality, and behavior implicated in, for example, both the concept "anger" and its close Ifaluk relative, the concept of *song* (justifiable anger). Without such explicit comparative treatment, the translations with which we tag indigenous emotion concepts have ambiguous status.

Let me give one example. On Ifaluk, *ker,* the rough equivalent of "happiness," is viewed as amoral, if not immoral. When I first sensed that the Ifaluk felt this way, my surprise signaled more than the fact that I had learned something about how they experience happiness. That surprise also signified that my implicit American ethnotheory of the person and emotion had been violated in one or more particulars—including, specifically, the notion that the pursuit of happiness is a commendable goal (so long, of course, as it is combined with the goal of avoiding inflicting pain on others). The process of translating Ifaluk emotion concepts into English, then, involved comparing the ethnotheoretical propositions affiliated with particular emotion concepts in both the United States and among the Ifaluk. The tendency to treat emotion concepts as conceptual primitives and universals has stood in the way of such explicit comparison in the past.

Emotion has only recently been studied through an examination of the use of language to create and negotiate socially its meaning and to reflect on it.[21] Our understanding of the emotional meanings communicated in social interaction and our understanding of the nature of emotional experience are enhanced through such attention to the speaking of emotions. Previous academic focus on nonverbal and physiological "signs" of emotion follows in part from cultural understandings in which language is considered the tool of logic par excellence, while emotion's "tools" are seen to consist of faces, gestures, and voice quality. Given the existing cultural meaning system, one of the last places we would expect Western researchers to look for emotion is in the speech behavior of individuals.

The methodology of the present study is concerned with bridging that culturally induced gap in our knowledge about the language of emotion. If emotions are to be treated as cultural, social, and moral phenomena, it becomes imperative that we look at the ways cultural groups have come to talk about emotional experience and how they make claims to emotional positions in social interaction. The study of emotion can proceed, as it did in the present study, by focusing on several kinds of speech, including natural discourse, interviews with adults and children on their emotional experiences, and folk definitions of emotion terms.

The study of naturally occurring discourse is coming to be seen as a fundamentally important entrée into a cultural world. This is particularly the case in cognitive anthropology (e.g., Hutchins 1980), where a concern with discourse has begun to replace earlier emphases on elicited language, which was experimentally "neat" but torn from the context of its production. Although tape-recording Ifaluk dialogues would have been ideal, this was impracticable given both my reluctance to intrude into what appeared from my perspective as "private" discourse (however public it in fact might be) and the fact that such interchanges occurred relatively unpredictably rather than within marked and delimited discourse frames. Wherever possible, however, I recorded statements relating to emotion verbatim in my field notes as well as the more general context of surrounding discourse, audience, and event.

A slightly less "natural" but instructive form of discourse generated included interviews with both adults and children on recent experiences that they had understood with the aid of local emotion concepts. The adult interviews, most of which were conducted with women, were transcribed as people spoke, while the child interviews were tape-recorded. People also told me stories prompted by two versions of the Thematic Apperception Test (TAT) cards (one with island scenes, the other with the often vaguely "Western" figures of the Murray TAT cards), and these were transcribed verbatim. The stories were replete with emotion language and repeated emotional themes that recur in Ifaluk myths as well as in everyday life.

The terms used in everyday speech to talk about the states of individuals and relationships are ones people can and do reflect upon and define quite readily. The ways people construe the task of providing a definition may vary widely across cultures and within cultures (see Boehm 1980). The ethnotheories of language and emotion subscribed to by an individual or cultural group will affect the way definitions are constructed. In the case of emotion words, some will use definitions to describe either the social situations or the physiological events, or both, correlated with the emotion concept, while others see a definition as an evocation of the essence of some "thing" referred to by the concept. Another influence will be the way the ethnographer's level of linguistic and cultural understanding is construed by the definition builder. Definitions of fifty-eight emotion-related terms were given to me by a number of people on Ifaluk.[22]

Finally, I learned, by running into painful reminders, of my failure to share emotional assumptions or commitments with the Ifaluk with whom I lived. The incident of the proscribed liquor just described is one example of the misunderstandings that can create understanding by bringing cultural differences to explicit attention. Devereaux (1967) and Crapanzano (1981) have demonstrated that the anxieties generated by human contact are "more productive of insight" (Devereaux 1967:xvii) than anything else. Similarly, Briggs (1970), Rabinow (1977), and Dumont (1978) illustrate how emotional "eruptions" mark progress in their understandings of others. What we might say in other terms is that the emotional response of the field-worker is a culturally informed interpretation—even if it is sometimes one of confusion over the seeming meaninglessness—of what is encountered.

While all these methods were useful, by far the most important was my daily listening to people as they described present and past events to each other and made emotional sense of them. Every ethnographer knows the awe which accompanies this listening, as another way of seeing the world and being with others is revealed, sentence by sentence, conversation by conversation. And so it was for me.

When the emotional content of everyday life is placed in the foreground, as it was by both Ifaluk interest and my own, virtually none of daily discourse and hence none of social life was displaced, as emotion talk ranged from warnings of the "justifiable anger" (*song*) of the chiefs at the violation of taboos by a fisherman, to the prompting of a teenager into acceptance of her new marriage by reference to the "fear/anxiety" (*metagu*) her husband must feel on entering a new household, to the use of declarations of "jealousy/excitement" (*bosu*) to force the redistribution of some tobacco or imported thread that had been in individual hands. Thus, these methods are not peculiarly or in the usual sense "psychological," designed particularly for the study of internal states, but rather they are more standard, ethnographic methods. To study emotion in this way is to study social life and the intense commitments that develop within it.

Let me begin, then, the task of outlining the relationship between emotion and culture by looking at the concept of "emotion" as a Western category. A large number of implicit cultural assumptions are embedded in that concept, and they have been used to structure both our understanding of ourselves and our anthropological descriptions of the people of other societies. Before moving on in further chapters to describe the emotional world of the Ifaluk, it is necessary to examine the paradigm with which Westerners approach the problem of identifying and evaluating emotion, because, as G. H. Mead observed of psychological development, "the others and the self arise in the social act together" (1932:169). Similarly, in the cross-cultural context, Western ideas about the nature of emotion have set the terms for descriptions of the emotional lives of cultural "others."

Taro gardens

Canoe house

A woman weaves an informal wreath for her son's head as she rests after grating coconut

A large group of men help a household move its place of residence

A man walks past a group of women at a feast, slightly *gabaroq* (bent over from the waist in respect)

A mother smiles at the fright of her daughter, who has been told that the photographer has a hypodermic needle in her carrying basket

PART 2

Two Cultural Views of
Emotion and Self

CHAPTER THREE
Emotion, Thought, and Estrangement: Western Discourses on Feeling

The emotion here is nothing but the feeling of a bodily state, and it has a purely bodily cause.
W. *James (1967:110)*

Emotions are the life force of the soul, the source of most of our values . . . the basis of most other passions.
R. *Solomon (1977:14)*

'Joy' designates nothing at all. Neither any inward nor any outward thing.
L. *Wittgenstein (1966:487)*

The extensive discussions of the concept of the emotions that have occurred in the West for at least the past 2,000 years have generally proceeded with either philosophical, religious, moral, or, more recently, scientific-psychological purposes in mind. This discourse includes Plato's concern with the relation between pleasure and the good; the Stoic doctrine that the passions are naturally evil; early Christian attempts to distinguish the emotions of human frailty from the emotions of God; Hobbes's view that the passions are the primary source of action, naturally prompting both war and peace; the argument of Rousseau that natural feelings are of great value and ought to be separated from the "factitious" or sham feelings produced by civilization; the nineteenth-century psychologists' move to view emotions as psychophysiological in nature, with consciousness seen less and less as an important component of the emotions.[1] One of the notable aspects of this discourse is its concern with emotion as essence; whether the passions are portrayed as aspects of a divinely inspired human nature or as genetically encoded biological fact, they remain, to varying degrees, things that have an inherent and unchanging nature. With the exceptions of Rousseau, to some extent, and of Witt-

Portions of this chapter originally appeared in *Cultural Anthropology* 1 (1987), no. 3, and are reproduced by permission of the American Anthropological Association.

genstein more recently, emotions have been sought in the supposedly more permanent structures of human existence—in spleens, souls, genes, human nature, and individual psychology rather than in history, culture, ideology, and temporary human purposes.

I begin here, then, not with a definition of what emotion is but with an exploration of the concept of emotion as a master cultural category in the West. An examination of the unspoken assumptions embedded in the concept of emotion is my first interpretive task for several reasons. It is necessary, first, because the concept of emotion is cultural, which is to say, constructed primarily by people rather than by nature. I explicitly went to conduct fieldwork among the Ifaluk to explore how the people of that atoll experienced emotions in their everyday lives. That concept, therefore, represented one of the primary cultural frameworks through which, or occasionally against which, my understandings of the Ifaluk proceeded. Exploration of the cultural "schema" with which any anthropological observer begins fieldwork provides a methodological key because translating between two cultural systems requires explication of the relevant meaning systems on *both* sides of the cultural divide. The cultural meaning system that constitutes the concept of emotion has been invisible because we have assumed that it is possible to identify the "essence" of emotion, that the emotions are universal, and that they are separable from both their personal and social contexts.

Second, to look at the Euramerican construction of emotion is to unmask how that schema unconsciously serves as a normative device for judging the mental health of culturally different peoples. Despite an assiduous rejection within anthropology of explicit value judgments in the description of other cultural systems, we necessarily import a variety of Western value orientations toward emotions (as good or bad things to have, in particular quantities, shapes, and sizes) whenever we use that concept without alerting the reader to the attitudes toward it that have developed in the West. Such attitudes are *necessarily* evoked in the anthropological audience when the claim is made that "the Xeno people are prone to anger" or that they recognize fewer emotions than do we.

The concept of emotion has this and other sorts of ideological functions; that is, it exists in a system of power relations and plays a role in maintaining it. As we will see, emotion occupies an important place in Western gender ideologies. In identifying emotion primarily with irrationality, subjectivity, the chaotic, and other negative characteristics, and in subsequently labeling women the emotional gender, cultural belief reinforces the ideological subordination of women. The more general ideological role that the concept has played consists in reinforcing the split between "facts" and "values," as cognition, which can theoretically achieve knowledge of facts, is dichotomized in relation to emotion, which is "only" an index of value and personal interest.

The importance of the concept of emotion to Western thinking about self, consciousness, and society is evidenced by the dense network of cultural theories or assumptions that are involved in everyday understanding and use of the word "emotion" and of the terms for the emotions, such as "love," "anger," and "boredom." These assumptions are evident in the number of sources of talk about emotion that the following discussion draws on, including both the everyday and the academic worlds. In examining the cultural foundations of thinking about emotions, I will point particularly to the shared cultural assumptions that unite disputing academic theorists of emotion with each other, and their theories with everyday thought. While there are some significant ways in which those two types of discourse vary, the more important similarities justify treating them equally as products of contemporary social conditions and of the long history of Western thought on the subject. And, although class and ethnicity are no doubt the sources of important variation in the contemporary West in conceptions of emotion, the focus here will be on what I take to be a middle-class Euramerican model.

In this and further references to Western or Euramerican culture, I am speaking about an amalgam of distinct cultural and subcultural traditions whose "unpacking" would allow a better understanding of diversity in beliefs about emotion. Gaines (1982), for example, has identified one important source of variation in theories of the person which is potentially very relevant to cultural beliefs about emotion; he notes two different kinds of understandings of the self and mental disorder, one of which he terms Protestant European and the other, Latin European. Where I do not specify a more precise locus for emotion beliefs (e.g., everyday thought, American academic ideas, etc.), I am hypothesizing a widely shared American ethnotheory of basically Protestant European, middle-class background, which is evident in social-science theorizing, everyday discourse, and clinical-psychological practice.

Emotion against Thought, Emotion against Estrangement

Emotion stands in important and primary contrast relationship to two seemingly contradictory notions. It is opposed, on the one hand, to the positively evaluated process of thought and, on the other, to a negatively evaluated estrangement from the world. To say that someone is "unemotional" is either to praise that person as calm, rational, and deliberate or to accuse them of being withdrawn or uninvolved, alienated, or even catatonic. Emotion is, at one time, a residual category of almost-defective personal process; at others, it is the seat of the true and glorified self. As we will see, these two views represent both a cultural contradiction and a necessary feature of any dualism whose simplicities cannot hold in the face of the demands social processes will put on it. Although each of these two senses of the emotional has played an important role in discourse, the contrast with rationality and thought is currently the more dominant in evaluative force, salience, and frequency of use. It is more often used to damn than to praise, and so I begin with an analysis of that contrast.

The split between emotion and thought goes under several other rubrics, including the more academic and psychological "affect" and "cognition," the more romantic and philosophical "passion" and "reason," and the more prosaic "feeling" and "thinking."[2] The distinction between them takes as central a place in Western psychosocial theory as do those between mind and body, behavior and intention, the individual and the social, or the conscious and the unconscious, structuring (as do those other contrasts) innumerable aspects of experience and discourse. Encoded in or related to that contrast is an immense portion of the Western worldview of the person, of social life, and of morality.

It is first important to note, however, that emotion shares a fundamental characteristic with thought in this ethnopsychological view, which is that both are internal characteristics of persons. The essence of both emotion and thought are to be found within the boundaries of the person; they are features of individuals rather than of situations, relationships, or moral positions. In other words, they are construed as psychological rather than social phenomena. Although social, historical, and interpersonal processes are seen as correlated with these psychic events, thought and emotion are taken to be the property of individuals. Thought and emotion also share the quality of being viewed as more authentic realities and more truly the repository of the self in comparison with the relative inauthenticity of speaking and other forms of interaction.[3]

The contrast drawn culturally between emotion and thought can be outlined initially by looking at the large set of paired concepts associated with the two terms and likewise set in contrast to each other. Thus, emotion is to thought as energy is to information, heart

56

is to head, the irrational is to the rational, preference is to inference, impulse is to intention, vulnerability is to control, and chaos is to order. Emotion is to thought as knowing something is good is to knowing something is true, that is, as value is to fact or knowledge, the relatively unconscious is to the relatively conscious, the subjective is to the objective, the physical is to the mental, the natural is to the cultural, the expressive is to the instrumental or practical, the morally suspect is to the ethically mature, the lower classes are to the upper, the child is to the adult, and the female is to the male. Although people in the West of course vary in the extent to which they would emphasize the connection between emotion and thought and any of these other paired associations, each pair appears as a cultural theme underlying much academic and everyday discussion of the nature of emotion. What is clear is that the evaluative bias in each of the associated pairs follows the bias evident in the distinction of emotion from thought itself, that is, as the inferior is to the superior, the relatively bad to the relatively good.

In the second major contrast set, emotion stands against estrangement or disengagement. The concept pairs that participate in the meaning of this contrast include life against death; community and connection against alienation; relationship against individualism; the subjective against the objective; the natural against the cultural; the authentic against the contrived; commitment and value against nihilism or morality against amorality; and the female against the male. While the emotional is generally treated as the inferior member of the set in the emotion/thought contrast, here the evaluation is reversed. It is better, most would agree, to be emotional than to be dead or alienated.

This sense of emotional is a Romantic one. The nineteenth-century tubercular patient is one cultural exemplar of the value placed then as now on feeling. Tuberculosis was the result of its bearer's "sensitive" soul: "TB was thought to come from too much passion, afflicting the reckless and sensual . . . [It] was celebrated as a disease of passion" (Sontag 1977:21). Emotionality in this sense may be tragic, but it is correspondingly heroic to feel. To be emotional is to understand deeply (even if too deeply) rather than to fail to see and know. If emotion in this sense is not necessarily affiliated with the notion of "rationality," it is at least a cousin to "wisdom."

Popular culture provides examples of the understanding of emotion as antidote to estrangement and of the fear, disdain, or pity often felt for those who do not feel. Science-fiction films and novels often present threatening aliens as characterized by a lack of emotion. In

The Body Snatchers, extraterrestrials take over human bodies, leaving their victims altered in only one fundamental way—they cannot feel.[4] The "cold fish" and the "coldhearted" are cultural types whose most important failing is a lack of warmth. A metaphor for emotionality, warmth is generated by action and feeling. The warm, live person has the heat of emotions; the cold, dead one feels nothing on either side of the grave.

It is natural that emotion is defined by its association with some of the same concepts in both contrast sets. The female, the subjective, and the natural define emotion in both its negative, unthoughtful sense and its positive, involved sense. In the context of the contrast between emotion and estrangement, however, these three qualities are defined and evaluated differently. Where emotion is life, subjectivity is glorified as the source of perception and individuality; the natural becomes the pure and undebased; and the female emerges as the repository of some of the most important human values, including the value of commitment to others.

While these two views of emotion—as the unthoughtful and as the unalienated—might at first appear to represent a logical contradiction, there are other more fruitful ways of conceptualizing the "problem" that the existence of these two contrasts presents. The two can be seen, in psychological context, as being formed by and creating the potential for ambivalence; the emotional is, for individual Americans, simultaneously good and bad, antithought and against estrangement, core of the self and residual effect. The two sets can also be seen as separately activated or drawn on for particular purposes in different contexts, as will be illustrated in a moment. Like their Ifaluk counterparts, these American notions are ideological practices whose meanings are found in the diverse uses to which they are put. The meaning of emotion is sensitive to the context, and particularly the social relations, within which its use occurs (see also chap. 8). The two contrast sets might also be viewed as evidence of, in Turner's (1967) terms, the multivocality of symbols (in this case, emotion) or as akin to the "structure" and "anti-structure" he finds in symbolic systems.

Another way of viewing the existence of these two contrasts is as a sign of the contradictions that pervade everyday life in modern America. We can link them to the contradictions which Crawford (1985) finds expressed in the prevalence of drug abuse, eating disorders, and the "health craze." He sees such things as anorexia and jogging as routes to the traditional self-control and productivity enjoined on us, in part, as a result of the need for properly socialized workers. In line with our role as consumers, we are contrarily expected to indulge ourselves and to see pleasure as a right, a cultural value that in many cases shades easily into substance abuse and binge eating. The conceptualization of emotions evidences the same contradiction between the emphasis on rationality, control, and order and the promotion of the pleasure *and* pain of emotion. Emotions can be viewed as good and natural "appetites," as consuming passions, or as impediments to the rational, anonymous organization of labor. Finally, the two views of emotions are evidence that any dualism cannot sustain itself in the face of the massive complexities of time, place, context, and purpose into which it is drawn. American culture cannot maintain a single account of emotion as the irrational or the nonthoughtful, just as it cannot consistently hold apart the dualistic poles of mind and body, self and other, male and female, or private and public.

We will see here and in further chapters that each element and combination of elements that make up the concept of emotion emerge out of everyday social practices in American society. These practices include bureaucratic activities, the separation of the family and the marketplace, relations between women and men, cultural pluralism, and the relative anonymity of much social interaction. In each, different pieces of the cultural system of emotional understanding come into use and help to form and re-form the nature of those social patterns. In circumstances such as formal schooling, the view of emotion as opposite thought comes more to the fore; in others, such as some relations in private, emotion is more likely to be set against estrangement. We can now explore in more depth these concepts that give the idea of emotion its complexity, its ambivalence, and its social utility.

Emotion as the Irrational

One of the most pervasive cultural assumptions about the emotional is that it is antithetical to reason or rationality. An evaluative concept, rationality is generally used to talk about actions and ideas that are "sensible," that seem sane or reasonable, and that are based on socially accepted ways of reasoning about problems. Rationality is closely related to intelligence, which in Euramerican thought is defined as the ability to solve problems, particularly those whose assigned parameters are technical rather than social or moral (Lutz and LeVine 1983). Rationality is, then, culturally associated more with practical action in the world than with contemplation or feeling. Both rationality and intelligence are taken as signs of mental vigor and of the potential for success in one's endeavors; both are morally approbated.

To be emotional is to fail to process information rationally and hence to undermine the possibilities for sensible, or intelligent, action. Mr. Spock of *Star Trek* fame, whose emotionlessness is part and parcel of his superior Vulcan intelligence, is one of many examples in contemporary popular culture which express the contradiction Americans see between rationality and emotion (D'Andrade 1981:190). While it can be said that a particular thought is irrational and that emotions in certain cases make sense, everyday discourse places much more stock in the ability of thought to contribute to rational action. Emotions tend predominately to lead either to erroneous judgments and hence senseless, irrational actions, *or* they remain internal feeling states which organize no action, initiate no problem solving, constitute no rationality. Although "reasons why" an emotion occurs may be posited, emotion is only rarely viewed as reasonable, as problem solving, or as rational. People tend to see emotion as a disruption of, or barrier to, the rational understanding of events. To label someone "emotional" is often to question the validity, and more, the very sense of what they are saying.[5] Even positive emotions are sometimes viewed as irrational. Interviews with Americans about their love for their spouses show that the reasons why one loves the other are sometimes not considered understandable. Said one man, "Why I should fall in love with Eileen and why she should fall in love with me, and why that should be so binding on our lives, has been something where there's not much of a rational explanation" (Quinn 1987:35).

It is clearly possible in this culture to make distinctions of degree with regard to the relationship emotion has with rationality (and with most of the other concepts described here). Some academic psychological research, for example, has made use of this less dichotomous view of emotion and reason in detailing how "intelligent" (or rational) performance of tasks is minimized only by an overly high level of emotional "activation" (e.g., Emde 1980). This tendency can also be seen in the psychologist Lazarus's (1977) emphasis on the coping and cognitive aspects of emotion and the philosopher Solomon's (1977) thesis that reason consists in reflection on emotion. What predominates in Euramerican discourse on emotion, however, is a more binary view of emotion. One either is or is not experiencing an emotion; emotion therefore either is or is not an impediment to rationality.

When emotion is devalued, its inherent irrationality leads to its association with the idea of chaos. While thought and rationality produce predictability and order, comparatively little rhyme, reason, or pattern are to be found in emotion and irrationality. This cultural notion is seen in common metaphors used for talking about feeling; we speak of having "tangled emotions," of emotions "swirling" inside us, of "exploding" in anger, of the grieving person "falling apart," or of being "mixed up" because of emotional experience. Emotion's chaos is, however, sometimes the base from which positive knowledge, rational maturity, and civilization itself emerge. The emotional chaos of Freud's unconscious mind and Durkheim's "collective effervescence" are the roots of the rational orders of the reality principle and social organization.

The chaos of emotion is linked with other features of the category beyond its irrationality. The chaotic energy of emotions makes them dangerous to anyone in their vicinity and weakens the person experiencing them, a notion we will explore in more detail in a moment. Emotion's chaotic nature is also the result of the culturally prevalent idea that, as Hillman notes, "emotion [is] simply excess, and as the excess of anything can be disordering, emotion [is] disorder" (1960:207).[6]

When the emotions are valued, what was their irrationality becomes their mystery. The mystery of love and other emotions is then not frustrating because unfathomably irrational, but romantic confirmation of the value of emotion in combating an overly prosaic and rationalized world. During the 1988 presidential campaign, Joseph Biden was interviewed by a reporter who confronted him with what she claimed was his reputation for being emotional—for being in some people's terms "a man of passion" and, in others', a "hothead." One political pundit the newscaster interviewed remarked that the Democratic candidate is typically "emotive" and therefore eschews "cool reason" and has less "command of the substantive issues" than others who instead favor use of "brain matter." In response to this commentator, who not incidently was a Republican opponent, Biden complained that "unless you're antiseptic and clinical, people think you're not thoughtful." This political exchange acquires meaning from the dualism of emotion and reason and the importance of emotion in both defining and evaluating the person; the basic disagreement is structured by the alternative ways of evaluating emotion we have been exploring. Biden symbolically associates an absence of emotion, not with problem solving or thoughtfulness, but with the rarefied, even "bloodless" world of the death-dealing hospital. He draws on the cultural association of passion with life; of its lack, with sterility and death. From this perspective, to be too clinical is to follow the medical model in its often culturally offensive form of diagnosing and treating problems rationally without any feeling for the person with the problem. His Republican respondent may have had the upper hand, however, in drawing on the more powerful notion, particularly in public contexts, that emotion blocks reason. In this view, the goal *is* precisely to aspire to the cultural style and stature of the cooly rational clinician.

Rather than viewing rationality as intelligence and natural order, however, we may define it more critically as the historically and culturally determined assessment of how a sensible, or fully mature, human ought to behave. Emotion, therefore, becomes a residual category used to talk about deviations from the dominant definition of the sensible or intelligible. For this reason, the rationality whose increasingly technical definition has been identified as one of the primary ideological underpinnings of the Western states is simultaneously a rationality from which the concept of emotion is excluded. When the emotional is defined as irrational, all those occasions and individuals in which emotion is identified can be dismissed, and when the irrational is defined as emotional, it becomes sensible to label "emotional" those who would be discounted. In this society, those groups which have traditionally "been conceived of as passional beings, incapable of sustained rationality" (Fleming 1967) include "infants, children, adolescents, mental patients, primitive people, peasants, immigrants, Negroes, slumdwellers, urban masses, crowds, and most of all, women" (Schudson 1978:129), as well as such contemporary additions as terrorists. Emotion becomes an important metaphor for perceived threats to established authority; the emotionality of repressed groups becomes a symbol of their antistructural tendencies. To the powerful, this is their chaos; to the groups themselves, it is their impulse toward freedom. The significance of this process will be explored below in relation to the culturally drawn connection between the female and emotion. The process takes on added importance when we consider in a moment that moral and critical impulses are often inextricably bound up with emotional ones. As a result, the cultural status of women and of moral critique becomes as endangered as that of emotion.

Emotion as Unintended and Uncontrollable Act

Emotion is conceptualized as something wild and uncontrollable, something whose occurrence is involuntary. In everyday discourse, we speak of being "swept away" by emotions, of those whose emotions "get the best of them," of being "under the influence" of one's emotions, and of being "helplessly" in love or "hopelessly" confused. These metaphors (cf. Lakoff and Johnson 1980) are consistent with the view of emotions as biological imperatives; external or internal events "trigger" our emotional switches virtually automatically. Although we are generally required to attempt to control their expression, emotions are conceptualized as resisting our attempts to do so. Thoughts may, in somewhat parallel fashion, "come to" us unbidden, but they neither move inexorably nor distort the self in the way that emotions are conceptualized as doing, and they are more easily disposed of. Thus, emotions, in contrast to thoughts, predominantly *happen to* the person and are, therefore, not fully intentional.

The notion of intentionality plays a central role in our view of the nature of individual responsibility. Any antisocial behavior that is less than fully intentional is less than fully reprehensible or punishable in both legal and more general cultural terms. The primarily unintentional nature of emotional response, then, has important consequences for American cultural interpretations of the emotional person. Although the executive or cognitive self may be called upon to rein in emotional responses (as when we advise other people to "get a grip on" themselves when emotional or to "stop feeling sorry for" themselves), if one is overcome by the material conditions of the self, which include emotions, responsibility is diminished. The dominance of the view of emotion as unintended and uncontrollable event is also clear in such phenomena as the readiness to acquit or countenance leniency for those accused of "crimes of passion." This divorcing of the emotions from mechanisms of control and from individual will has been bemoaned by observers from Sartre to Kagan who note that this view of emotion tends unnecessarily to absolve the individual of responsibility for that behavior which results from emotions (Averill 1974; Kagan 1978; Sartre 1948; Solomon 1977).[7] It is important to note, however, that responsibility does not evaporate in the face of emotional experience and behavior. The general cultural devaluation of emotion has also meant that the person who displays emotion may sometimes be held accountable for that display. Those individuals, for example, whose failure to control emotion is viewed as characterological in origin are seen as having a weakness which, however congenital, is nonetheless blameworthy.

A clear and interesting dilemma or contradiction is present in these cultural views. On the one hand, emotion is conceptualized as based in a physical reaction much like a sneeze or a burp; it cannot be controlled by thought which, being immaterial, is seen as operating in a separate realm of existence. Alternatively, we sometimes speak as if emotion *can* be reasoned away. This cultural ambivalence is evidenced in the academic and clinical psychological literature, where "cognitive" therapies (Beck 1967; Ellis 1962) compete with drug or cathartic treatments for emotional disorders. In the former, painful emotions are conquered by the individual's altering the way he or she thinks, cognition being more easily controlled and thereafter "trumping" (Bailey 1983) emotion. In the latter, externally induced organismic or subsequent emotional changes provide the main route to elimination of emotional pain, with the person's only responsibility being to "submit to" therapy.

Emotion as Danger and Vulnerability

Emotion is related to vulnerability in two ways. First, the emotional person presents a threat to the thoughtful person, and second, the emotional person is him- or herself made vulnerable by the experience of emotion. Let us explore each of these cultural twists in turn.

Because a rational individual does what is "sensible," she or he is also predictable and, therefore, safe. The danger of emotion for the person observing it in the other lies in the belief that someone who is acting on the basis of emotional impulses is being led by an unreliable and senseless guide. Emotion is said to "blind" people (and we are blinded by both love *and* rage). Those individuals can be expected, as a result, to stumble crazily through social life, potentially harming the delicate and proper social coordination that has been achieved by the application of reasoned thought.

The danger of one person's emotion for the other also derives from the fact, just explored, that people who are emotional cannot be said to be in control of or responsible for their actions. Behavior that is not under the control of the executive self is behavior that can be expected to be less than fully socialized and, therefore, to be dangerous. The underlying assumption here is that the unsocialized self consists, in the main, of antisocial, self-serving, and aggressive impulses. The emotions are dangerous because they push against the restraints of the socialized, cognitive self. This image, elaborated in Freud's writing and in everyday discourse, is consistent with the association of the emotions with all that is precultural and presocial, which is to say, with the natural in its brutish and Darwinian forms.

Emotion also creates, or derives from, vulnerability in the subject. People are conceptualized as being "overpowered," "buffeted," "eaten away" by or "at the mercy" of their emotions. Emotions act on the individual rather than vice versa; the person is thereby dominated—his or her weakness is both produced and demonstrated by that emotion. People who experience emotion are also weakened because their behavior, being unreasonable, cannot advance them in the pursuit of sensible goals.

Emotion's being linked to weakness is an expression of the ideological role of the culturally constructed split between emotion and thought. It is the "weak" who are emotional, and although that weakness is often defined characterologically, it is the dominated members of this social system (such as women, children, and the lower classes) who are primarily defined as experiencing emotion, both in general and to excess. This purported emotionality, given its association with weakness as well as irrationality, is used to justify the exclusion of these individuals from positions of power and responsibility and to legitimize their disadvantaged social and economic positions.

It is also important to point out that by virtue of having what we conceptualize as physical force, emotion can be seen as creating a feeling of strength rather than weakness in the individual. Sartre (1948) points to this phenomenon when he characterizes the emotions as "magical transformations of the world." This view of emotion, although not culturally elaborated to any great degree, is culturally comprehensible within the framework of the more positive social evaluation of emotion that occurs when it is counterposed to estrangement. When emotion is viewed as a source of life, it is also viewed as having the *powers* of life, as being the source of all personal energy. The disengaged or alienated person, on the other hand, is one who has lost the energizing and interest-forming force of emotion. In losing this, she or he has lost access to the fundamental source of movement, purpose, and power in the world.

Emotion as Physicality

The concept of emotion bears a somewhat paradoxical relationship to that of the physical. It draws in the first instance, on the mind/body dichotomy that pervades Western thought, and is identified with physical feeling and the body in contrast with thought, which is seen as purely mental. This cultural view is evident in the predominance of physical images in talk about emotions ("his stomach knotted up," "she was fuming," "his eyes popped out of his head"); in the emphasis on the link between emotions and hormones; and in the linked contrasts of emotion and energy with thought and information. Images of emotions as so many BTUs (and hence of an earlier, more primitive

65

industrial age) contrast with images of thought as computer processing (and the more contemporary and advanced information age).[8] Although both sets of images can be seen as reifying, thought is overall viewed less physically than emotion. When combined with the idea that it is through the mental that we have distinguished ourselves from lower forms of life, this factor represents another way in which emotion is devalued.[9]

The emphasis on this association between the emotional and the physical is especially strong in twentieth-century academic psychology. Take, for example, the definition given by Tomkins, whose view of emotion is one of the most influential of the contemporary psychological theories: "Affects are sets of muscular and glandular responses located in the face and also widely distributed throughout the body, which generate sensory feedback that is either inherently 'acceptable' or 'unacceptable'" (1980:142). Lévi-Strauss also draws on this cultural connection when he writes, "Emotions . . . are always *results* either of the power of the body or the impotence of the mind" (1963:71). Although cognitive theories of emotion have been developed more recently (e.g., Beck 1971; Lazarus 1977; Mandler 1975) in an attempt to balance the other view with a concern for the ways cognition regulates emotion, "feelings" or perceived physiological state changes remain central to the definition of emotion in these theories as well. An example of this is found in the work of Kleinman, who defines two types of emotion, including "primary" affects, or "uncognized universal psychobiological experiences" (1980:173), which are transformed into "secondary" (and culturally specific) affects through cognitive processes of perception, labeling, and evaluation.[10]

Although this way of looking at the relationship between the emotions and the physical predominates in American culture, emotions are associated, in their positive but secondary sense of the engaged, with the spiritual and the sublime. To have feelings is to be truly human, which is to say, transcendent of the purely physical. Whereas emotions stand in close relationship to the instinctual when contrasted with cognition, they emerge as opposed to the animalistic and physical connotations of the instinctual when contrasted with what can be called the spiritual death of estrangement.

Emotion as Natural Fact

Closely related to the Euramerican view of emotion as a physical event is the idea that emotions are more natural, and hence less cultural, than thought. This view of emotion is obviously dependent first upon the nonuniversal distinction, elaborated in particular forms in the West, between nature and culture (Wagner 1981; MacCormack and Strathern 1980). Culture or civilization is seen predominantly as a conscious, cognitive process; emotion then takes its place as the natural complement to cultural processing—as material which culture may operate upon, but which is not culture. We speak of emotions as "raw," as "wild," and as "primitive forces"; they are the natural, aboriginally untouched by the cooking, taming, and civilizing of culture. Needham, for example, sees the diverse vocabularies of emotion developed in many societies as necessarily "wrong" about the feelings they purport to describe; this is so, he claims, because feelings, being natural and universal, exist at a level that is unaffected by the cultural modes of thought expressed in those vocabularies (Needham 1981:23). The emphasis on emotion as physical feeling means that the transformations wrought by culture on the affective base (as on the physical base) become "secondary," as in Kleinman's formulation (see also Levy 1984). An interest in the emotional aspects of culture—in raising the (for us, paradoxical) association of the two concepts—has necessitated the introduction by some anthropologists of the idea of "sentiment," or culturalized emotion, and the sharp distinction between it and private, natural feeling or emotion (see, e.g., Fajans 1985).[11]

The ambivalent or multivalent stances taken toward emotion in the West result in part from variation across individuals and across time in the conceptualized relationship between, and evaluation of, nature and culture. Strathern has noted about this variability that "at one point culture is a creative, active force which produces form and structure out of a passive, given nature. At another, culture is the end product of a process, tamed and refined, and dependent for energy upon resources outside itself. Culture is both the creative subject and the finished object; nature both resource and limitation, amenable to alteration and operating under laws of its own" (1980:178). Emotions are seen in fundamentally the same way. Thus, emotions are alternately the pliant material on which acculturative and cognitive forces have their way (e.g., in the theories of Beck 1967 and Hochschild 1983),[12] or they are, almost literally in many theories of emotion (e.g., Zajonc 1980), the energy which animates otherwise lifeless cultural forms. These two possibilities may help account for the observation that emotions are "sometimes . . . treated [in the American folk model] as things 'triggered' by experience, and at other times as things 'created' by experience" (D'Andrade 1987:127).

It is the view of emotion as creative energy that is particularly drawn on when emotion is being discussed in contrast with alienation. Here, the unemotional or disengaged is seen as an unnatural or cultural mode of being. While emotional response is still taken to be natural, the evaluations attached to the natural have taken on a much more positive tone. In the Romantic tradition, the natural (including emotion) is depicted as synonymous with the uncorrupted, the pure, the honest, the original. Nature and emotion are seen as fountains of high truths, while culture, conscious thought, and disengagement are all viewed as disguise, artifice, or vise—as themselves the limitations which are more commonly seen as characteristic of nature and emotion. When emotion is seen as natural in this positive sense, thought and its offshoot, social speech, come to be seen as less authentic and less "really real." It is only uncognized, unexpressed emotion that is truly natural, then, as it has not been reached and disturbed or warped by cultural conventions for the conscious experience or display of emotion.

This cultural view is evident in the speech presidential candidate Jesse Jackson made at the 1984 Democratic National Convention. Attempting to apologize for remarks insulting to Jewish voters, he asked that the public "Charge it [the mistake] to my head, not to my heart." Jackson was saying not only that he "thought" rather than "felt" the insult but also that the attitude revealed by the remark was not his "real" attitude, not his natural way of approaching the world. His apologetic appeal could only be understandable if things of the heart (the emotions) are commonly seen as the true, real seat of the individual self, and things of the head (thoughts) as relatively superficial, socially influenced aspects of the self.

It is important to add a secondary proviso to this characterization of Jackson's apology. While his statement is consistent with and revealing of these American cultural views of emotion as the site of the true self, the appeal that it entailed may have had limited success in convincing his audience because of some other aspects of those cultural views. In particular, Jackson, like Biden, may have disregarded the fact that such positive views about emotion and the implied denigration of thought are not appropriate for males in this society. A failure of the appeal to convince most Americans is probably likely, as well, given the dominance of the more negative model for understanding the emotion/thought relationship.[13] Finally, black men, like women of all races, are more liable to be labeled emotional in the negative sense. Both blacks and females in the public domain can refer to emotion positively only at some risk of being further discounted.

The view of the naturalness of emotions is evident in psychological theory where, for example, Tomkins defines as "pseudoemotion" any emotion which is at all socially constrained or suppressed, which is not "unconditionally free[ly] vocalized" (Tomkins 1979:208). Elsewhere, in Freud's theories, emotion plays the role of the natural counterpart to the civilization of thought; for him, emotion is generated within its own domain, and thought (like culture) emerges, in Strathern's terms, as "finished object." It is also evident in an important strain of academic and popular art theory in which "aesthetic emotion" is seen as the authentic and natural response to the image and intellectualization as its cultural threat (Burgin 1986:31). A natural, unmediated taste or feeling for art is valued over a cultivated and cognitive one.

The culturally constructed "naturalness" of emotion has also had the effect of making Westerners less reticent about attributing universal emotional abilities to others than they have been about ascribing particular cognitive abilities to all humans. This tendency to infer more readily what non-Westerners are "really feeling" than to claim that they are really thinking something other than what they claim to think is in part the result of the belief that natural processes are more invariant than cultural ones and, therefore, that emotions are both more uniform cross-culturally, and less culturally malleable, than thought. This view is developed most fully by those universalists for whom emotion's naturalness has been further confirmed by such theories as the sociobiological or psychodynamic. Spiro (1953), for example, claims that the Ifaluk really feel anger or hostility, though they mask it with fear. Freeman (1983) sees the occasional angry displays of Samoan orators at the island's competitive speaking events as demonstrations of the natural rage that any creature feels after dominance attempts by others. Freeman's analysis of Samoan behavior makes use not only of this assumption of the invariance of the natural features of humanness but of the idea that emotion is both natural and ultimately uncontrollable. In speaking of Samoan aggression in warfare, Freeman approvingly quotes from the ethnologist Krämer, who, at the turn of the century described how the "violent passions" of the Samoans were "set recklessly free" in wartime (Krämer 1903, quoted in Freeman 1983:166), turns of phrase which obviously imply the naturalness—weakly controlled—of emotions. For Freeman, the natural (like the emotional) is the more active member of the nature/culture set; the following quotation makes evident his implicit use of the cultural idea that nature's emotions are also a dark, animalistic force.[14]

> On some occasions the chiefs I was observing would, when contending over some burning issue, become annoyed and then angry with one another. By intently observing their physiological states . . . I was able, as their anger mounted, to monitor the behavior of these chiefs in relation to their use of respect language. From repeated observations it became evident that as chiefs became angry they tended to become *more and more polite*. . . . Occasionally, however, the conventions of culture would fail completely, and incensed chiefs, having attained to pinnacles of elaborately patterned politeness, would suddenly lapse into violent aggression . . . [T]he conventional behavior is replaced, in an instant, by highly emotional and impulsive behavior that is animal-like in its ferocity.
>
> (Freeman 1983:300–301)

In sum, emotions are primarily conceived of as precultural facts, as features of our biological heritage that can be identified independently of our cultural heritage. Although there is variation in the *evaluation* of the effect of culture and the natural substrate of our emotions on each other, the element of natural emotion counterposes itself to either the civilization of thought or the social disease of alienation and forms the basis for much everyday and academic talk about emotions. The questions that are then asked concern the relationship between a natural fact—the affective response—and the cultural facts, including cultural beliefs and social institutions.

Emotion as Subjectivity

Emotions are viewed as constituting subjectivity in several of the senses in which the term "subjective" is used.[15] In the first instance, they are subjective in the sense of biased. To say of individuals that they are acting emotionally is to say that they are acting on the basis of a personal interest which is inconsistent with the wider interest they ought to consider. From this perspective, emotion necessarily creates bias in a way that thought does not; while thought may be subjective in the sense of being individual and unique perceptions, it does not by its nature distort judgment, as emotion does. Emotion, as we have noted, blinds the individual to judgments that she or he *ought* to make, causing thereby both a failure of perception and potential social disruption. As bias pushes individuals to pursue goals that accord *only* with their own views, the emotional/subjective person may thwart the attainment of more global, social, objectively determined, and valid goals.

This view of emotion as subjective is related to the notion that ideally one can and should know the world best by achieving a timeless, transcendent, decentered, and unpositioned knowledge. This, the knowledge of positive science, is not seen as the only way to know, but it is seen as the most effective, the most mature. Objective knowledge can be "seen" by all in a way that the emotional cannot; objective knowledge is absolute and unchanging, while the emotional is particular to a time and place and embedded in the individual's moment and point of view. This is in contrast to many other cultural systems which emphasize the irreducibly person-centered or relationship-centered nature of knowing (Shore 1982). The Western views of rationality, as we have already seen, and of morality, as we will see, participate in this same system which is crucially connected by the view of emotion as subjectivity.

The second sense in which the emotions are subjective consists in the idea that emotions constitute the perspective of the individual on events. This notion has several implications which are more positive than those associated with bias. In particular, the subjectivity of emotions in this sense gives them a fundamental—even sacred—role in individuating the person. Given the importance, in the American value system, of the individual personality, this aspect of emotions elevates them to a special place.

The emotions create the possibility for this individuality in at least two ways. First, they constitute individual opinion. It is only I who have these particular emotions, opinions, and values. From this perspective, emotions are *Me* in a way that thoughts are not. Because thoughts can be objective, they will be the same in whatever mind they appear. Feelings, however, are subjective; they therefore are not completely communicable, and very possibly are uniquely my own. It is, then, impossible, in the parlance of this culture, to speak literally about "*our* emotions" or, conversely, to speak of someone as an individual who is not unique, a uniqueness which is achieved in part through his or her emotions.

Second, the emotions stand for individual privacy or inviolability. Feelings, it is thought, cannot truly or absolutely be known except through self-revelation, that is, except through a decision on the part of the individual who experiences the emotion to discuss it. It is not possible to ascertain conclusively what someone else is feeling solely on the basis of observation. Americans will in fact often react vehemently to any attempt that is construed as "telling me what I feel"; only the subject can truly know his or her own emotions. Self-revelation of emotion is made both necessary and problematic, first, by the fact that it is considered much more difficult to communicate accurately one's feelings than one's thoughts (since thoughts can be objective) and, second, by the fact that the emotions are treated as the private property of the self. Individuals are sacred only insofar as each of them "owns" his or her particular and distinct set of emotions. Belief in emotion's privacy is somewhat qualified by other ideas which outline how it *is* possible to know what someone else is feeling without the other's telling us or even wishing us to know. Faces, body gestures, and tone of voice are then foregrounded as relatively involuntary indices, or "leakages," of the person's internal states.

The subjectivity of emotions is clearly connected to both their irrationality and their problematic morality. One cultural domain in which this is articulated is journalism. In a social history of American newspapers, Schudson (1978) shows how an ideal of objectivity arose in newswriting by the turn of the twentieth century, an ideal which entailed the separation of facts and values as well as a shift from a story-based to an information-based type of reporting. The new journalism was not supposed to arouse passions but rather to feed the mind with facts and information. Many papers then and now continued, however, to publish stories that were construed as emotional and moral-laden. The contrast between the objective *New York Times* and the subjective *New York Post,* for example, can be seen as a "moral division of labor between newspapers" which "may parallel the moral division of the human faculties between the more respectable faculties of abstraction and the less respectable feelings. People control themselves to read of politics in fine print; they let themselves go to read of murders or to look at drawings of celebrities. Information is a genre of self-denial, the story one of self-indulgence" (Schudson 1978:119).

We can also note with Schudson, however, that taste (whether for types of human faculties like thought and feeling, or for newspapers) is not only cultural in origin but also class specific. Those who prefer the subjective and emotional journalism of the *Post* tend, at least by reputation, to be middle and working class, while the *Times* from its inception has cultivated an upper-class or upwardly-mobile-class readership. The moral struggle between affect and thought was drawn into, then, the moral struggle between objective versus subjective journalism and social science; both kinds of oppositions are drawn on in the struggle between social classes.

Emotion as Female

American culture brims with images and discussions of the emotionality of women. Women are much more likely than men to be portrayed crying in movies and smiling broadly in advertisements. Similarly, the classic justification for the traditional exclusion of women from the office of the American presidency has prominently included the notion that women are "too emotional." Attitude surveys have demonstrated that Americans believe that women are both more intrinsically emotional and more emotionally expressive than men. Women are also thought to be better able to control or manipulate their feelings consciously—"to have the capacity to premeditate a sigh, an outburst of tears, or a flight of joy" (Hochschild 1983:164). Studies also show that men, who in general hold more extreme gender-role stereotypes (Rubin, Provenzano, and Luria 1974), see women as more emotional than women see themselves. This belief may do much to organize important social evaluations. Intense and sometimes adverse public speculation arose, for example, when Jacqueline Kennedy did not cry at her husband's funeral. More striking was the scorn that greeted the report that Edmund Muskie cried publicly in the midst of his presidential campaign.[16]

American cultural belief does not deny that men may become emotional. It docs, however, engender expectations that men will experience only certain types of emotion, notably, anger. Women are expected to experience the entire range of emotions, with the possible exception of hate and anger, more frequently and deeply. Hochschild has pointed out that men's emotions are also interpreted differently from those of women. A man's anger will usually be seen as more *important* (i.e., as requiring attention) simply because he is culturally defined as a more important person. The emotions of men are also seen as more *explicable* in terms of the situation in which they find themselves (i.e., the anger is seen as "called for" by the context in which it occurred) (Hochschild 1983:172–73). While women's emotion is seen as characterological, men's is seen (when it occurs) as situational and, hence, sensible.

These cultural beliefs are also found in force in the clinical and academic psychological communities. Garai, for example, claims that women are "naturally" more emotional than men, that "the stronger aggressiveness of males and the greater susceptibility of females to fear appear to have a genetic origin" (1970:126). An experimental study by Broverman, Broverman, and Clarkson (1970) found that clinical psychologists in the United States describe "healthy" women as more excitable and emotional than men, as having their feelings more easily hurt, and as being less objective (and for that reason disliking mathematics and science). Moreover, the traits seen as indicative of mental health in a male not only diverged from those considered normal or usual in a female but were virtually indistinguishable from those seen by the clinicians as healthy in an adult whose gender was unspecified.

From the more general cultural theories about the nature of women and emotion, Parsons and Bales (1955) drew the categories with which they characterized male and female roles in the family. This study, one of the most widely cited in the post–World War II sociological literature on gender, describes women as "expressive" (or emotional) and men as "instrumental" (read pragmatic, utilitarian, rational, cognitive). Parsons and Bales claim that a woman's expressiveness is linked to and required by the necessity that she be a "willing and 'accommodating' person," thereby being supportive of the male in his role of "technical performer" (1955:51). This cultural order of concepts is presented by these sociologists as the scientific, or natural, order of things.[17] Such "naturalization" of *any* social fact is the ideological strategy par excellence; this is evident in the academic and everyday portrayal of the sources of gender roles, of performance on IQ tests, and of the formation of socioeconomic classes.

Most of the concepts associated with emotion, including particularly irrationality, are implied by the statement that women are more emotional than men. When women are said to be emotional, their inferiority is also generally asserted, given the general cultural devaluation of emotion. It should be noted that I am not claiming that the negative evaluation of emotion leads to a negative evaluation of women because women are (objectively) emotional but rather that the ideologies of gender and of self and emotion reinforce each other on the question of where weakness and inferiority are to be found. The socially and ideologically weak position of women is indexed by the company that they keep when emotion ascription takes place. For example, Havelock Ellis (1929) noted that among women, "as among children, savages, and nervous subjects," the emotions are dominant reflexes. Although his statement is dated, it mirrors the common and contemporary cultural associations among the female, the subordinate, and the emotional.

The association of the female with the emotions is reinforced by the "naturalness" that the two purportedly share. The view of men and of cognition as each more cultural and more civilized con-

74

trasts with the primeval associations of the concepts of the female, the emotions, and nature, each of which is simpler, more primitive, and more antistructural than the male, cognition, and culture. Women's greater naturalness is thought by many in this culture to derive from their child-bearing and child-rearing roles (e.g., Ortner 1974). More important, the portrait of the natural woman is painted with the implicit cultural assumption that the achievements of nature are overshadowed by the achievements of civilization.

The dual interpretations that have been applied to the concept of nature take on the same important role here in constructing the female. Women, like their emotionality, have been seen alternately as pure or as debased by virtue of their naturalness. On the one hand, nature is weak, making women (and emotion) weak. We speak of "fragile ecosystems" and of a distraught woman being "in a fragile state." The weakness of women, nature, and emotion, then, requires protection and control. A woman's emotionality, originally attributed to the greater internal mobility of her bodily organs, and particularly her uterus, is today associated with the hormones. A woman's naturalness may make her, on the other hand, strong and dangerous, although no more positively evaluated; shifting uteri and hormones wreak the same havoc as thunderstorms, avalanches, and other natural phenomena. Nature, it is said, has less fury than a woman scorned, that is, than a woman who is emotionally upset. The ambivalence that the association between women and nature generates is clear in contemporary Euramerican thought, as it was in the discourse of eighteenth- and nineteenth-century Britain and France, a discourse that Jordanova says characterized women as at once "tougher *and* softer, more vulnerable *and* more tenacious of life than men" (1980:49).

Contrast the ideologically dominant view of the relationship between women and emotion that I have been discussing up to this point with the cultural perspective that emerges in those moments and groups which emphasize the emotion–estrangement dichotomy. Here, women's greater perceived capacity to experience emotion is seen as an index of their spiritual superiority and of the lesser degree of their alienation. The ideological placement of women in the domestic sphere in nineteenth-century Europe and America and the association of men with the disenchanted world of industry was accompanied by the notion that women's more sensitive emotional nature was the family's treasure and resource (as, e.g., in Parsons and Bales 1955). Here, the concept of nature takes on its Rousseauian sense and, as a consequence, women are evaluated relatively more positively because of their emotionality.[18]

Contemporary feminism has, in particular, developed this theme, which had remained a relatively minor one in the culture at large. Women's emotionality is celebrated, either explicitly (e.g., Chodorow 1978; Ruddick 1980) or implicitly (e.g., Smith-Rosenberg 1975), as a sign of women's closer approximation to the natural state of human beings, which is to be in relationship with others; it is these relationships—this interpersonal *engagement*—that produces affect. Men's diminished emotionality has been seen as the result of a socially learned or produced suppression or excision of those natural emotional capacities which women evidence. Ruddick (1980), for example, identified "resilient good humor and cheerfulness," "attentive love," and "humility" as among the central features of maternal virtue that follow from (rather than precede) the task of mothering and, by frequent correlation, the task of being female. Here, as in most feminist writing, the natural is not the biological so much as it is the positive or correct state of affairs. Women's greater emotional expressiveness is seen as natural, which is to say, as both effortless and good, but not as a natural *fact;* the gender differences in emotionality are seen in much feminist discourse as constructed by women's and men's experiences in a particular social world.

Emotion as Value

The double-edged character of the Western cultural conceptualization of emotion is nowhere more evident than in the way the emotions are related to value, morality, and ethics. While emotions are fundamentally devalued themselves—as irrational, physical, unintentional, weak, biased, and female—they are valued by some individuals and in certain contexts as "good" aspects of the person. Associated, on the one hand, with all that is amoral—our physical, animal heritage, the unconsidered and uncontrolled, the irresponsible—the occurrence of emotion may ensure immoral behavior or even relieve the person of moral responsibility. As we saw when examining affect's subjectivity, emotion is associated with self-indulgence; thought, with discipline and self-denial. To the extent that morality is culturally defined as self-control in the interest of a higher good, emotion's culturally defined self-indulgence is antithetical to it.

On the other hand, emotions are also sometimes considered to be an expression of personal values. Emotion is, in this case, conceptualized as the means by which value is apprehended or perceived in the world. We experience emotion when we focus on the values involved in a particular situation. Here, morality requires emotion because affect provides the motivation for taking particular moral positions toward events. There is another sense in which morality requires, or even is, affect, and it is raised by Foucault. He notes that, through time, "not always the same part of ourselves, or of our behavior, is relevant for ethical judgment," but that currently "you can say, in general, that in our society the main field of morality, the part of ourselves which is most relevant for morality, is our feelings" (Foucault 1983:238). The centrality of affect to morality derives from the role of feelings in indexing the true self. If one's heart is in the right place, one's behavior (however damaging to others) can be portrayed as justifiable and moral. The dominant view of the relation between morality and emotion, however, has the two operate in radically different, even opposed, ways.

To understand the cultural contradiction between these two senses of emotion (as constituting value and as its antithesis), we need to recognize that the concept of "morality" is, like "emotion," culturally constructed. The concept of morality depends, for instance, on the concepts of the person and of knowledge dominant in a particular society if we begin with the premise that morality is a particular way of being human in the world. One cultural concept of the Good which contrasts with what we more specifically mean by morality in the West is evident in M. Rosaldo's description of the Philippine Ilongot view of why people behave in the way they do: "When Ilongots see their interests as potentially opposed, issues of forcefulness and strength . . . and not of guilt, or personal desire and restraint, are likely to determine moral choice" (1983:141). Morality is, for the Ilongot, not a nexus of decisions for the individual, nor a struggle between the antisocial individual impulse and the wider social good, but the achievement of the valued state of affairs (e.g., the elimination of violence or selfishness between kin) "by fiat, dominance, or gift exchange . . . for cooperation to proceed, no more is necessary than the correction of imbalances by which men are divided" (1983:141). For many Samoans, morality is not transcendent but always embedded in the need to sustain relations with others (Shore 1982).

What appears to be at the root of the paradox of Euramerican attitudes toward the morality of emotion is the tradition of positivism. By splitting the world into objective and subjective domains and into matters of fact and matters of value, and by associating detachment and cognition with the former, positivism eliminates passionate involvement with and commitment to a way of viewing and acting in the world. Science, which defines itself as seeking the most important kind of knowledge, is declared value free (or at least ideally so). With the erosion of faith in positivism in the more recent history of social science and of this culture generally, there has been concern with reincorporating the concept of morality into the pursuit of knowledge and into social science. The new positions attempt to relate science to value by legitimating criticism and commitment in the pursuit of an understanding of social life, or rather by making the goal of knowing the world subserve the goal of eliminating injustice in it (Geuss 1981).

These views of knowledge as permeated with value and interests, however, continue to speak of segregating emotion from the process of critical understanding. This view is represented in a recent collection of articles on the relationship between morality and social science. The introduction to that volume states that all the included authors agree, in their critique of positivism, "that social science has an intrinsic connection with the moral and political life of a society," that this recognition makes us "better able to *cognitively* understand the reality that we confront," and that there is an "obligation of the social scientist to view reality as *dispassionately* as possible" (Bellah et al. 1983:16; emphasis added). While they would appear to allow that it is not possible to eliminate emotion from all scientific deliberations by their proviso that we expunge only as much as is possible, it is clear that they view minimal emotion as the ideal in attempts to understand reality. The continued emphasis on the incompatibility of moral awareness and emotion would appear to occur because the concepts of emotion and morality remain themselves unexamined. Given the dominant cultural meanings assigned to these terms, there are too many reasons for the positivists to save the technical rationality and resultant legitimacy of their enterprise from the critique of either morality or emotion and for the postpositivists to rescue morality from the subjectivity, irrationality, and chaos implied by emotion, if we take into account the positive valuation of the former concept and the negative view of the latter set.

The contradiction between this dominant perspective on emotion as antithetical to morality and the perspective in which emotion and value are intertwined can be viewed as the result of subcultural variation within the Euramerican tradition in understandings of the concept of morality, variation identified by Gilligan (1982) as gender related. Specifically, Gilligan argues that morality is sometimes conceptualized in two different ways by men and women and that the male definition has dominated in social-scientific (and other "official") discourse in our culture. The predominately male definition of morality focuses on the competing rights of individuals, on "fairness," and on the application of an abstract moral code to particular cases of ethical choice. The conception of morality which Gilligan found to dominate American women's thinking centers on notions of the conflicting responsibilities facing the moral decision maker and the primacy of caring for others as the most adequate guide for behavior; this female view of morality puts relationships rather than individuals, and concrete contexts or relationships rather than abstract codes, at the center of moral questions. Gilligan exemplifies this contrast between the two versions of morality by reference to "the biblical Abraham, who prepared to sacrifice the life of his son in order to demonstrate the integrity and supremacy of his faith," thereby "sacrific[ing] people to truth." Abraham stands "in implicit contrast to the woman who comes before Solomon and verifies her motherhood by relinquishing truth in order to save the life of her child" (1982:104–5). The male morality of "rights and noninterference" may seem to women a "potential justification of indifference and unconcern," while the female morality of caring and responsibility may seem to men "inconclusive and diffuse, given its insistent contextual relativism" (1982:22).[19] The former morality seems "heartless," the latter "too subjective." Given our dualisms, there may seem no way to a "complete" morality, a complete person.

If the masculine definition of morality is used implicitly in the dominant ideology of self and affect, emotions will be seem as having little to do with the mature exercise of the ethical sense. Moral development becomes cognitive development; and value, an abstract code or set of rules. And in particular, given the individualistic view of self in males that goes hand in hand with this morality, emotions are events which happen exclusively inside the individual and are conquered there. The morality which characterizes American women, on the other hand, has much to say about discourses on emotional development, as it is in the ability to experience the emotions necessary to caring for others, which include compassion most especially, that moral development proceeds. Given the relational view of the self that more commonly characterizes women, according to Chodorow (1974), Gilligan (1982), and others, we might expect that emotions will be spoken about by them as an aspect of relationships rather than of individuals.

Morality, in sum, bears a contradictory relationship to the concept of emotion. This contradiction can be illuminated both by reference to the underlying and different contrast sets (cognition and estrangement) in which emotion participates and by reference to subcultural variation in the conceptualization of morality, particularly as it is evidenced in the moral views of American men and women. To speak of the relationship between emotion and value, then, we have needed to deconstruct these various and shifting senses in which the two concepts can and have been used in Euramerican discourse. In the long run, this allows for the claim that emotions ought to be seen as central to morality and culture because the particular form of rationality and critique that they represent is central to the regulation and preservation of social relationships. To make this claim is to draw on the traditions in which morality is primarily nurturance rather than rights and in which emotion is the necessary result of relationship with others more than the unfortunate breakdown of individual cognitive functioning.

In explicating the cultural assumptions embedded in the concept of emotion, this chapter has attempted to reclaim the language of emotion from the unexamined terms of the dichotomies—of thought and estrangement—in which it has participated. It is also intended to undermine, to some extent, the ideological functions the concept of emotion has served. And finally, by demonstrating the nature and extent of the Western cultural construction of the central concept which concerns us here, it is possible to move on to contrast these conceptions with some Ifaluk cultural constructions of phenomena that we now only gingerly term "emotional."

CHAPTER FOUR
The Ethnopsychological
Contexts of Emotion: Ifaluk Beliefs
about the Person

Recognizing emotion as a cultural rather than a natural category leads us to ask some general questions about how the Ifaluk experience and talk about related personal phenomena. We work initially from our own sense of the person as divided into a thinking part and feeling part, which is private and set off distinctively from a social world of others, from whom we are ideally markedly independent. The emphasis on the distinction between mind and body and the view of the person as above all a sovereign individual help structure the concept of emotion as commonly used by Americans and help organize experience itself. In contrast, the ethnopsychological beliefs that surround and structure Ifaluk emotional life include the notion that the person is first and foremost a social creature and only secondarily, and in a limited way, an autonomous individual. Daily conversations on Ifaluk are pervaded by the assumption that people are oriented primarily toward each other rather than toward an inner world of individually constituted goals and thoughts. This social orientation of the person has fundamental implications for the way emotions are conceptualized, and it includes the practice of viewing emotions as

Parts of this chapter were originally published as "Ethnopsychology Compared to What?" in *Person, Self, and Experience,* edited by Geoffrey White and John Kirkpatrick (University of California Press), ©1985 The Regents of the University of California.

more public, social, and relational, and necessarily more dyadic than do we. One person's anger (*song*) entails another's fear (*metagu*); someone's experiencing grief and frustration (*tang*) creates compassion/ love/sadness (*fago*) in others. As we will see, motivation is portrayed in several ways, but through its relation to the social more than as an independent internal force that generates behavior. The notion of something like individual will is not absent (it is termed *tip-*), but its muted or secondary place in Ifaluk thought marks at once the sameness and the difference between the Ifaluk and American ethnopsychologies. Moreover, virtually inseparable connections are drawn in Ifaluk belief between what we distinguish as thought and feeling and as mind and physical being. Our "insides" are, in the Ifaluk view, relatively undivided. Common, natural thought (*nunuwan*), like idiosyncratic desire (*tip-*), is emotion laden. The distinct emotional concepts of "compassion/love/sadness" (*fago*), "justifiable anger" (*song*), and "fear/anxiety" (*metagu*) that will be examined in the three chapters to follow each draw part of their meanings from these more general views of self and relationship.

In describing the ethnopsychology of the Ifaluk, this chapter also outlines the important links between this interpretive system and cultural values. The connection between cultural images of the good most clearly take form in the image of the good *person*. Ifaluk ethnopsychology, like our own, articulates those values through character or trait terms, through norms for child development, and in many other ways. The adoption practices, threatening spirits, and quiet voices on Ifaluk all have much to do with cultural definitions of normal—which is often to say, virtuous—personhood. Virtue, emotions, and other aspects of ethnopsychology are related because the cultural construction of moral social relations is at least partially dependent on the understanding that permits virtue or the virtue that permits understanding. For the Ifaluk, those values include egalitarianism in wealth, respect for rank, sharing, nurturance for the weak, and interpersonal gentleness. If emotions are conceptualized analytically as an index of social relations, they cannot fail to be reflected in cultural definitions of the ideal ways of being with others.

Cultural beliefs about emotion are intimately related to broader cultural theories about the nature of the person and of social relationships. Any local theory of emotion will fundamentally reflect the more general views that are held about why and how people behave, feel, think, and interact as they do. To understand how the Ifaluk talk about emotion, therefore, we must examine the ways people on the atoll think about the nature of personal organization (including consciousness and the body), about morality, about individual capacities, and about why individuals vary among themselves and across the life cycle. We can begin with some general considerations of definition and method in the study of ethnopsychology.

Ethnopsychology as a Domain of Study

The description of ethnopsychological knowledge systems is predicated on the belief that people in every society have developed some shared understandings about aspects of personal and social life, aspects which for heuristic purposes may be termed "psychological." As has been the case in the study of indigenous conceptualizations of such things as plants, history, and medicine, however, it has been necessary to recognize the danger—which is involved in naming a domain—of setting rigid, a priori, or culturally alien boundaries to indigenous thought systems. Although we may find the rubrics "ethnopsychology," "ethnosociology," or "ethnoepistemology" useful starting points for ethnographic analysis, given our understandings of the "domains" of knowledge, boundaries between such fields may be nonexistent or differentially construed in other cultural systems. A number of ethnographic studies have in fact demonstrated the interpenetration of concepts of the person with virtually every aspect of cultural knowledge, from that concerning the division of labor, to notions of time and history, to ideas organizing politics (e.g., Geertz 1973; Heelas and Lock 1981; Marsella, DeVos, and Hsu 1985; Kirkpatrick 1983; Myers 1979, 1982; Rosaldo 1980; Shore 1982; White and Kirkpatrick 1985). The term "psychology" is appropriate, however, insofar as we are concerned with cultural constructions of particular persons as well as of human nature. I will begin, then, with the definitional premise that ethnopsychology is concerned with the way people conceptualize, monitor, and discuss their own and others' mental processes, behavior, and social relationships. All ethnotheories explain some aspect of variability in the world; ethnopsychologies explain inter- and intrapersonal variation, and they both construct and derive from people's observations of changes in consciousness, action, and relationships.

Ethnopsychological knowledge in human cultures arises from at least two sources, including the need to anticipate and make sense of others' behavior and the need to evaluate social relations. Theories about human nature and human variation enable people to make "inferences about the interrelation of actors' goals, intentions, and abilities" and "to formulate probable courses of social action" (White 1980:767). In this way, ethnopsychological theory makes the behavior of others more predictable, although this may facilitate either social coordination or conflict. The importance of ethnopsychological theory is also indexed in Hallowell's argument that self-awareness and concepts of the person are universal and at the same time cultural phenomena (Hallowell 1955, 1960). Without some notion of the self as distinct from other selves and objects, the creation, perception, and enactment of a human social and moral order would be impossible. However, cultural variability appears to exist not only in the contents of self-awareness and person concepts, but also in the degree to which this awareness is itself monitored, emphasized as salient, and explicitly discussed in everyday discourse.

Before I go on to describe this knowledge system among the Ifaluk, several methodological issues need to be raised, including that of the nature of the evidence for the existence of indigenous psychologies. The methods that can be used to investigate and describe ethnopsychological theory are neither less varied nor, as Rosaldo has pointed out (1980:62), more complex than those that can be used to investigate other aspects of culture. The task of ethnopsychological study is to examine what people both say and do in everyday life which indicates that a cultural knowledge system for interpreting self and other is at work.

The ethnographer's acquisition of language skills is the first and most significant way that access to local ethnopsychological knowledge is obtained. Several aspects of language are methodological entrées into such cultural knowledge systems. First, the lexicon of the self and interaction provides evidence about the concepts underlying ethnopsychological understanding. In the present study, the question of the meaning and translation of the terms for those concepts was taken as the primary and logically prior one. The similarities and differences between, for example, the Ifaluk state term *fago* and the English terms "compassion," "love," and "sadness" are at the core of ethnopsychological description and comparison. Also of interest is the centrality or salience of particular ethnopsychological concepts within the wider cultural system. Quinn (1982) has shown the value of an analysis of the "key words" of particular knowledge domains in demonstrating the range and depth of meaning such words can communicate. When we describe ethnopsychological concepts, it is important to note the salience or resonance of particular words in the knowledge system.

Beyond the lexicon of the self, the metaphors and modifiers used in talking about human functioning are important entrées into an understanding of ethnopsychological conceptualizations. Lakoff and Johnson (1980) have argued that use of metaphors constitutes one of the most fundamental ways people understand the world. When we link concepts that are experientially vivid, such as the spatial and ontological, with abstract or poorly understood concepts, understanding is enabled or enhanced. As ethnopsychological concepts are often abstract to a degree which plants and colors are not, metaphors will be frequently used in attempts to understand and communicate the experience of self and other. For example, D'Andrade (1987:145) has noted in American ethnopsychology, "One can say that thoughts are like things one says to oneself, or images of what one sees with one's eyes."

Finally, and perhaps more problematic, is the ethnopsychological proposition (Lutz 1987). Words descriptive of self and other constitute the primary elements from which ethnopsychological statements are built. These statements may be heard in natural conversation, or they may be presented to the ethnographer. They may be either general in form ("Some people are hot-tempered") or particular ("Lelam will go crazy if you hit her"). Speech is naturally shorthand, however, there being many unspoken assumptions involved in conversations about self and others. These assumptions serve as the basis on which the hearer (including the ethnographer) makes sense of discourse. Thus, ethnopsychological knowledge is evident both in what is said and in what is not said (Tyler 1978). Since the inferences people make on hearing a statement are based on culturally provided knowledge (Hutchins 1980), the attempt to understand why one statement (or action) follows another is a crucial method for the study of ethnopsychology. Where some of the most vexing methodological problems arise is in validating our descriptions of implicit ethnopsychological propositions. A too-ready explanation of the supposedly implicit ethnopsychology of a people runs the danger of becoming culture and personality in a new guise, with our own ethnopsychological inference-making abilities taking over. On the other hand, the use of implicit knowledge can be convincingly demonstrated by reference to commonly occurring sequences of verbal and nonverbal behavior in everyday contexts.

In what contexts are ethnopsychological propositions evident? We most readily observe ethnopsychology, Black (1978) fruitfully has pointed out, in the course of public attempts to modify deviant behavior, as, for example, during dispute settlements. Given the ubiquity of deviance and of concern with defining and dealing with it, this is a particularly important theoretical and methodological framework for examining ethnopsychologies. Black (1985) has also noted that it is the negotiation of meaning that is observed by the ethnographer. What is usually at issue, then, is not the validity of the ethnopsychological tenet itself, but rather the applicability of particular propositions about self and other *to a particular case*. This is not to say that ethnopsychological propositions are absolute, unchanging, or unambiguous "rules" to which people unambivalently subscribe; culture is obviously structured by events as well as structuring them. Observing such negotiations, we can begin to understand both the criteria for making decisions about the applicability of widely shared propositions as well as the emergence of ethnopsychological meaning.

Additional methodological issues include the description of cultural and cognitive diversity in this domain and elucidation of the uses of ethnotheory, or the contexts in which it is produced and the purposes for which it is used. Questions of method surround the following aspects of particular ethnopsychological propositions: (1) the degree to which they are shared by all or some members of the community; (2) the historical context, or the manner in which propositions develop and change with changing environmental conditions and resultant changes in the issues that the domain must address; (3) the restriction of their expression or change in their meaning in some particular contexts in a society as opposed to others (Kirk and Burton 1977; White 1978); and (4) the degree to which they are salient and in daily use or, conversely, a post-hoc response (however culturally appropriate) to the ethnographer's concern with the subject.[1] Each of the above issues can fall under the rubric of the ecology of ethnopsychological knowledge because they all concern its context-sensitive appearance. The systematic way the ecology of interpersonal behavior has been researched (Whiting and Whiting 1975) might be duplicated in this realm.

Person, Self, and Other: Categories of Agents and Variation in Consciousness

Ethnopsychological knowledge was initially defined as those ideas used to explain variation within and across persons in behavior and consciousness. It will be helpful to begin, then, by describing the class of actors whose behavior is explained in everyday life. Second, the universal distinction between self and other can be explored by an examination of differences in ways of speaking about the two.[2] And finally, variation in individuals' conscious experiences is noted in Ifaluk ethnotheory and can be described as an aspect of self-awareness.

Personhood

Three fundamental types of actors inhabit the behavioral environment of the Ifaluk, including "human persons" (*yaremat*), "spirits" (*yalus*), and the Catholic God (also termed *yalus*, or more occasionally, *got*).[3] The human person is said to come into existence at about the sixth or seventh month after conception, as, at this point, I was told, a miscarried fetus first looks physically human. The term *yaremat*, however, is not used primarily to contrast this period with the earlier fetal period. Instead, the contrast is drawn between human persons and spirits, and there is great concern to distinguish any particular actor as a member of one of the two categories. This is indicated by the question frequently asked in legends by protagonists in their encounters with others, "Are you a spirit or are you a human person?" A very few anomalous individuals who are not considered as falling clearly into one category (e.g., an albino woman resident on a neighboring atoll) have been the topic of much discussion and some anxiety. The need to distinguish between human persons and spirits follows from differences in what one can expect from encounters with each of the two.

Spirits differ from the human person primarily in their power and intentions. Although particular spirits may be either benevolent or malevolent, named or unnamed, ancestors or not, in general they are much more likely to intend harm or cause fright than are humans. They do, however, share many of the motivations and traits of people. They can be envious, righteously indignant, or compassionate and, in the case of ancestor spirits, retain the personal characteristics that they were identified as having when alive. The Catholic God, on the other hand, can be expected to behave consistently in an exemplary way that epitomizes Ifaluk values of sharing, concern for the welfare of others, and benevolent authority. In these respects, God is conceptualized as being motivated in much the same way as are chiefs on the island.

Although people attempt to minimize contact with spirits, the thoughts and feelings of both human and nonhuman actors are believed to be fairly easily transmitted and to affect others readily. The special power of the spirits means that such interpsychic communication and influence tend to run in one direction, that is, from spirits to humans. Spirits are known to cause certain types of dreams as well as certain illnesses. The arenas of illness and of the dream are not enclosed within the self (although it is the self which is aware of them), and spirits can therefore freely enter those arenas and influence the course of events. As we will see, other human persons can likewise cross what are considered private and less penetrable boundaries in Western conceptions.

The term "human person" (*yaremat*) is most frequently used in simple reference to individuals, as in "Who are those 'human persons' over there?" The term is also used rhetorically in situations where an individual feels that she or he has not received the treatment to which all persons are entitled. For example, Letachibel, a middle-aged woman, sat nearby as a group of people ate from a bowl of taro. She implicitly complained of having missed an invitation to share when she asked a sympathetic listener, "Aren't I a 'human person'?" Human persons are not, therefore, simply the class of human agents but are also those to whom certain types of actions, including particularly nurturant and other inclusionary practices, *should be* directed. Although varieties of people are recognized, some of whom are seen as having mild to severe character and performance defects, ideally each would be considered a human person.

Within the class of persons, then, how are self and other distinguished? The point at which the self stops and the other begins is neither fixed nor conceptualized as an impermeable wall. It is considered natural that one person's thought should influence another's. People are frequently characterized as "following the thoughts/feelings" of others; in doing so, they take on the attitudes, angers, or plans of the other. Similarly, the sources of behavior are seen as multiple and interpersonal and are not to be found exclusively in any independent or central part of the self. Although, as will be seen, an important source of behavior is the individual will (*tip-*), the mature self is one that is moved quite directly by others. Pronoun forms in language can take on psychological and symbolic importance as markers of the boundary and relations between self and others (see White 1985). Through these forms, people on Ifaluk place strong emphasis on perceived or desired similarities between self and other. In relation to agentive pronouns, most striking is the frequent use of "we" (inclusive) where "I" might have been used in American-English discourse. During one of my first weeks on the island, I asked a group of young women visiting my hut, "Do you (all) want to come with me to get drinking water?" Faces fell, and I realized after later experience and reflection that my pronouns were at fault, failing, as they did, simply to assume an isomorphism between myself the speaker and the hearers. The usual and more correct form of this question would be, "We'll go get water now, O.K.?" The use of the first-person plural is nearly as common as that of the first-person singular in statements about mental events. On observing something unusual, a person would be more likely to say, "We [speaker and listener] don't know what's going on here" rather than "I don't know what's going on here." "We are worried" is as likely to be heard as "I am worried." The emotion word *fago* (compassion/love/sadness) is more often preceded by the first-person plural than by any other class of pronoun.

First-person pronouns are, by definition, egocentric. They are used by the speaker to frame all statements from his or her own viewpoint. When the "we" rather than the "I" form is used, as it frequently is on Ifaluk, this is strong evidence that the relevant viewpoint is taken to be that of the group rather than the individual. The implications of this distinction may be variable across contexts and cultures using the same pronoun forms. For example, in the case of the use of the term "compassion/love/sadness," which refers to a very socially desirable emotion, to say "I feel 'compassion/love/sadness' for that person" may risk the interpretation of that statement as a boastful one, which puts the self apart from and above others. In another of the above examples, to say "I am going to get water" may communicate an intention of striking out on one's own, without regard for the needs of others, either for water or for companionship. It could also result, in fact, in one's going for water alone, a prospect associated with boredom, loneliness (people are assumed virtually always to want the company of others), or fear (of spirit encounters). Although the "interconnectedness" of self and other that White (1985) infers from A'ara pronoun use may be seen as an aspect of each of the examples here, a further differentiation by the context of statements of this sort reveals how several ethnopsychological principles can interact in producing the linguistic forms.

Material objects have a social life and so also a relationship with the self (Csikszentmihalyi and Rochberg-Halton 1981). Ethnopsychological propositions may emerge as people address the problem of things in their everyday lives. Take, for example, the values and practices surrounding property on Ifaluk. A stress on resource egalitarianism and sharing means that a person smoking a cigarette will pass it around to as many people as are present. Any great show of magnanimity in sharing is, however, frowned upon, as this putting forward of self is seen as denigrating of the other. Any behavior that appears to make a gift out of what is seen as a shared resource is condemned, suggesting as it would that the item was given freely as a matter of choice. Rather, the item should be seen and treated as something that was "ours" rather than "mine" to begin with. Food, in particular, is invariably spoken of as "our food." On the other hand, things that everyone possesses to an adequate and equal degree, such as clothing and bush knives, are generally not shared. Such objects take on special significance in marking out areas of autonomy and assertion of self.[4] Unlike time, labor, or food, these things can be disposed of only by their owner. This aspect of Ifaluk self-awareness was particularly dramatized by the exaggerated extent to which one of the mentally ill men on the island used the possessive in a visit to the house I lived in. His entire conversation consisted in a listing of his possessions, as he pointed out, with emphasis, "*my* lighter, *my* knife, *my* basket."

Wider symbolic meanings surround possessions. Consumable items such as food and tobacco, which are commonly shared and referred to as "ours," are strongly tied to sociability and emotion. To say that we eat together is to say that we are intimates. Clothing, on the other hand, not only marks off the physical boundary of the person but also, as Turner (1980:112) has eloquently shown, "the frontier of the social self as well." For the Ifaluk, clothing connotes sexuality and so requires treatment consistent with the fact that the sexual person is both socially problematic and culturally constituted. Certain terms for male and female clothing, for example, are taboo in mixed company, and people take care to keep clothing from being seen by those of the opposite gender when it is not being worn. In some respects, sexuality is seen as divisive, possibly creating competition and jealousy as opposed to sociability.

Although people talk about themselves and others in ways that assume similarities and easy communication between them, it is nonetheless possible to identify differences in how self and other are spoken about. Other persons are sometimes described by a term from the domain of words that describe enduring characteristics of persons (see below).[5] In contrast, it is extremely rare to hear people talk of themselves in terms of their own traits or mannerisms. Only a small number of trait terms is used with any regularity, however, to describe others. The more frequent descriptions of both self and others focus on the immediate situational sources of action, as in, for example, "She didn't invite me to her birthing because she followed the advice of her husband," or "The child walked away because he is irritated." With this outline of the nature of the person and of the self/other distinction as it is seen and expressed, we can go on to ask in more detail about the nature of self-awareness.

Talking about "Our Insides": The Undivided Self

"Introspection" is the term most frequently used in English for self-examination and its resultant self-awareness. As ethnopsychological knowledge arises in the context of goals, it should first be pointed out that introspection is valued only for certain purposes rather than as an end in itself. In contrast to our own notion of introspection as a potential voyage of self-discovery, valid in its own right and as a key to self-knowledge, the Ifaluk stress the moral, self-monitoring role of introspection. People are often explicitly advised to "separate the good and the bad" in their minds in order to behave correctly, and this requires a type of introspection. Absent is the notion that, on basic principle, one should "know oneself" or that one *can* even know oneself outside the moral and social constraints that sometimes make introspection necessary. The asocial definition of thought and its positive evaluation in Euramerican culture give introspection connotations not found among the Ifaluk, given their conceptions of the person. As will be seen, thinking is, in fact, sometimes seen as more troublesome than not, and people are advised in such cases to avoid introspection or dwelling on a thought. Of a girl who was homesick for her brother on another island and who went off alone to cry and to think about him, I was told by a somewhat exasperated observer, "She *wants* to think about him."

At the core of Ifaluk ethnopsychology is a set of beliefs about the structure of persons which portrays them as basically undivided entities. In marked contrast to Western ethnopsychology, sharp distinctions are not made between thought and emotion, between the head and the heart, or between a conscious and an unconscious mind. Although some other distinctions can be and are made, both theory and use place more emphasis on the essential internal unity of the person than on her or his compartmentalization. While the Ifaluk clearly have a set of terms we would characterize as emotion terms, such as "justifiable anger" and "disgust," there is no superordinate term that translates as emotion, nor do people show much concern with contrasting those kinds of phenomena with others less "heated" or more cognitive in the set of senses I have already explored in chapter 3. The two major terms used to talk about aspects of the self, *nunuwan* and *tip-*, can both be said to be potentially emotion laden. What central distinction the Ifaluk *do* make is subtle but important and centers on the need to talk about more socially standard personal processes (*nunuwan*) and those (*tip-*) more individual or idiosyncratic (although not therefore of necessity antisocial or immoral). Both are subsumed under the category "our insides" (*niferash*), the most general term used to describe internal functioning.[6] To say "My insides are bad" (*Ye ngaw niferai*) may mean one is either feeling physically bad or experiencing bad thoughts and emotions, or both, the exact meaning, as with the English phrase "I feel bad," being determined by context.

Let me begin by tracing some of the processes by which my understanding of these central terms emerged. The following attempt to describe the meanings of *nunuwan* (thought/emotion) and *tip-* (will/emotion/desire) should *not* give the impression that the terms are seen as referring to two distinct "entities." In response to my questions about the differences between them, people most often began by saying that the two were very similar. *Tip-* and *nunuwan* are difficult to distinguish from each other because they are seen as referring to aspects of the same phenomenon. *Nunuwan* refers to mental events ranging from what we term thought to what we term emotion. Although the first and tentative translation that *nunuwan* brought to my mind was "thought," the inadequacy of that gloss soon became evident. The Ifaluk see mental events as value-laden, ideally moral stances, and they do not, for this reason, separate evaluative and emotional responses from nonevaluative and cognitive responses to an environmental event. Thus, *nunuwan* may be translated as "cold through hot thought," "hot through cool emotion," or, more simply, as "thought/emotion." The following excerpts from field notes illustrate the range of uses of the term:

> Malemang says that people who tease others and children who throw rocks at others do so because their *nunuwan* is bad.

> Pakemar says that some people are short-tempered because their *nunuwan* is not good. Their *nunuwan* is not long.

> Lemalesep [a woman whose son had just died] asked for Ilemai's infant in adoption. Although the baby has already been promised to someone else, Ilemai said, "Our *nunuwan* will be good if we give the infant to Lemalesep."

> Ilefagochang said that if we have bad *nunuwan*, we will have bad insides, and if we have good *nunuwan*, we will have good insides.

> [I was] sitting on the ocean side of the island with Ilefagochang, and after some silence she said, "I have lots of *nunuwan* when I look out over the sea" and then talked about how she doesn't know what she's going to do about adopting out her son who's been promised to a woman on [a distant island].

Ilemarelig said that Ilemai [a pregnant woman] has lots of *nunuwan* because the health aide is leaving on the next ship which is coming, and she [Ilemai] *nunuwan* that there will be trouble with the delivery of the baby.

It is not simply that thought evokes, or is accompanied by, an emotion; the two are inextricably linked. *Nunuwan* is included in the definitions of various words that we would consider emotion words. For example, *yarofali* (longing/missing) is the state of "continually *nunuwan* about [for example] one's dead mother." The emotion words themselves may be used to describe *nunuwan* when the latter is used as a noun, as in the example "My thoughts/emotions are justifiably angry" (*Ye song yaai nunuwan*).

As several of the above examples illustrate, *nunuwan* is extensively involved with local ideas about morality and maturity. A mature, exemplary person is sometimes characterized as one who has "many *nunuwan*" (although the same turn of phrase can also refer to the state of being burdened with many thoughts and feelings and attendant indecisiveness). Children and the mentally ill, on the other hand, are said to have "only one *nunuwan*." Deviant behavior may also result from a dearth of *nunuwan*; in explaining the morally reprehensible behavior of one particular woman, someone told me that "She doesn't *nunuwan* behind her. She doesn't *nunuwan* that people will be justifiably angry at her, so she just does what she wants. She thinks[7] that her *nunuwan* is the same as [other people's] *nunuwan* [but it is not]."

Tip- (will/emotion/desire) is the second major term descriptive of "our insides." This concept is similar to that of *nunuwan* (thought/emotion) but is distinguished by its stronger connotations of desire and movement toward or away from an object. Like the Western concept of will, *tip-* implies preference and independent choice. A typical definition given me is the following: "Our *tip-* is what we want, like to chat with someone or to go visit another village." One of the most common uses for *tip-* in daily conversation occurs in the context of rank and obedience. Superordinates are regularly asked for permission to do something. If the elder knows of no rule or has no preference to the contrary, he or she will say, *"Ye shag tipum,"*[8] which is literally "It's just your will," or, in other words "[In the absence of external constraints] it's up to you." Where social rules or values are not at stake, the person's *tip-* is granted free reign. *Tip-* is not seen as intrinsically dangerous, however; individual will or desire is not seen as inherently antisocial or necessarily amoral but rather as one of the most important sources of action of all kinds. One's *tip-* may motivate conversation, dancing, or working in the taro gardens. On the other hand, personal preference can by no means be the only thing a person considers in making a choice. Failure to behave correctly may be attributed to *tip-*. For example, a young girl of eight was scolded for failing to visit her sick relative and was told that her behavior (and the possible consequences) were due to her *tip-*.

Tip- is at once the capacity for emotion as well as the capacity for will. As is the case with *nunuwan,* one's *tip-* may be characterized as "happy" or "angry." The fusion of emotion and will in *tip-* is not the result of a failure to differentiate the concept; rather, the concept is a seamless one, because the act of desiring or willing something implies for the Ifaluk either its fulfillment or frustration. The individual will may be thwarted or not. Emotion is not produced as a result, but is inherent in the experience of *tip-*.

"Thought" and "will" are not adequate translations for *nunuwan* and *tip-,* respectively, because neither of the latter is seen as emotionally neutral as are the former. Both are motivating and thus help in accounting for behavior. The fact that the Ifaluk distinguish at all between the overlapping categories of *tip-* and *nunuwan* indicates, I believe, their concern with a distinction between unsocialized, unmanipulable, or idiosyncratic mental events and socially generated mental events. *Tip-* refers to those aspects of the self seen as more fully one's own. That these concepts are seen in this way may also be indicated by the fact that only *tip-,* and not *nunuwan,* takes a direct possessive suffix. The possessive suffix, taken also by body–part and kin terms, may occur for items which are more tightly bound up in personal identity. Moral decisions and choices are more in the province of *nunuwan,* and "social intelligence" (*repiy*) is associated more with the latter than with *tip-*. As people are not considered to be fundamentally antisocial, however, what people desire, or their *tip-,* is neither immoral nor even amoral.[9]

Other aspects of "our insides," distinguished from both *nunuwan* and *tip-,* are the states of hunger (*pechaiy*), pain (*metagi*), and sexual sensations (*mwegiligil*). These states are considered to be universal and unlearned human proclivities. Although their occurrence can lead to thoughts and feelings, they are considered an entirely different class of events. The Ifaluk further distinguish among these three states of physical sensation and the corresponding desires or drivelike states that follow upon the sensations. These include "wanting food [or a particular food]" (*mwan*), "wanting pain to end" (*gar*), and "horniness" (*pashu*). American folk models of mind do not make these distinctions (D'Andrade 1987).

There appears to be considerable variation in the conceptions Oceanic peoples have of the place of physical processes in relation to mental or social ones. While many appear to use disrupted physical process (illness) as an idiom for talking about wider-ranging disruptions in psychosocial life, the use of normal physical process in metaphorical or literal understandings of mental or social process seems more variable. For example, the Baining of New Britain experience hunger as a sentiment rather than as a physical sensation (Fajans 1985). Although food is closely tied to sociability among both the Ifaluk and the Baining, the Ifaluk associate the sharing of food, rather than the consumption of it, with ties between people. The Tobians described by Black (1985) share many cultural features with the Ifaluk but nonetheless appear to be much more reticent in speaking about such physical states, the fear being that such revelation would lead to manipulation (Black, personal communication). People on Ifaluk frequently and openly talk about hunger and pain, both as feeling states and as associated drive states. This is not considered an embarrassing irruption of the natural into the cultural arena but as a predictable state of affairs over which no one is expected to have control.

Metaphors in common use for describing normal and abnormal psychosocial functioning shed light on the way the processes of the person and of self/other interaction are conceptualized. "Thoughts/emotions" (*nunuwan*) are often spoken of as "coming out" or "coming up" from "our insides." The spatial metaphor here is consistent with the traditional view of thoughts and desires as originating in the gut. When these things arise within the person, they are then followed. That is, people act in accordance with them. Thus, the relationship between mental occurrences and behavior is conceptualized as relatively nonproblematic in normal adults. The term *nunuwan* is appropriately glossed as "thought/emotion" in part because the concept entails what we mean when we speak of emotion in contrast to thought, which is to say, an internal event that strongly motivates behavior as opposed to one that does not.

The thoughts/emotions of a person, as already noted, are also sometimes said to be followed by others. This may occur because the other naturally wishes to follow, or because a specific request has been made, as in the form, "Sweetheart [a polite form commonly used in making requests], you will follow my thoughts/emotions."

After the woman who was my adoptive mother found that a close relative had given birth without her being asked to attend, she told me, "Follow my justifiable anger and so do not visit [the confined mother and infant]." The implication is always that the "follower" will behave in keeping with the other's thoughts and emotions and with the definition of the situation that they imply. The leader-follower image evoked here is a powerful one in the context of the value placed on obedience in all aspects of Ifaluk life. A request of this kind, like all requests, is taken seriously; it can also be taken as a sign of desired intimacy between self and other.

Speech is attributed great power and importance throughout Ifaluk culture. Some examples: talk rather than mute example or physical discipline is seen as the primary vehicle for the enculturation of children; the chiefs, in speaking at periodic islandwide meetings, believe that their words exhorting the people to act ethically will result in behavior change; spoken prayers are one aspect of Christian ritual that has been most enthusiastically adopted; and great value is placed on the use of good or polite talk in interaction with others. Such talk is considered to be at the root of pleasant social relationships, one of the most important bases for compliance with requests, and a mark of fine character.

Consistent with those attitudes toward language and toward the following of thoughts/emotions is the view that the overt expression of mental events is a mark of maturity. Children and the mentally ill are said to be marked by problems with such expression; they do not talk about their thoughts/emotions and "their insides do not leave them."[10] Here, the act of expression is metaphorically conceptualized as a physical act, with the internal event spoken of as a separate entity with independent movement. Mature people, in the Ifaluk view, verbally express what they are thinking and feeling. The mature are also capable of ridding themselves of unwanted thoughts and feelings, and this is said to be done primarily through verbalization of what is occurring in one's insides. This is in contrast, of course, both to the American middle-class ambivalence over the value of expression and to the widely shared sense that the inside and the outside of the person are radically separate.

Internal processes are seen as acquiring their significance in relation to social processes. The psychological event is neither denied in favor of the social nor is it defined outside the social. As "thought/emotion" is defined as a truly *psychosocial* act, so is expression seen as serving psychosocial goals. Expression is allowed and encouraged, although neither as an aggrandizement of the self nor as a praiseworthy expression of a unique self. Rather, expression is seen as a natural concomitant of an external event, whereas the lack of expression is seen as a possible precursor to illness or as a sign of mental incapacity. The single important exception to the general permissiveness in expression is an absolute sanction against the physical expression of inner events in violence or, to an important but lesser extent, in loud or impolite words. For this reason, it is said that a person may not look angry or irritated, but may still have angry thoughts/emotions. Men, in particular, should and do suppress their anger.

The term for this suppression is *goli*, which is literally "to hide." One may also hide laughter or tears in an inappropriate situation, but such masking is observable to others. The object of keeping a state an internal one is not to conceal the fact that one is experiencing a particular emotion, but rather to avoid conflict or other unpleasant social consequences. In general, however, there is little emphasis on the masking of emotion. It is frequently said that one can always tell what the internal state of the other person is from facial, gestural, or situational cues. The role of speech looms large here as well, as indicated by the answer to my frequent question about how one can tell if a person is experiencing state *X;* the response was often, "She [or he] tells you." Occasionally, however, people would protest, to my questioning, that "we cannot see our insides" and so cannot be absolutely sure about what is going on there, and particularly so in the case of others' insides.

Several other ideas in common use point out the importance of ridding oneself of unpleasant or disruptive thoughts/emotions and the role of the will in expediting this. "We divide our heads" (*Gish si gamaku chimwash*) is a phrase which is both an aphorism and a form of advice which is given, primarily by and to men, when someone is experiencing potentially socially disruptive thoughts/emotions. It is, they say, as if there were two halves to the brain, one good and one bad. People are advised to separate the good from the bad, or "divide the head," and then to "throw away" disruptive thoughts/emotions. This is universally the advice to the troubled, while at the same time, advice is given to express verbally one's thoughts/emotions as a preliminary step in ridding oneself of them.[11]

When someone is troubled by unpleasant thoughts/emotions, it is said that they will not "leave my insides." When some problem or conflict results in such a situation of unresolved, unpleasant thought/emotion, the person involved will go to another with the express purpose of "saying my thoughts/emotions so that they will leave me." Similarly, when one is experiencing grief over a death or home-sickness, the advice given is to stay among people so that one will not "think/feel" about the loss.

To express one's thoughts/emotions verbally, therefore, is both a sign of intelligence, as this is the natural course of events, and the route to relieving the unpleasantness of those mental states. Although the will would appear to play a part in this process, by enabling the self to "divide the head," the emphasis is more on control of behavior than of thoughts/emotions. Although the latter are never bad in and of themselves (as they may be in the West, with its concepts of sin and bad intentions), they can be disruptive, uncomfortable, and may cause illness in the self or others. What is important and valued, however, is to prevent the thoughts/emotions from leading to aggressive or socially disruptive behavior. The individual will, in ethnopsychological thought, can play a primary role in preventing this.

The Body

Any discussion of conceptions of the person must touch on the role the body plays in the cultural system. Is the body a little-valued "container" for more metaphysical and consequential events? Is it one, or perhaps the only, aspect of persons which consistently distinguishes them from others? On Ifaluk, as elsewhere, the body's structure and well-being are seen as involved in an inseparable and systematic way with psychosocial well-being. What we might call the "emotional mind" of Ifaluk ethnopsychology is solidly embedded in moral and social life, on the one hand, and in the physical body, on the other.

The physical structure of "our insides" is divided into *ubwash* (our upper torso), which includes the heart and liver, and *sagash* (our gut, our stomach), which includes the stomach and abdominal region. The heart, liver, and stomach, as well as the brain, are implicated in ethnopsychological beliefs about the origin of specific psychological and physical processes, beliefs which have undergone much change through the influence of Japanese and American ethnopsychologies. Traditionally, all thought/emotion (*nunuwan*) and will/emotion/desire (*tip-*) were believed to be experienced in the gut, and most people, especially older adults, speak of thoughts and emotions as being located there. The Japanese colonialists, however, constantly told the island boys who attended their schools in the prewar period to "use their heads." There may also have been a period, during Spanish colonization, when the heart was more often seen as the seat of thoughts/emotions. One term for the heart (*corasonai*) is a variant of the Spanish, and this idea is also prevalent today. Many younger people, and most especially the men, now include the brain as one of the seats (and sometimes as the only seat) of thoughts/emotions. There is much diversity of opinion, however, including the following post-hoc synthesis given to me by Ilefagochang, a woman in her twenties: "It is uncertain whether 'thoughts/emotions' [*nunuwan*] and 'will/emotion/desire' [*tipash*] come from the heart along a large vein to the brain, which then sends them out so that we speak." The liver is also implicated in thought and emotion, specifically in relation to *rus* (panic/fright/surprise), which is said to cause that organ to jump.

The links between emotional-mental and physiological functioning are explicitly spoken about by the Ifaluk. The gut, as the traditional seat of thought, feeling, and will, is seen in a very real sense as the link between mind and body, or, more accurately, as the core of the self in both its physical and mental functioning. Food, which holds a primary place in the Ifaluk value system (see Burrows and Spiro 1953), is the foundation of both physical and emotional states, positive and negative. The presence of plentiful fish or taro is often the occasion for exclamations of "our insides are good," by which is meant both good mood and physical feeling. Food provides by far the greatest satisfaction, and its lack produces the greatest upset.

Appetite is the one physical function most often seen as symptomatic of physical or emotional upset. Loss of appetite occurs for many reasons, including homesickness, fear, and weariness. "Food does not taste sweet" when one is upset; when one has many thoughts/emotions and is unsure about what will happen in the future, one feels "full from thoughts/emotions" and loses appetite. Such explanations are often sought for weight loss in others, as exemplified by the following incident. When a young woman, Ilechangemal, became thin, a variety of factors were blamed. One woman said it was caused by Ilechangemal's having many thoughts/emotions because she had much work to do, yet her adoptive daughter constantly whined and needed to be carried. Another woman, however, said the weight loss was due to her being "lovesick" over a brother who had gone away to school on Ulithi.[12] The stomach area is also seen as the region of the body first affected by strong negative thoughts and emotions. People describe their extreme grief over a death or loss by saying "my gut is ripping." Those experiencing loss are advised not to "hate your gut," implying that the sufferer ought to "feel compassion" for himself and follow traditional advice for alleviating the state of grief, as, for example, by staying in the company of other people.

Emotion, thought, and body are seen in ethnotheory as intimately linked through their roles in illness. Emotional upset and physical illness are conceived of and treated in parallel ways. Both illness and unpleasant thoughts/emotions must "come out" in order to alleviate the trouble they can cause. In addition, emotion not expressed may cause illness. One term (*gachip*) is used in talking about therapy for both kinds of problems; in the case of emotional upset, it means "to calm down" and in the case of illness, "to cure."

Individuals are constantly advised to "throw out" their thoughts in order to avoid illness. At funerals, relatives of the deceased are advised to "cry big" in order to avoid later illness. This advice is meant to be taken sequentially, that is, the grieving person should scream and wail for the twenty-four hours of the funeral and then stop thinking about the deceased, or risk becoming ill. At the funeral of a five-year old, I was also advised to "cry big." Observing my somewhat surreptitious tears, several people approached me and said, "You should not cry like this [imitating my stifled style and stiff posture] but should cry big, or you will be sick." The father of the child was told that he should not think/feel about the dead child, as he would then not be able to take care of his other children. The ability to throw away these bad thoughts/emotions is a sign of "social intelligence," but this should only be done after the intense mourning of the funeral period has been able to act as a prophylactic against possible illness. The mother of the child in the case above became ill after the funeral with headaches and numbness in her arms and legs. This was diagnosed (by the island's health aide) as being caused by her thinking/feeling about the dead child. This woman had, in fact, been the one close relative who had not "cried big" for extended periods at the funeral (see chap. 5).

Emotion in the self can cause illness in the other as well. This most often occurs with a confined mother and infant and with relatives living on two different islands. Those who are homesick for another will cause the latter to become ill if they continue to focus their thoughts/emotions on the missed person. Such homesick people may themselves become ill, through loss of appetite, as described above, or, as in several reported recent cases, they may become "crazy" (*bush*). Counsel to an individual who is homesick sometimes takes the following general form: "Don't cry [although crying out of homesickness is not frowned upon]. Forget those thoughts of your relatives. You will soon see them again. If you continue to feel homesick, your relatives will know this, and they will become sick."

In the confined mother–infant pair, this process is somewhat more complex. An infant will become sick and cry excessively if its mother has "bad thoughts/emotions." As Ilefagochang told me, "It is said that it is like the baby knows the thoughts/emotions of its mother and becomes 'sick and tired/bored' [*nguch*] of the mother." The confined mother is particularly susceptible to the latter emotion, and this may lead to irritability or hot temper. She is also more likely to be "worried/conflictful" (*waires*) about work around the house or garden which may be going undone. All these thoughts/emotions in the mother may result in the child's becoming sick and "always crying" (*tangiteng*). The child is given "medicine for *gos*" (*taffeyalgos*), with *gos* being the name of the condition of both the mother and child.[13] The spirits may also be involved in causing a mother to become hot tempered, which also makes the infant ill. In one such case, Talemangemar, an old man, heard his next-door neighbor's infant crying at night. The crying was recognizable as "some different kind of crying" (*semat tang*) and was said to be due to the spirits of the infant's mother's mother's brother and mother's mother which "ran into the 'thoughts/emotions' of" (*riglog lan yaal nunuwan*) the mother, causing her to be hot tempered and quarrel with her husband. Ilefagochang said in partial explanation of the mother's irritability that it was difficult because there was no one to take the infant when she wanted to work in the taro gardens. Talemangemar made "spirit medicine" for the infant.

This set of ethnopsychological beliefs serves as warning to people in the household and to other relatives of the confined mother; it is their responsibility to see that work is done around the house and garden and that the mother is occasionally relieved of caretaking for the infant. It is also notable that the mother with negative thoughts/emotions is not blamed for the infant's subsequent illness as much as are other relatives around her, including the spirits of deceased relatives. Blame is attributed quite explicitly in these cases, with it being said of the case above, for example, that "her sister did not 'think/feel' about [the confined mother], that she needed help with the infant," and so illness resulted. This is but one example of the general principle that the mental state of *any* mature individual is seen as having fundamentally social roots. Others can then be held responsible for the social conditions that produce the state. In so talking about the relation between emotion in self and other, the Ifaluk emphasize that feelings come from social relations, that their emotional lives *are* their social lives.

Explaining and Evaluating Behavior

The question of the origins of behavior must be problematic to some extent in every society. This issue is not a philosophical one but arises in the context of the goal of changing behavior that transgresses cultural norms and of duplicating behavior that exemplifies them. The behaviors that are seen as worthy of explanation are those identified as deviant, as Black (1985) points out; they are "marked" in relation to generally unspoken notions of normality (Fajans 1985). Although ethnotheoretical ideas about the causes of behavior are elaborated particularly around negatively evaluated behavior, they also are concerned with praiseworthy behaviors. The universal, evaluative dimension of perception (Osgood, May, and Miron 1975) is evident in the state, trait, and behavioral descriptors in use on Ifaluk and elsewhere (e.g., White 1980). The strong evaluative weight on terms for feeling and acting indicates that the role of ethnopsychology is not simply to describe and explain but also to evaluate behavior vis-à-vis cultural values, and thereby to begin to exercise some control over that behavior. Although cultures will vary both in the sheer number and range of behaviors lexicalized and evaluated and in the emphasis on control (as opposed to a more laissez-faire attitude toward state or behavior change), the recognition of at least some degree of interpersonal behavioral variation will necessitate both some explanations and some sanctions. Both vices *and* virtues are outlined because some control over the occurrence of both will be universally desirable.

Causality in Behavior

Most everyday explanations of behavior on Ifaluk are concerned with the situational causes of particular acts and their associated mental states. Emotion states are often the medium by which people talk about those situations, as particular situations are necessarily linked to particular emotions (see Lutz 1982) which are linked to particular actions.[14] The first question that unexpected behavior raises often concerns the incongruity between the situation and an emotion. Sitting by the channel which separates two islets of the atoll, the woman I was with noted a mother wading across with her baby in her arms. She called out, "Why don't you have him in a carrying basket? Won't you be regretful if it rains?"

A person's behavior is not, however, attributed to either wholly external or wholly internal sources, as the terms "situation" and "emotion" respectively connote. The cause of behavior is not conceptualized as located in an inner wellspring so much as in environmental "triggers." The most important facets of these situations, moreover, include the behavior of other actors. Typically, statements about the cause of behavior would take the form, "He did X, and so I did Y," or (in explaining others' behaviors) "He did X, and so she did Y." When the question arose, for example, of why a particular young girl had not come from her adoptive home to visit her biological parents for some time, it was said that "she is 'afraid/anxious' that her younger brother would hit her."

The extent to which other people are sometimes seen as the ultimate sources of one's own behavior often means that the responsibility (i.e., the cause and therefore occasionally the blame) for one's internal state lies with the other. Many emotion words can, with the addition of a causative prefix (ga-), be used to talk about the causes of both emotion and behavior. "He made me justifiably angry" (Ye gasongayei), "They caused fright in me" (Ihre gametagayei), and "She is needy" (Ye gafago), or literally, "She causes compassion," are examples of frequently heard statements. The mature person, we have already seen, expresses his or her internal states. The state is itself seen as having a reasonable situational explanation. Thus, the person who leaves valuable possessions out in view of visitors is to blame when someone becomes "excited/jealous" (bosu) as an inevitable result. The host in such a case would be criticized by saying that he or she was "showing off" (gabosu), or literally, "causing excitement/jealousy."

Other types of explanation for behavior exist. An individual's will/emotion/desire (tip-) is occasionally spoken of as the reason for an action, as in "Why is she making breadfruit instead of taro?" "It was her tip-." As the thoughts and emotions of others can have a powerful influence on one's own behavior, such influence is often taken as a satisfactory explanation for someone's actions. In one such case, Tewasemar, an older man, was leaving to visit another island despite the advanced state of his daughter Ilefagomar's pregnancy. As kin should ideally fear for their relative's life at the time of childbirth, and as they should want to give help to the new mother—that is, as Tewasemar's actions did not correctly correspond to the situation—his behavior required explanation. It was decided, after much discussion, that he had "followed the nunuwan [thoughts/emotions]" of his wife (who was his second spouse and not the mother of the pregnant woman) to leave the island.

The concept of "craziness, incompetence" (bush) is used in a wide variety of contexts to explain the actions of some people. "Craziness" is the opposite of "social intelligence" (*repiy*) (Lutz and LeVine 1983) and is used to talk about any behavior that shows a lack of mental and social competence. Crazy people behave in ways that indicate they have incorrectly perceived the situation they are in and so do not feel, think, or act appropriately. A person may be crazy in several senses. Some people are born crazy and, although their primary failing is their inability to perform adult work, they also often engage in much otherwise inexplicable behavior, such as violence, shouting, or a lack of table manners. There have been cases in the past in which a person was said to have gone crazy for months or even years and then returned to a socially intelligent state. In some cases, the cause of the episode was said to have been an intense emotional experience, such as homesickness or panic, although in other cases there appeared to be some reluctance to talk about the reasons behind it.

People who are otherwise socially intelligent may sometimes do things which earn them the label of craziness on a very short-term or even metaphorical basis. For example, a woman who left her son for much of an afternoon at her household in order to engage in the much-maligned activity of "walking around" (which implies strutting around and a failure to do one's work) was disparagingly called crazy. Thus, the term can be used to describe anyone who is behaving in an irrational and unadult manner. To say that someone is crazy is to say that his behavior has no other reasonable explanation. It is also at least temporarily to write that person off as one whose behavior is beyond the pale.

In a few special cases, crazy behavior occurs for what are seen as somewhat more understandable or elaborated reasons. Senility is the "craziness of elders," while excessive grief, which in one case I observed led to pushing and shoving to get near the corpse at a funeral, is the "craziness of 'tears/grief'." An intoxicated person who misbehaves usually has his actions explained simply by reference to his drunkenness. Occasionally, however, people speak of particularly misbehaving drunks as being "crazy from toddy." In extreme and rare instances, spirits can cause behavior. I observed this only once, in the case of Gachipemar, a young man whose serious illness had been diagnosed as spirit caused. One afternoon, after a week of illness, his arms began to sway up from his sides, and he talked "as if he were crazy." Unlike true craziness, however, his behavior was explained as being due to the entry of a spirit into his body and its control of his insides.

A final type of explanation for behavior is one made in terms of enduring personal traits such as hot temper or calmness. These will be explored after a discussion of ideas about child development.

The Ethnopsychology of Development

Examination of the life course can make two important contributions to the description of an ethnopsychology. In the first instance, the course of development is explicitly conceptualized, classified, and explained in most, if not all, societies. These notions about development frequently point out the infant or child as not yet fully a person. The ways children are seen to differ from adults will often reveal important ethnotheoretical dimensions which might otherwise go undiscovered. In addition, the process by which development is thought to occur is revealed in talk about the life course, including conceptions about which human behaviors are changeable and about how that change may be caused. Such conceptions thereby often point to the hypothesized origins of behavior. Ethnotheories of human development also recognize divergent outcomes, such that behavior and other aspects of personhood vary within and across adults. This variation may be explained with trait or behavioral descriptors, descriptors which fundamentally entail statements of values.

Second, an examination of the life course reveals how a culturally specific self-awareness is built up. Following Hallowell (1955), we may ask about the behavioral environment of the emerging self. By the efforts and example of the socializing other, the child begins to construct a self. The acquisition of ethnopsychological notions is a process that can be observed in both verbal and nonverbal communicative acts.

On Ifaluk, strong taboos prevent speaking of the unborn as a "child" (*sari*). It was also formerly taboo to speak of a stillborn child, or one who died in the birth house, as a child. Rather, one said in such an event, "The water has been thrown out," and the infant was buried without tears or ceremony. Catholic missionaries in the postwar period, however, encouraged graveyard burials for these fetuses and very young infants, and there is now some mourning at a birthhouse death.

Naming practices can provide insight into a people's ethnopsychology, as, in the act of linking a person with a label, the individual is particularized or identified in relation to other persons (see Goodenough 1965). The name may symbolize the location of the person in space and time and in relation to other objects in the environment (Geertz 1973). The Ifaluk name the infant (and begin to refer to it as a child) only after the mother has returned from the birth house after a ten–day period of seclusion. Although the infant has been a "person" (*yaremat*) since several months prior to birth, it is at this point, after the period of greatest life threat is passed, that children gain their full social identities. It is better that a newborn who dies do so nameless; without a name, I was told, there is less to forget. Names are given to the child by any one or more persons (kin or otherwise) who have taken an interest in the child, frequently including the child's adoptive mother or father, if there is one. The act of name giving is seen as an important statement of connection with the infant, and people will often give accounts of the origins of their names. The linguistic label itself is always a unique one, as a name can never be that of an ancestor, for to mention the name of an ancestor is to call forth his or her spirit. Each syllable, however, may be taken from the name of a different ancestor. Thus, naming is seen as creating a bond between the child and both the creator of the name and the ancestors whose names were in part used.

From the earliest period, infants are capable of certain emotions, but in general they must be protected from them. Concern with infants' states begins at birth. At one delivery I attended, the first two comments about the infant were "It's a girl" and "It's hot tempered [*sigsig*]." Infants may "feel good inside," be "hot tempered," or experience "panic/fright/surprise" (*rus*), a state which has serious implications as, in excess, it can lead to illness. Parents therefore make serious attempts to protect the infant from *rus* by avoiding loud noises and rough handling of the child and by placing a ball of cloth close to the child's chest while it sleeps.

Crying is considered the primary way children express their needs. It is to be avoided at all costs, and mothers sleep in close contact with infants in order to respond to their cries. Infants who cry while lying down are first assumed to be uncomfortable because of the impressions being made in their skin by the cloth or the mat on which they are lying. If moving children to another position does not stop the crying, they are held and fed until they sleep. Infants are bathed if their cries are interpreted as meaning that they are hot.

Until they reach the age of five or six, the most fundamental ethnopsychological fact about children is that they are socially incompetent or "crazy" (*bush*). As noted above, they share this label with the mentally retarded and mentally ill, the deviant, and the senile. Young children, being crazy, are not considered responsible for their actions. Children are considered not to know right from wrong, and the resultant aberrant behavior must, therefore, be ignored or tolerated. From about one year of age onward, however, children may be called *gataulap* (naughty). This term can be glossed as "naughty," as it connotes bad behavior, but behavior which, being more or less expected of someone at that age, is more annoying than reprehensible. Infants at the crawling stage may be naughty if they climb onto things or touch objects, but the quintessential naughty child is the toddler. "Naughty" toddlers empty out adults' personal baskets and touch knives or weaving thread. At three years, their naughtiness consists of running around, throwing things, or hitting others, or always whining to be given such things as knives or baskets.

It is near the age of weaning at two years that adults must begin to *garepiy* (cause to become socially intelligent) their children, despite the fact that their educability is seriously limited. Learning theories on Ifaluk give a prominent role to both the parents (adoptive and biological) and peers. Bad behaviors are said to be most frequently learned from peers, although it is the parents' responsibility to counteract the bad example of children's age-mates. Although children are believed to learn through watching the behavior of others, a very strong stress is placed on their ability to hear and to listen. The older, weaned child is sometimes instructed on proper behavior through parents' stylized "preaching" (*folog*). In these lectures, an axiom of proper behavior is gone over quietly but repeatedly. Obedience is highly valued, and children are believed to obey *when* and *because* they listen and understand language; intention and knowledge become virtually synonymous in this system. It is assumed that correct behavior naturally and inevitably follows from understanding, which should follow from listening. Although the concept of independent will is not absent (this is represented in the concept of *tip-*), the greatest stress is placed on the connections among language, listening, understanding, and correct behavior. This differs from emphases in common Western models, where "if one desires or intends to do what is good, then one must be able to conceive of what is good" (D'Andrade 1987:144).

Physical punishment does not play a prominent role either in the ethnotheory of learning or in practice. Lecturing is preferred to spanking, in line with the important roles given speaking and listening. People sometimes voice the fear that children who are hit, rather than spoken to, may "go crazy." Physical punishment may be a source of great embarrassment to parents when they engage in it, as gentleness in all matters is highly valued. Children are also said to learn by the examples given through socialization techniques. Those who are hit, and who are not spoken to politely, will grow up to be short-tempered and will not know how to engage in "good speech," or polite talk. Some fear is also expressed that children who are hit and shouted at may aggress against their parents in return or possibly even kill themselves.

As children approach the age of six, they are first considered socially intelligent, that is, they are seen as capable of a significant number of thoughts/emotions. In contrast to the Bimin-Kuskusmin of Papua New Guinea (Poole 1985), who use metaphors of directionality, solidification, and straightening to talk about the development of social sense in children, the Ifaluk speak primarily about an increase in the quantity of thoughts/emotions and about their value (good or bad) as they occur during childhood. Social intelligence consists in both the knowledge *and* the performance of mature and valued behaviors, such as subsistence work, respect toward the more highly ranked, and compassion for others, and these are now expected of the child. The amount of time parents spend casually instructing and formally preaching goes up dramatically. Adults believe that their words will now have an important effect on children, although, in the first few years of being socially intelligent, children are believed to forget parts of the lectures. If children have not been periodically lectured during the earlier years, it is said that they will not be used to such lectures. They will, therefore, become hot tempered when they are lectured at a later age.

When children reach the age of social intelligence, they are considered capable of learning some adult economic tasks. At this time as well, certain trait and behavior labels first become applicable to the child. Foremost among these is "laziness" (*gagu*). The state of "compassion/love/sadness" (*fago*) is fully possible in the child beginning only at this period. The things which constitute naughtiness change from the younger years and now include being loud and disruptive at school, being uncooperative around the household, and causing younger children to be noisy by getting them excited or by making them laugh. In the last instance, children begin to learn that they are responsible for the emotional states of others.

The development of individual differences is believed to arise from the various forces at work on the child. All children are believed to be basically the same until they become "a bit socially intelligent." Young children have only one thought/emotion, which is to eat. When they reach the age of two, they begin very slowly to acquire more and varied ideas. It is consequently only then that individual differences arise, as the number and nature of these thoughts/emotions begin to diverge in different people. Among the several factors said to cause differences are gender and sibling order.

Beliefs about innate sex differences are minimal. One of the only distinctions made between male and female infants concerns their crying; male cries are louder, stronger, and more constant, while female cries are softer, with more breathful pauses in between. Male infants are also said to drink and eat more than girls. Boys' crying is considered more problematic at later ages, and if a boy is labeled *tangiteng* (constantly crying) he will be given medicine which should solve the problem by the time he reaches adolescence. The position within the family of youngest and only children explains, in local theory, their being different from others. In infancy and early childhood, they are likely to be "constantly crying" because there are no younger siblings competing for their mothers' attention. These children also frequently grow up to be somewhat "bad hearted" and "hot tempered."

"Bad-hearted, jealous" (*lalongaw*) and "constantly crying" (*tangiteng*) children are recognized as different from others and are seen as particularly troublesome. Bad-heartedness is a much disliked trait in both children and adults. Children are not born bad-hearted but may become so when, for example, a new child is born and sibling rivalry erupts. I was told that the child "wants to be alone with the mother, and thinks that only the infant will be cared for by her." Bad-heartedness is only possible in children once they are somewhat socially intelligent and are capable of thinking such thoughts. Constantly crying children are dealt with by being encouraged to verbalize their internal states. If they cry because someone has taken something from them, they are told to go and ask for it back; the verbal expression and action should substitute for tears.

The most important point of discontinuity in the life cycle in Ifaluk ethnotheory occurs with the gaining of social intelligence at around age six. Although still called children, they are treated just like adults in many respects. Although it is considered silly to try to converse with a child before that age, the socially intelligent person of any age is incorporated in group conversation. In contrast to the more differentiated marking of stages and the particular elaboration of ideas about the nature of teenagers among some groups, such as the Marquesans described by Kirkpatrick (1983), the Ifaluk downplay changes which occur in early and later adulthood. When "elder" (*tugofaiy*) status is reached, however, sometime in the late forties or early fifties, certain personal traits are said to become more prominent in some people.

Older persons are said to be more likely to be "easily and often frightened" (*garusrus*) and are also more likely to be "playfully happy" (*metau*). Although senility is known and named, it is not considered to be a necessary or common concomitant of old age. Neither is physical debilitation considered naturally to follow aging, although the several seventy-year olds who continue to work in the taro fields and climb coconut trees are seen as commendable.

Just as daily discussions on Ifaluk about the varieties of living persons elucidate some of the most important dimensions of personhood, so do deaths become "occasions for dramatic public statements about the meanings of particular lives and of life in general" (LeVine 1982a:26). The Ifaluk mourn each death massively with wailing and sung laments which tell of the pain of bereavement and the beauty or skills of the lost one.

> I will lose my mind with missing her.
> She was like a flower,
> Like the quick-growing tumeric;
> She grew fast, but no sooner grown than she died.
> To her mother she was like a flower;
> I wanted to wear her in my hair;
> But she has died and left me.
> I am worn with sorrow.
>
> (Burrows 1963:300)

People do not simply die; they "die away from" the living. The loss of the elderly is said to be no less painful than the loss of children. My question whether the imminent death of an eighty-year-old woman would be seen as putting her "out of her misery" was greeted with some incredulity; the death of a person of any age tears a hole in a wide-ranging network.

Death is the point at which persons become spirits. It is as spirits that the deceased are dealt with from then on, and people reminisce little about them as persons; taboos on speaking their names support this practice. Although it is believed that those who have been good during their lives will become good spirits and those who have been bad will become bad spirits, these two prospects are not seen as reward and punishment as much as a continuation, in another form, of life as it was led in this world. Relatives who have died will be seen in the next world, and this fact is often given as counsel to those who are grieving over the death of another.[15] The exception is accidental or sudden death, which is a "bad death," because the deceased will become a particularly malicious spirit. The prospect of such a death for oneself or another is especially feared.[16] Death, both accidental and otherwise, stirs up the spirit world for a period and leaves the living both fearful and lonely.

In sum, ethnopsychological beliefs about development on Ifaluk are related to parental goals about the type of child desired (Lutz 1983). The good child is depicted in ethnopsychology as one who has the correct emotions as well as the correct behaviors. Children should grow up to work well and consistently and not be lazy or short-tempered. The child should grow into social intelligence, which is to say, able to think, feel, and behave like an Ifaluk person. A more detailed discussion follows of those qualities that are valued.

Interpersonal Variation and Conceptions of the Good

To speak of one set of terms which the Ifaluk use to talk about interpersonal variation as "personality" trait descriptors is misleading insofar as it connotes the range of ideas associated with that term in English, including ideas about the importance of traits in explaining much of the everyday behavior of individuals. Although the Ifaluk ethnopsychology of traits shares several notions with Western theory, such as a belief in the origins of some traits in early experience and learning, the emphasis is on explaining behavior rather than explaining individuals. In indigenous theory, people do have tendencies to feel, think, and behave in certain predictable ways, but in practice, it is only in exceptional cases that people are consistently or permanently identified with particular trait terms. Goodenough has identified this phenomenon on neighboring Truk, and he has noted that the permanent ascription of invidious labels to a large proportion of the population of nonmobile, face-to-face communities may be counterproductive for continued cooperation within such groups.[17] On Ifaluk, trait terms are used to explain and evaluate behavior only when it cannot be explained by solely emotional, which is to say, social situational, criteria. Thus, the ideal explanation appeals to what the Ifaluk see as universal human proclivities rather than particularistic ones. The latter are, however, sometimes necessary. While both state and trait terms are evaluative (and interrelated by their common reference to the same cultural value system), the use of trait terms may be less compatible with the goal of *changing* than that of simply identifying or labeling behavior.

To use a trait term on Ifaluk is, almost invariably, to make a moral statement. In speaking about other people, both in interviews and in the daily round of conversation, the Ifaluk consistently speak in the same breath of the good and the bad, traits, and the emotions.[18] Many traits are defined by the predominance in a person of a particular emotional style, while the behavioral implications of both temporary and permanent personal states are explicitly judged by the criteria of cultural values. Two logical statements can describe the broad outlines of Ifaluk beliefs about the connections among their values, traits, and emotions: (1) The good person is "calm" (*maluwelu*) and "afraid/anxious" (*metagu*) and is not "hot tempered" (*sigsig*). (2) The bad person "misbehaves" (*gataulap*), is not "afraid/anxious," and is "hot tempered."

The highest compliment that can be paid to a person is to say that he or she is *maluwelu,* or gentle, calm, and quiet. Used to describe either the lagoon or the wind when calm, the term also denotes a personal style unrippled by offensive actions or emotions. The root of the word (*maliuw*) refers to looseness, such as that in a slack cord. Connections between this trait and the emotions are direct and multifaceted, the primary ones being that the calm person is *not* hot tempered and *is* fearful. One woman described calm children to me in the following way, emphasizing the trait's origin in the child's relationship with his or her mother:

> Children who are calm stay with their parents and are *metagu* [afraid/anxious] among people. If one came here, she'd bend over in respect, talk slowly, and not make loud noises. They only go other places with their mothers. They are like this because they take after their mothers who also don't walk around. They are used to their mother's way and so are 'afraid/anxious.' If there is a feast, and the mother tells the child to go get her some tobacco [from another person], he won't do it because he's 'afraid/anxious.' The child who is not 'afraid/anxious' will stand right up and do it.

The seeming contradiction between obedience and calmness in the quote above is also evident in daily life. Although obedience is absolutely expected of older children, noncompliance is both tolerated and even positively sanctioned if it derives from the timidity associated with being calm. In all other areas, however, the calm person is obedient. Their "kindly talk," respectfulness, and even temper are the basis for the judgment that calm persons are pleasant companions. Children are sometimes told that they should be calm "so that others will like you."

112

The state of "fear/anxiety" (*metagu*) plays an important role in calmness as it is seen as the most important response to the potential justifiable anger of others at one's misbehavior. It is the potential for offending others (and provoking moral outrage or even violence) that leads to fear/anxiety and from there to the trait of calmness. I do not translate *metagu* as "shame," however, even though both concepts entail the inhibition of behavior in public; *metagu* involves a balance of self-consciousness and other-consciousness that shame does not. In addition, it is often the person who *has* misbehaved who is ashamed; it is the person who is conscious of the danger involved in potential misbehavior who is fearful/anxious (*metagu*) and acts calmly. The trait of calmness, then, arises not so much from an inner tranquillity (although calm people are not easily irritated) as from a sensitivity to and knowledge of cultural norms. The height of social intelligence, in fact, consists in large part of the thought, emotion, and behavior patterns characteristic of the calm person.

Calmness is seen as antithetical to a number of traits which are characterized by "show-off" behavior. Many words describe people who strut about, "thinking they are 'number one.'" People who are *gaiseus* walk with their shoulders thrown back and do not sit all the way down among a group of people. This manner of walking and sitting is seen as marking a lack of respect and an attitude of superiority. People who are *gatinap* constantly talk about their skills or intelligence; a *gatinap* man brags about the number of fish he has caught and often thinks that many women like him. *Gabosbos* refers mainly to people who show off their material possessions and is often used for those who come from other islands with radios or new clothes and with knowledge of the outside world. These show-off traits are very disliked because they are seen as painful to watch, stirring up jealousy or affronting another's rank. The number and constant use of terms descriptive of this constellation of traits is evidence of the high value placed on both egalitarianism and respect. In sum, the most highly valued trait on Ifaluk is calmness, as it results in harmonious, cooperative interaction. Opposed traits involve hot temper, misbehavior, and immodesty and are maligned for the social conflicts and bad feelings they create. Despite the presence of a hierarchy of clans and lineages, Ifaluk is a relatively egalitarian society. Rank ideally should be nonobtrusive, and jealousy about differential fortunes, where such exist, should be minimized. Even, or perhaps particularly, the atoll chiefs should show humility and calmness. Their hereditary leadership is spoken of as a service role, and it is duty rather than special skill that incumbents put forward as a rationale for their position.

Construing labor as work and as nurturance rather than as a personal achievement is consistent with other central Ifaluk values, including diligence and skill in work and generosity. Careful, diligent, and patient work is highly praised, and many words describe traits related to it. "One who is always working" (*tauyengang*) is considered an ideal marriage partner; such a person likes to work as much as possible, either at gardening, weaving, fishing, or canoe building. *Laloolai* describes the patient, even-tempered person who enjoys work and does not become upset by interruptions. *Sheowefish* are people who are industrious and take great care in their work. As with those who are *laloolai*, the secret of their success is in performing a task slowly and patiently, rather than doing it haphazardly or simply to finish. Like calmness, these traits are defined by the absence of irritability or hot temper.

The opposite characteristic is "laziness" (*gagu*). Although this common epithet is used especially with children, it also describes any adult who shirks duties, whether familial or communal. This trait is related to the emotion of *nguch* (sick and tired/bored), which occurs when one does not want to work. People will never characterize themselves as lazy but rather will say that they feel *nguch*. While the former is very negatively sanctioned, the latter is not. A self-proclamation of *nguch* may, in fact, prevent the attribution of laziness. "I am *nguch*" is a statement that my failure to work is merely a temporary reaction rather than an enduring personal trait, and people are at pains to avoid being seen as a poor worker by disposition.

Another set of personal traits are those connected with the value of generosity. *Mweol* (generous/friendly/obedient) describes a person who offers food, tobacco, and help freely and who personifies the value placed on sharing. Opposed and commonly used epithets for those who will not share include *farog* (stingy/selfish) and *lalongaw* (bad hearted). A related accusation is involved if one is called a "big eater" (*mongolap*). Periodic food shortages on the atoll mean that one person's eating more will entail another's eating less. Here the unmarked trait, in Fajans's (1985) terms, involves restraints on consumption such that an equal share of resources may be taken at all.

Several trait terms are specifically emotional types, that is, they describe a person in whom a particular emotion predominates. The two most common are *sigsig* (hot tempered/always angry) and *garusrus* (nervous/excitable/always fearful) (see chap. 7). A third and more general emotional type is *tangiteng,* which describes a tendency to cry often. Normal adults will cry only if someone has died or gone away or been lost at sea, and it is said that all people cry sometimes; "It is not possible," several people told me, "that someone would never cry." The person who is *tangiteng* tends to experience a stronger than usual "compassion/love/sadness" (*fago*) for others or is "hot tempered" (*sigsig*). People who are *tangiteng* will also cry when they are "happy/excited" (*ker*). Children are *tangiteng* for many reasons, but the most serious among them is the emotional state of the mother, as we have just seen. It is said that women, more often than men, are *tangiteng*. The person who was most often given as an example of a *tangiteng* person, however, was a man.

The types of virtues and vices that trait terms refer to are intimately related to Ifaluk values of cooperation, nonaggression, the minimization of jealousies, and sharing. Given these general values, it is not surprising that the ideal person is seen as calm, generous, hard working, and modest, and that these traits are lexicalized and discussed. The relationship between these traits and thoughts/emotions in ethnotheory is also evident and involves (1) the absence of hot temper, which disrupts both interpersonal relationships, personal equanimity, and work habits, and (2) the presence of a good amount of fear/anxiety, which works to encourage obedience and calmness and to discourage negatively valued behaviors, including aggression and showing off. Both trait and state attributions on Ifaluk are not simply statements about the characteristics of sovereign individuals. They are not the private property of the self. Rather, they explicitly link characteristics of persons to situational and social-moral considerations. The traits of a "good person" are those that create valued emotions in others and otherwise serve social ends.

Conclusion

The purpose of this chapter has been to describe the theories that the Ifaluk use to describe and explain human nature. Like the ethnopsychologies of all cultures, these Ifaluk beliefs are used to think and talk about people—their behavior, consciousness, and fundamental orientations in the world and about the nature of variation across individuals and across the life cycle. In broad outline, the Ifaluk speak about themselves as persons who are relatively undivided, either internally or from their social context. Thought and motivation, word and deed form more nearly seamless units than is the case in Euramerican ethnopsychology. The Ifaluk can, in fact, be characterized as having endowed themselves with an "emotional mind" that understands events in a way that is, in our terms, simultaneously cognitive and affective. Moreover, that consciousness, while localized by the

Ifaluk "in their insides," ideally serves not simply to understand the world but necessarily pushes the person to act in it. Consciousness has this latter element in part because people are characterized as oriented primarily toward other people rather than toward an inner world of individually constituted goals and thoughts. From the Ifaluk ethnopsychological perspective, it is not presocial individuals who confront the community, but rather persons who are profoundly influenced and defined by it.

Finally, we have also seen that the most central Ifaluk values are explicitly involved in their views of persons and in their descriptions of behavior. The people of this atoll have created an ethnopsychological knowledge system that can be used to make moral judgments— not only to predict what others will do but also to evaluate (and thereby, it is hoped, go some way toward controlling) the behavior of their kin and neighbors. In thinking and talking about persons, behavior, and consciousness, the Ifaluk are clearly involved in a *moral* discourse, and the outlines of the value system to which they subscribe are thereby highlighted.

Although this knowledge system has often been described here in the form of a general cultural code, it is in fact a system whose existence is verified and justified in concrete, everyday discourse, where it serves the immediate and pressing needs that people have to understand and justify their actions to each other, to interpret and evaluate ongoing events, and to solve occasional problems in the functioning of themselves and of others. This knowledge system is, in other words, the basis for much everyday social interaction; as Wallace has pointed out, any ethnopsychological frame of reference "is not merely a philosophical byproduct of each culture, like a shadow, but the very skeleton of concrete cognitive [and, we might add, emotional or evaluative] assumptions on which the flesh of behavior is hung" (1970:143).

PART 3

Need, Violation, and Danger: Three Emotions in Everyday Life

Need, Nurturance, and the Precariousness of Life on a Coral Atoll: The Emotion of *Fago* (Compassion/Love/Sadness)

The implicit poetry in Ifaluk emotional understandings is nowhere more evident than in the concept of *fago* (compassion/love/sadness). In their use of that word, people on Ifaluk communicate a central part of their view of human relationships; they impart their sense of the place of suffering in their lives, of the naturalness of interpersonal kindness in the face of that pain, and of their feeling that maturity consists, above all, in the ability to nurture others. *Fago* speaks to the sense that life is fragile, that connections to others both are precious and may be severed through death or travel, that love may equal loss. *Fago* is uttered in recognition of the suffering that is everywhere and in the spirit of a vigorous optimism that human effort, most especially in the form of caring for others, can control its ravages.

My sense of what people were saying when they used the term *fago* emerged only slowly over the course of my stay on the island. The concept required, more than did most other Ifaluk emotion concepts, an effort to disentangle my own native emotional understandings from theirs. From the perspective of the implicit notions entailed in the American-English terms—including compassion, love, and sadness—that together best translate *fago,* the concept involves some basic internal contradictions. In particular, love and sadness differ in valence, in behavioral consequences, in the sense of empowerment they bestow, and in feeling tone. Love is positive and activating, sadness negative and enervating; the loving person is strong, the sad person weak. The ethnotheoretical notions surrounding the emotions with which I had come to Ifaluk created the structure of bafflement that I felt at seeing the diverse contexts within which the term *fago* (compassion/love/sadness) was used. The following accounts of several events I either observed or participated in exemplify the problems encountered in translating *fago*.

Ilefagochang, a woman in her late twenties, walked with me past the church one early evening as the sounds drifted from a group of women singing at daily vespers. Ilefagochang recognized the voice of her younger friend Lauchepou in the chorus, and said in the sentimental tone that people typically use to express affection, *"Mawesh Lauchepou"* (sweetheart Lauchepou).

Ilefagomar asked me one day if I had ever seen a person who had no toes. I replied by describing the somewhat more horrible condition of a man I had seen in New York City some years before. This man, I explained, had no legs but propelled himself along the city streets on a low board outfitted with wheels. To this, another woman who was listening exclaimed, with much intensity in her voice, "I would *fago* him if I saw him." She then immediately asked me where his family was and why they were not "taking care of" (*gamwela*) him.

As we sat listening to a love song on the radio that was tuned to a Guam station that played American music, Ilefagochang indicated that she had goose bumps and added that they are caused by, among other things, our *"fago* for the person who is singing."

A young married man, Gachipemar, became very ill. His relatives attributed the illness to his excessive drinking, which they had earlier advised him to limit for his health's sake. When his stomach swelled out and the problem appeared to be a serious one, the standard and elaborate scenario for caring for the sick (to be described in a moment) began. Several weeks later, the interisland ship came and took Gachipemar, in the care of Pakesowel, his older brother, to be treated at the hospital on Yap. The brothers returned on the next ship, because the younger's condition had improved. Pakesowel told his relatives on his arrival, however, that Gachipemar had, against his advice, begun drinking again as the illness had receded. Pakesowel reported that he had rebuked Gachipemar for this behavior on Yap, saying to him, "You do not *fago* my thoughts." He reminded Gachipemar, he went on, that he (Pakesowel) had taken him to Yap's hospital even though it meant leaving his young son, for whom his *"fago* is strong" and on whose account he was homesick on Yap. By way of final reprimand, he told Gachipemar, "You do not *fago* your own breath [or life]."

On another occasion, I was sipping early-morning coffee with Ilefagomar when she told me that she had heard her younger brother singing as he fished from his canoe in the lagoon the previous evening. As she heard him, she said, "I had a bit of *fago* for him."

The field ship was making a daylong stopover at Ifaluk. It had gotten dark and the time was nearing for the boat's departure. I was sitting near the shore with Getachimang, an older man, when his twenty-five-year-old classificatory son, who was to leave on the ship, came to bid him a formal goodbye. The two men spoke in especially serious and quiet voices, calling each other father and son, terms that are rarely used in addressing (rather than simply in referring to) one's relatives. They held hands for some time, as Getachimang said several times to his son, "Be careful." The younger man reciprocated by speaking of his *fago* for the father.

These episodes indicate that the translation of the concept of *fago* (compassion/love/sadness) requires an understanding of the way the Ifaluk conceptualize positive relationships with others. *Fago* is used to alert others to the strength of particular relationships, to talk about the pain involved in the severance of those relations by death or travel, and to signal a readiness to care for the other. To explore in more detail the daily events that set the stage for *fago* is to examine the relationships that matter to people on Ifaluk, *how* precisely they matter, and the kinds of action—including primarily nurturance—that the relationships with others are felt to demand.

The Forms of Need and Nurturance

The primary contexts in which *fago* occurs are those in which the person confronts another who is somehow *in need*. The link between *fago* and "neediness" (*gafago*) is indexed in the form of the latter term; the causative prefix *ga-* is added to the emotion term *fago* to produce the term which can be translated as "needy" or "poor" (*gafago*). Thus, the person who is needy is one who literally "causes compassion" in others. The idea that neediness *necessarily* produces nurturant feelings and actions in mature others is not only seen linguistically but is also a deep and consistent theme running through Ifaluk culture more generally. This assumption—that a durable and automatic link exists between the suffering of one person and the nurturing of others—lies at the heart of Ifaluk emotional and moral life.

The *gafago* (needy, poor) are those individuals who are lacking one or more of the necessities for a good life. The needy are identified by the Ifaluk as those who are sick or dying; those who must leave the island and their families for some period; those who lack the ability to procure their own food, such as children, the aged, and the infirm; and those who lack the mental abilities or social status that would enable them to make decisions and move as autonomous agents in the world. Thus, the needy are the foodless, the landless, the kinless; they are the unhealthy and the socially subordinate.

While need provides the most fundamental pretext for *fago,* the emotion also arises in quite different circumstances. *Fago* occurs in one's relationship with people who exhibit some of the most culturally valued personal traits. People who are "calm or gentle" (*maluwelu*), generous, or more generally "socially intelligent" (*repiy*) are particularly apt to encourage feelings of *fago* in others.[1] As we will see, such people resemble the needy in an important way because both activate similar scenarios of nurturance, invoking a script that calls for active caring for the other.

Let us look, now, at the various kinds of contexts in which the concept of *fago* is used by the Ifaluk to understand events and to constitute their relationships with others. In the process, we will look at aspects of the emotional meaning of illness, death, hunger, children, social hierarchy, and good citizenship.

Illness

The use of emotion words in everyday life can be said to mark or acknowledge the existence of particular kinds of relationships. One of the most common kinds of relationships that *fago* points to is that which exists between the sick and the healthy. What makes the concept of *fago* an appropriate marker is the expectation that the sick person is suffering and in need, not only of recovery, but of elaborate and constant care by others. In addition, the concept of *fago* is often used in these situations to indicate concern that the sick person will die or, in other words, one's sense that ultimate separation and loss are imminent. Ifaluk's experience with sudden and devastating epidemics and the inadequacy of the island's cosmopolitan health care system help to explain the intense expectation that illness will lead to death.

The scene that occurs at the bedside of an ill person on Ifaluk is a dramatic one from the perspective of someone like myself, whose previous experience was restricted to some middle-class American patterns of treatment of the sick. If the illness is considered a serious one, people begin measures such as those taken for the young man, Gachipemar, mentioned earlier. When his stomach suddenly swelled, leaving him prone and in great pain, his sisters and father went to visit him at least twice daily for the first few days of his illness. Divination was carried out by one of the few older men who had the skill, and the family was advised to move the patient from his wife's household to his natal land if his condition did not soon take a turn for the better. The move was made, but the patient was later returned to his wife's homestead for the next several weeks of his illness.

Several family members who knew the recipes for medicines thought to be potentially helpful for Gachipemar's condition went out into the bush to collect the necessary ingredients, and each brought and administered his mixture to the patient. The recipes for particular medicines on Ifaluk are privately owned, and individuals maintain secrecy about their contents. The use of such valued knowledge in attempts at curing is considered one of the most important expressions of *fago* for the ill person. Gachipemar's older sister, Ilefagomar, was one of those who donated medicine. On several subsequent occasions, I heard her describe to others how she had given her brother the medicine, emphasizing explicitly each time that she did it out of her *fago* for him.

When Gachipemar's condition did not improve, his large extended family began to move their sleeping mats and mosquito nettings to his wife's household. Such moves by the patient's family are common during long-term and serious illnesses, for several reasons. First, the change of residence allows those involved to be available for the extensive twenty-four-hour patient care that is required. The move also is motivated in many cases by the fear that the patient's death is impending. Since one of the most important goals of every adult on Ifaluk is to be at the side of close relatives at the moment of death, continued residence at home poses a great risk. The move also allows people to communicate to others the extent and degree of their *fago* for the patient, involving, as the move does, no small amount of effort and inconvenience.

Several weeks passed, with continued provision of medicines and daily massage treatments. Each day would find Gachipemar lying on his mat with from at least two or three to many more individuals attending to his needs. If one counted household members and those who had come from elsewhere to be with the patient, more than fifty individuals could be found in and around the house during any one day. One, two, or even on some occasions ten people sat next to him fanning away the heat and flies. If Gachipemar wished it, his head and shoulders would be propped up on the lap of someone who sat behind him. He would be gently carried down to the lagoon several times a day for elimination and bathing. Fresh flower wreaths were constructed for his head, and he was anointed with coconut oil. The early morning hours would find several people at his side who had remained awake caring for him throughout the night.

The primary person involved in coordinating Gachipemar's care was his older brother, Pakesowel. When Gachipemar was eventually evacuated on the ship to the Yap hospital, Pakesowel accompanied him there. It was primarily women who fanned and fed him, with his mother's sister, wife, wife's mother, and brother's wife caring for him most actively. Although they were in near-constant attendance and although they brought medicine, Gachipemar's three sisters tended to stay at a small distance, given the taboos that regulate the brother-sister relationship (see chap. 6). Thus, the nature of the expression of *fago* reflected both the culturally induced formality and the intensity of relations that exist between the sick and the healthy.

As Gachipemar's illness worsened, including several episodes of spirit possession, people came to expect his death. His name was rarely used, this in partial parallel to the taboo on the use of the names of the dead, and he was instead usually referred to as "the sick person." Tears became more frequent in those who waited on him; his brother Pakesowel wept quietly as he propped up his head, his wife's father cried as he talked about moving him into his own sleeping house in case he died, and his sister Ilefagomar had tears in her eyes as she reported the instructions they had received by radio not to feed Gachipemar until the ship arrived for him.

The treatment accorded Gachipemar, who eventually recovered after his evacuation to Yap, was seen on the numerous other occasions when people became ill. In the shorter or milder cases of illness, the special attention might be restricted to a mother's staying awake through the night and bathing her fevered child or to a brother's visiting his sister whose diarrheal bout had diminished her appetite and his expressing concern that she try to eat. Conversely, when the possibility of the death of the patient becomes a certainty, the expression of *fago* intensifies beyond even that shown in Gachipemar's case. As one elderly man slowly died of tuberculosis, he was dressed in a bright, new, blue loincloth, anointed with imported perfume, and bedecked daily with multiple freshly woven flower wreaths. Several villages sent collective gifts of drinking coconuts to his household, and nearly everyone on the island made a visit to him at one time or another during the last few weeks of his life.

Death

The dying person is the prototypical object of *fago*. When I asked people about recent experiences with *fago,* many spoke of death. As one woman, whose elder relative had recently died, said,

> The last time I [experienced] *fago* was when our 'mother' died two days ago. We really felt bad inside. It was like our insides were being torn. We beat our chests and scratched our faces because our *fago* was so strong, because there is no other time that we will see her.

A man whose classificatory brother had recently died in a fall from a tree said,

> At the time, I felt like I was going to cry all the time, every time I remember what we did together, like drinking and fishing together, and then I feel like I will cry.

The *fago* that begins in illness is intensified when death occurs, and the experience is described as that of a "ripping stomach" (*ye tewasi segai*).[2] From a young age, children also recognize death as overwhelmingly central to the meaning of the concept of *fago.* An eleven-year-old girl spoke about the meaning of the word *fago* by reference not only to death but also to the specific kinds of relationships whose potential loss would most concern her:

> Sometimes I *fago* someone from my family who has died. I really *fago* him [or her]. I feel bad. If a man died, I would *fago* a lot . . . If we were sisters, I'd cry.

The response to death that the adult woman above refers to was, like the scene that accompanies illness, a dramatic and even shocking one for me, given that I, like most young Americans, had neither observed death nor encountered anything but the subdued ritual of one funeral.[3] My first view of the emotional response to death on Ifaluk occurred when Tomas, a five-year-old boy, contracted a sudden, high fever (most probably as the result of meningitis) and was comatose within twenty-four hours. People began to gather at the house of his biological parents, where he had been brought by his adoptive parents when he first became sick. The usual routine of washing a child's feverish body was followed by several women through the morning until it became clear that such pragmatic expressions of *fago* were futile. Expecting death, and anticipating its timing, the close male relatives took turns holding his semirigid and rale-shaken body. Tomas's two fathers, his biological father's brothers, and his several adult half-brothers wept as they cradled him. His biological mother, in a dazed state, lowered from the rafters the bundle of lavalavas and grave goods (known as the *tugtugal mas*) that each household keeps prepared for the deaths of close relatives.[4]

At the moment of death, a great wailing went up. The dead boy's biological mother, seated on the floor mats near him, rose to her knees as if she had been stabbed and pounded her fist violently against her chest. The adoptive mother, a woman of about sixty (and the boy's father's sister), began to scream and throw herself about on the ground. Others rushed forward to restrain both of them from hurting themselves, and the biological mother was soon sitting in stiff shock. The house filled with crying, from low moaning to loud, wrenching and mucus-filled screaming to wailingly sung poem-laments, and continued without pause through the night. Both men and women spent tears in what seemed to me equal measure. It is customary that people take turns coming forward (or rather being invited forward by the closest relatives) to cry in the immediate circle around the body. A careful choreography of grief generally requires that those who are "crying big" (or loudly and deeply) do so closer rather than further from the body, and that those who are not crying move back from it.

The next morning, the body was placed in a coffin that had been built by the men of the village. Objects from the *tugtugal mas* were placed in the box alongside items given by other relatives and neighbors as visible signs of their *fago* for the deceased. Lavalavas were also brought for the family of the child. As a final gesture, close family members cut their hair into the coffin (in some cases nearly shaving their heads). The box was then carried to the graveyard and lowered into the ground; an uninscribed wooden cross was added to mark the site.

Traditionally, the Ifaluk buried their dead at sea (Burrows and Spiro 1953:311). Land burial was encouraged by the Catholic missionaries who proselytized on the island in the 1950s, and the last ocean burial was in 1963. Some people complained, however, of their unhappiness with the use of the graveyard because it serves as a constant reminder of the death of loved ones. Sea burial, they maintain, made it easier to do the necessary forgetting of the deceased. The graveyard stands in contradiction to the several cultural practices which are designed to aid in this forgetting (such as taboos on speaking the name of the dead person). Although Tomas's family would return to weave flower garlands for the grave the next four mornings and evenings and although his mother's brother would "cry big" on the gravesite on his return from another island, in general this and others graves are avoided.

For the next four days, Tomas's family would do no work. They "cried big" again the morning after the funeral and spent much of their time lying down, as is customary. Relatives and neighbors frequently came to visit over the next days and months in an explicit effort to help them "forget about" the dead child. "Kindly talk" was in much more frequent use than usual in talking to those who were grieving.

A two-sided approach to dealing with the loss of death is promoted on Ifaluk. On the one hand, people are advised by others to "cry big," particularly at the funeral, and told that those who do not will likely become sick afterward (see chap. 4). On the other hand, the grieving person is told to think of the living and in essence to refocus her *fago* on those who are in need of nurturance, such as her children. In talking to me several months later about the death of her son, Tomas's biological mother, Lemalesep, said,

> I didn't think he was very sick at first, that it was just the flu. But then he didn't speak. When he couldn't open his mouth, then I got *rus* [panicked/afraid/surprised]. I just lay down here; I didn't know what the people around me were doing. My head hurt, probably because my thoughts and feelings [*nunuwan*] came up from my insides to my head. I couldn't walk because my legs hurt. But they talked to me to think about my other children and to take care of the baby and I thought, maybe it's true [that I ought do that].[5]

At the funeral and in the weeks following it, several people repeatedly advised the principal mourners (the four parents) to try to forget about the dead child.

The pain nevertheless continues. One woman described the *fago* that lingers after death by talking about a hypothetical person whose daughter has died:

> They will see the taro-patch planting of their dead child and cry and leave. Or they will see the flower wreath worn by their dead child and they cry and wrap it up carefully in a new cloth to keep. Or they will see their child's friends and be reminded. They are not hungry.

Fago is not the only response to death. The *rus* which accompanies the initial shock of a death (and particularly an unexpected one) can, as we have just seen, linger after the event. For others, the long-term emotional meaning of death centers on the notion of *nguch* (sick and tiredness/boredom/irritation). Lemalesep spoke more about her *nguch* than her *fago* when reflecting on the aftermath of her son's death:

> These days I am often *nguch* because of my child that died. I think that maybe he will just walk up the path. I remember his manner[6] when he was alive. He was not skinny like [his younger brother], but rather was big. I can't sleep. I don't like people to bother me [a typical index of *nguch*]. Then I walk around so my *nguch* will leave. Then I can sit down.

The concept of *nguch* is used to talk about frustrating situations which must be accepted despite the difficulty. For the Ifaluk, illness produces primarily the active emotion of *fago* in others, while death also induces the emotions that derive from a realization that nothing more can be done.

The person who dies is said to "die away from" the living. This turn of phrase reflects the fact that death is seen not so much as the end of an individual life but as the end of a set of relationships. In some cases, it is also a "dying toward" the spirit world; certain deaths are said to be caused by the spirit of a deceased relative who had strong *fago* and *pak* (homesickness, missing) for the dead person. The emotion of *fago* marks the existence of a valuable relationship, including a relationship that is threatened by death.

To Be without Kin

Perhaps the worst fate that most people on Ifaluk can imagine is to be without kin—either through a combination of demographic chance and death or by travel from the island. In the last two circumstances, the concept of *fago* is used to communicate the importance of those missing relatives. In daily conversation, people speak of their *fago* for those relatively rare individuals whose kinship networks are small or are missing crucial members. By use of the concept, the islanders also announce and renew their kin ties to the increasing number of people who leave the atoll for schooling, health care, wage labor, or marriage.

One's kin represent both companionship and social and economic support and survival, as they do in most preindustrial societies, and on Ifaluk the companionship and support are spoken of in the idiom of nurturance and, particularly, of food. People without kin on Ifaluk are said to have no one "to take care of them [*gamwelar*]"; they are, above all, people without food. The man who has no sisters can be in the precarious position of being without access to taro gardens and their fruits; the old woman without sons is said to be pitiable as she has no one to bring her fish. The tragedy of being without relatives is also that one then eats alone, and for the solitary diner, "food does not taste sweet." Each meal is a reminder that one is denied the opportunity of sharing food with the relatives who are either permanently or temporarily missing.

Let us look in turn at each of these two related contexts for *fago*—the traveling relative and the permanently missing one. Most of Ifaluk's people were born, live, and will die within the boundaries of the atoll's one-half square mile. The ties to other people that result from this embeddedness are multiple, strong, and enduring. Although travel from the atoll has always occurred, as men have sailed to distant atolls for trade or marriage, it has dramatically increased in the more recent colonial past as young men have left for schooling or, in some cases, wage or nonwage labor. Travel now is not by canoe but by the interisland steamer which arrives approximately every six weeks. An emotional cycle runs parallel to the ship's schedule as people are taken away to visit sick relatives on other atolls, to high school on Ulithi, or to work or hospital on Yap.

In the days before the ship is to arrive, both men and women talk explicitly about the impending loss. People who are leaving may comment on their own imminent homesickness (*pak*) or speak about their *fago* for those who will be left behind in some neediness, without recourse to the traveler's help. Here, as elsewhere, the use of a particular emotion concept may be used to rule out other, less favorable definitions of the situation. Thus, initially one teenage boy said he was afraid (*metagu*) to go back to high school on Ulithi because he would be labeled "dumb" there. Several days later, he was saying instead that he would not go because he had *fago* for his needy family, who required his help.

The relatives whom the traveler leaves behind more commonly speak about their *fago*—both for the person who will suffer in homesickness once they leave and for themselves in their own loss. As one woman told me, "Every day I *fago* my relatives who are away. I *fago* them, that they might be sick, and because I don't see them." *Fago* for the traveler is based on the horribleness of homesickness. One man described the consequences of homesickness as follows:

That person will sleep a lot. And talk a lot about his island. He'll get sick. [Actually] he'll just pretend to be sick but is not really sick. Taliyag was homesick on Ulithi and went crazy [*bush*]. He couldn't sleep or eat. He thought people were after him. There was a man from Yap who went to Harvard and went crazy because of his homesickness. There were no other Micronesians there. He's still crazy.

That part of *fago* caused by the loss itself is often described as due to the thought that one might never see a relative again.

The evening before the ship is to arrive, those who will leave travel to the homes of their relatives to say a formal goodbye. Night visiting is otherwise rare on Ifaluk and thus marks the occasion as particularly special. As we saw in the episode recounted at the beginning of this chapter, these leave-takings are marked by especially quiet, polite, and sentimental talk. When one boy came to say goodbye to the family with whom I stayed, both the elder man and woman of the house "spoke kindly" (*kepat gach*) to him and each kissed his hand.

An informal set of norms is attached to the moments of leave-taking. A wife may not touch her departing husband, and many will not speak or overtly acknowledge the parting. Taboos in the brother-sister relationship continue to apply here, but other relatives may kiss a departing child or adult.[7] Generally, both the traveler and those being left behind should strive to avoid crying at the shoreline, this constraint being especially important for the person leaving. At parting, however, there is often weeping on all sides, with people occasionally running back toward the houses to hide their tears from the object of their feelings.

One young man who was leaving for high school on Ulithi told me that he and his classmates would get drunk before they left so they would not cry. Like many men, he spoke spontaneously and openly (and more frequently than did women) about those occasions on which he had cried in the past; when he first went to high school, he said, he wept every night.[8]

After the ship has left with its Ifaluk passengers, people speak again and again about the missing. Sitting around at work or rest, someone will spontaneously remark, in reference to the person who is gone, "that sweetheart" ("*maweshe iy*"). For those closest to the traveler, the experience of *fago* is as painful as it was for one woman whose two brothers left on the ship:

When [my brothers] went away to high school, I *fago*. Maybe because I was used to them always coming here to eat. When they left, my *fago* made me unable [to function]. That night, the ship stayed for a while and I could hear the engine and I couldn't get to sleep. I was incapacitated with my *fago*. I sat up, opened the doors, and smoked outside. I just cried and cried. My back hurt so I lay down. . . . In the morning, I didn't want to see the house where they slept.[9] Now it [the *fago*] has calmed down a bit because it's been a long time.

While travel creates one kind of kinlessness, demographic variation creates another. Couples may be childless, a man may have no sisters, a household may have no men. To understand the *fago* that people express for the barren woman, the only child, or the man without sisters, as well as the *fago* felt for one's existing kin, is to understand how the Ifaluk kinship system is experienced by individuals. *For whom* people feel *fago* is an index of which kin relations are seen as most necessary to the quality of life. *Why* the emotion is felt for each type of relative indicates the kinds of duties and benefits attached to that relationship. Ifaluk ideas about what people need, and about how relatives serve to fill those needs, are evident in the concept's use.

Several relationship types can be explored by examining the way in which *fago* is used to articulate their meaning. The parent–child relationship is, along with that between sisters and brothers, the one most frequently understood with the concept of *fago*. The child is the quintessential needy person—vulnerable to illness and death and unable to get his or her own food—the ultimate subordinate and the ultimate object of *fago*. In needing the parents' care, the child needs the parents' *fago*. Children are often named in accordance with this emphasis on their vulnerability and the nature of their relationship with the adult world. There are, for example, women on Ifaluk named Lefagochang and Lefagoyag and men called Fagolimul and Fagoitil, names which may be translated respectively as "love and desire," "love binding," "love and generosity," and "love quickening."

When Ifaluk parents talk about their *fago* for their children, it is frequently when the child is sick. Their use of the term to describe the situation is an attempt to communicate their sense that the child is helpless and may die. Fevers in particular are cause for both alarm (*rus*) and *fago*. Again and again, people would recount their children's illnesses and, in so doing, would describe the thoughts and behavior indicative of *fago:* "I didn't sleep all night"; "I bathed my baby in cool water"; "I thought she was going to die." Healthy children are also recipients of *fago,* which is seen as a parent fans away the heat or gently captures mosquitoes as they alight on her sleeping child or carries a four-year-old on his back.[10]

131

On the other hand, the parent also needs the child, both for its eventual contribution to the household labor pool and to the parent's care in old age and for the enjoyment and fullness he or she brings to the home. To be without children, then, makes the adult an object of *fago*. To give a child in adoption to such a person is a commendable act of *fago*. Although nearly every household on Ifaluk has adopted children, the rate of adoption is much higher among barren couples, with several having adopted four or five children. A woman who loses a child to death is sometimes given another child in adoption soon afterward, people say, "because we *fago* her." As parents reach infirm old age, the emphasis shifts from their *fago* of the child to the child's *fago* for his or her mother and father. When conflicts arise over the extent to which the child is fulfilling obligations to an aging parent, however, the failure may be discussed by the elder as an emotional failure.

The complementarity and central importance of the relationship that exists between brothers and sisters on Ifaluk is reflected in the *fago* expressed between them and the pity bestowed on those who have no cross-siblings, particularly men in such a position. Women often speak of their *fago* for their brothers, as, we noted above, Ile-fagomar did after hearing her brother sing as he fished in the lagoon. Ilefagomar's statement draws on the notion that women need brothers (and men, more generally) to fish for them. Her statement also had the pragmatic effect of praising her brother for his diligence and skill in fishing, for, as we will see, the word *fago* is also used to talk about situations in which someone exhibits exemplary behavior.

In talking about adoption, a woman will commonly say that she has taken in her brother's children "because I *fago* my brother, and therefore take care of his children." In feeding these children, she in effect gives her brother access to the produce of her gardens. In addition, a man's sister will often send him cooked taro or breadfruit as an explicit sign of her *fago* for him. Implied here is that the man is needy in not having any gardens of his own. Although he eats from his wife's gardens, in a sense, it is only at the latter's pleasure that he does so. A man has tenuous ties to taro land, and so is pitiable; his most solid ties are through his sister, however, and she feels her obligation, expressed as *fago*, to send him food and to feed his children. One man in his fifties was frequently spoken of as an object of *fago* because he had no biological sisters. This man was an only child, and although it is pitiable to have no brothers, people much more commonly remarked on his lack of sisters. The gifts of food that were frequently sent to him by his clan sisters and those sisters' children were signs of their *fago*. The recognized complementarity of men and women (both brothers and sisters as well as husbands and wives) is revealed in the attempt people make to put together a household, through birth and adoption, of both genders. One woman whose marriage had been barren remarked that she had followed the common wisdom in adopting both boys and girls. The boys, she said, "will take care of the girls, getting them fish and coconut sap, and climbing for coconut and breadfruit," while the girls will get taro.

In crisis, it is cross-siblings who, out of their *fago* for each other, most forcefully come to each other's aid. When Tamalekar's ten-year-old son threw a rock at the island's psychotic, Tamalekar's sisters hurried to his house with gifts of cloth goods to be given, by way of apology, to the family of the "crazy" man. It was particularly Tamalekar's shame and embarrassment (*ma*) over his son's behavior that elicited his sisters' *fago*. Similarly, when Ilefagomar's father and sister abandoned her to travel to another atoll just before her giving birth, it was her brothers who rushed to her side to comfort her and assure her of their *fago* and added help (see chap. 6).

The relationship between two sisters is also a very close one on Ifaluk. Frequently, sisters will spend their entire lives together under the same roof, eating from the same pot, weaving at adjacent looms, and tending each other's children. Although the relationship is at least as central to their everyday lives as any other, the concept of *fago* is not used by women as often to talk about their sisters. This seeming paradox might be explained by the fact that relations between sisters do not share two of the important characteristics of the other relationships which are marked by declarations of *fago*, that is, clear differences in rank and a cultural and objective sense of the vulnerability of the relationship. In contrast with cross-siblings and parents and children, sisters are relatively equal in status, and social structural arrangements place them solidly in alliance and proximity. The concept of *fago* is used to mark relationships whose inequality highlights the need for nurturance and whose vulnerability to loss is more likely owing to death or social arrangements, conditions which do not normally exist for sisters.

The solitary anthropologist in the field must represent, virtually everywhere, a somewhat anomalous type of human being because he or she lives without kin. Despite the anomaly, the whole complex of Ifaluk ideas about the relationship between *fago* and kinlessness was activated to understand my position in the community. People frequently remarked that they had *fago* for me because I was so far from my family and because I must be terribly homesick. My adoption by an Ifaluk family and their feeding of me was understood as an expression of *fago*—as the normal and necessary response to my vulnerable situation.

Although I was in fact homesick during my stay on the island, use of the concept of *pak* (homesickness) to understand the situation came more slowly to me than it would have to an Ifaluk person in a similar situation. This contrast corresponds to that between Ifaluk's political economy and our own; the survival value of strong and enduring ties among people on Ifaluk has made the paired concepts of *fago* and *pak* central to their emotional understandings of the meaning of separation from kin. The necessity for a physically and emotionally mobile labor force under industrial capitalism, on the other hand, has been one factor in the minimal cultural elaboration around the emotions of (at least temporary) separation in the United States. Discussions of the field experience in the anthropological literature reflect this by failing to mention it as a possible, much less a central, element in the field-worker's response.

When the Ifaluk say that they *fago* the person who is without kin, they say that people need, above all, to be embedded in a network of others who "take care of" them. No person can survive alone, either physically or emotionally. No person ought to be denied the opportunity of being dependent on the judgment and caretaking of others. Perhaps paradoxically to the Western observer, the idea of being taken care of by others suggests one is in a comfortable position. The incredulity expressed over the story of the legless man on a New York City street was not due to the repulsiveness or the anomaly of his physical state. What astonished the women who heard about him was that a man in such need was not being taken care of by his relations. While the Ifaluk value their relatives as bulwarks against loneliness and for access to the wealth of larger numbers of taro gardens and fishing expeditions, these advantages are transcended by or subsumed within the notion that kin, through their *fago,* alleviate suffering and need.

Other Forms of Need

Several other types of need are emphasized in Ifaluk thought and spoken of in terms of *fago*. People speak about their *fago* for those who suffer social embarrassment or discomfort. As we will see in chapter 7, one of the most unpleasant experiences for people is being the center of attention for any reason, especially, of course, being an object of critical attention. Ilemochang, a woman in her fifties who had adopted her brother's daughter, was scolded by him for allegedly failing to teach the girl how to work. A woman who had observed his harsh words to his sister said that she had *fago* for Ilemochang, who had at first tried to protest but finally "did not know what to say."[11]

Men, however, are said to be more susceptible to being shamed or embarrassed (*ma*) than are women, and as a result I more often heard statements expressing *fago* directed toward shamed men. Marriage is frequently the occasion for this emotion because a man must cope with the shame that can occur if the woman rejects him, as well as with the anxiety of coming to live with relative strangers in his wife's household. Ilefagomar told a small group of women and me the story of the attempt made many years earlier to marry her to Torogoitil. To show her opposition to marrying, she threatened to starve herself to death. Despite concerted efforts to gain her compliance with the arranged marriage, she ran off into the bush. Then, she said, one old man had such strong *fago* for Torogoitil that he himself ran into the woods in another direction.[12] As a result of both these actions, "the men got Ilemelemar [a prepubescent girl] for him [as a wife] so he wouldn't be ashamed [*ma*]."

A shamed person does not always prompt prople to *fago* him. When someone's misbehavior has resulted in their own shame, others may declare themselves "justifiably angry." Shame may also simply draw laughter from others if they choose to focus on the faux pas that has produced the shame. The use of the term *fago* (rather than *song* or laughter) in these contexts involves a process of social negotiation. Which emotion term is used is dependent on what people individually would like to see happen to the affected person (e.g., either relief or social ostracism) and how those goals are influenced by social forces and counterbargaining by others.

The discomfort associated with being the center of attention is also considered to be painful enough to warrant *fago* in mature onlookers. Lauchepou was sitting and talking with her sisters about the boys who had just gone off to high school on Ulithi when she remarked, "We *fago* the new students [the freshmen] because they aren't used to Ulithian custom, and they don't know all of the taboos that exist there." Implied here is that the boys must be anxious or afraid (*metagu*) in the new and unfamiliar setting. The Ifaluk assumption that it is *very* unpleasant to be with relative strangers could be inferred from the use of the concept of *fago* to explain how others ought to respond to newcomers. This was implicit in a discussion involving Lesepemang, a woman who was rejecting her new husband. Lesepemang's adoptive mother appealed to her capacity for *fago* when she asked, "Wouldn't you be 'afraid/anxious' [*metagu*] if you came to eat in a strange place [as your husband has]?"

Fago is also seen as an emotion that can prevent violence. If one feels *fago* for a potential victim, the desire to hurt is short-circuited. In socializing children, a parent's appeal to *fago* is often made as a way of promoting gentle (as well as generous) behavior. I observed an example of the teaching of the ethnotheoretical tenet that *fago* and consistently gentle behavior are linked as I sat with a small group of women in the cleared area in front of their house, preparing food for the next several days. The women, who included two sisters and the teenage adopted daughter of the elder, were using much muscle and sweat to grate coconut. Some taro they had harvested in the cooler sun of that morning boiled nearby in a large pot once used by the Japanese Army in the 1940s on nearby Woleai. They discussed with animation the ongoing conflict among some people in a neighboring household and concluded, as had others in the village, that the problem could be traced to the perennial hot temper of one of the older men of the house. As they chatted, they casually kept an eye on their toddlers who played at making kites out of the large breadfruit leaves that lay about the yard. Suddenly, one of the young boys picked a small piece of coral rubble off the ground, aimed it at the other two-year-old (his mother's sister's son) with whom he had been playing, and stood for some moments with the stone raised behind his head in a stereotypical gesture of threat. As was almost always the case when small children made aggressive moves, the nearby adults responded immediately. "Gatachemai," called out one of the women to her stone-wielding son, "Don't you *fago* your 'brother'?"

Similarly, people have seen Western movies (brought on shore occasionally by the personnel of visiting U.S. Navy vessels) in which characters are killed, and in recounting those viewings the narrator often mentions his or her *fago*. As one woman said, "I turn away [from the screen] because my *fago* is very strong for the ones who are killed." The middle-aged woman Lemalesep described *fago* to me as something that happens "if you see someone getting hit or having his hands tied together. You'll *fago* and think you'll go untie them, because he's *gafago* from that person." While violence is extremely rare on Ifaluk, anticipation of it is not, and the concept of *fago* is called on in planning one's response to it.

Fago for the self can also prevent suicidal violence, which is very common in the Central Carolines and in Micronesia generally (Rubinstein 1983). There had been two suicides (both committed by men) on Ifaluk in the twenty or so years before the fieldwork period, several suicide attempts, and many more suicide threats. After telling several stories about men who had killed themselves (which as we will see is often attributed to the justifiable anger of the suicide), Ilefagomar said, "Even if I was very *song,* I could never kill myself because I *fago* myself."

Drinking, which is taboo to women and nearly universal among men, is an additional context in which need is perceived and *fago* used. Men who become very drunk will often say that they *fago* themselves ("*Gang i fagoayei*"). It is said that some men feel this *fago* because they think that they will die. A man's more sober companions may also *fago* him in his very inebriated state; I saw, for example, one man hold up another who was intoxicated, lead him to his house, and attempt to get him food to eat. Because drunks more often inspire panic (*rus*) and flight or avoidance in women, whatever nurturance they receive is usually from other men.

What most of these diverse situations have in common is, in the Ifaluk eye, that they all leave a person in a state of need. People must be in a setting that is familiar, that is free of violence, and that does not make them objects of unwanted attention. Someone who is without these basic conditions may, and usually will, become an object of *fago*. The concern with these human needs emerges from a particularly Ifaluk set of emphases and constitutes one way cultural concerns are reflected in a society's emotion concepts.

The Good and Gentle Person

While most the contexts in which the word *fago* is used represent major or minor disasters for those involved, the emotion is also importantly linked to encounters with people whom the Ifaluk define as exemplary in crucial kinds of ways. As one person told me, "You *fago* someone because they do not misbehave. You *fago* them because they are calm and socially intelligent." This use of *fago* was exemplified in the following case. When the interisland ship arrived late one afternoon, it carried as passenger a young Trukese man who came ashore to visit Tamalekar. Although they had not met previously, their shared clan affiliation made the visit an appropriate one. They and the rest of Tamalekar's family spent the evening in quiet talk, with the Trukese speaking with respect and politeness. The visitor also distinguished himself by bringing a gift of a carton of cigarettes. The evening wore on past the point at which the family usually retired, and when the young man stepped out for a moment to relieve himself, Tamalekar said to his family, "We *fago* this one because he's calm [*maluwelu*]. Even though we're sleepy, we'll stay up and talk with him [until he's ready to go back to the ship]." Later, when the man was about to leave, Tamalekar gave him something from the locked cubicle in which he kept his most valued possessions.

Time and again, people would link the concepts of *fago* and *maluwelu* in their speech. The calm or gentle person is the epitome of the good person on Ifaluk (see chap. 4); no higher praise can be accorded someone than to say "She is *maluwelu*." The number of ethnopsychological inferences that Ifaluk adults can draw about the emotional world of the *maluwelu* person are many. Indigenous theory posits two types of connection between the trait or behavior of calmness or gentleness and the emotion of *fago*. In the first instance, people who have *fago* for others will be calm and gentle as a result; their behavior emerges from the emotion. Stated another way, calm people demonstrate, through their behavior, their compassion for others. What is compassionate about calmness is primarily that the calm person does not frighten others. He or she speaks quietly and politely and behaves gently, actions that most Ifaluk see as necessary for putting people at ease and relieving the fear that might otherwise result from being around others.

The relationship between calmness and *fago* for others was a frequent topic for discussion on Ifaluk. Several individuals in the village in which I lived were identified as *maluwelu*. Lepoulimai, they said in the same breath, is *maluwelu* and has *fago* for people. Conversely, people would remark on those who showed their lack of *fago* for others by their rough, uncalm behavior. After one of the island's chiefs went to scold the women of Woat village for teasing a young woman from Burag, someone remarked that the teasing was primarily led by Lemafagomar, "who does not *fago* people." Teasing is literally that which makes the other angry (*gasong*); the person who knows how to *fago* others acts in the calm ways which avoid making others *either* frightened or angry.

This context for use of the concept *fago* shares an important characteristic with the other, less pleasant ones that we have already examined insofar as it also refers to need. In this case, the *maluwelu* person fulfills the culturally constructed need for peaceful interaction with others. Here, however, it is not the perception of need but its alleviation by the *maluwelu* person that prompts declarations of *fago*. To be calm is to be giving, and giving ought to be reciprocated with compassion if possible.

A second ethnotheoretical link between the two concepts is that the calm person creates the emotion of *fago* in others. In other words, everyone loves those who are *maluwelu*. Lesepemang relied on my making these inferences when she told me, in the midst of a conflict with her mother's mother's sister, "I am justifiably angry with Laufelichou [her MMZ] because she talks sharply and abruptly to me. She doesn't talk *maluwelu* like [our adoptive mother], who we therefore *fago* and obey." It is important to add, however, that Lesepemang's praise of her adoptive mother was strategic, being used to dramatize her condemnation of Laufelichou. When she was, on other occasions, displeased with her adoptive mother, Lesepemang complained to anyone who would listen that her mother was hot tempered (*sigsig*), a trait which we saw in chapter 4 is diametrically opposed to both calmness and to *fago*.

Both of these senses in which *fago* and calmness (as well as generosity) are linked were drawn on when one young women answered my questions about when she experienced *fago* and how she knew when others did. "I *fago* you because you give me things. . . . If I take care of you, give you things, and talk to you, I'll know you *fago* me. You'll talk calmly to me and give me things and I'll know [that you *fago* me]."

These, then, are situations or contexts most centrally associated with the category *fago* in Ifaluk discourse. Categories, it has been demonstrated (Rosch and Lloyd 1978; Lakoff 1987), are organized around prototypic cases rather than by a set of properties or criteria shared by all members of a category. A shift is under way in many disciplines from the latter Aristotelian view of concepts which would lead us to ask, in this case, about the necessary and sufficient criteria for inclusion of events, feelings, or relationships in the category of *fago*. Instead, we are led to note that death and the parent-child relationship represent better examples, in the Ifaluk view, of *fago* than does the calm person. The new view of the nature of categories also leads us to look for the roots of category structure in underlying cultural goals and cultural models, as Quinn (1982) and Lakoff (1987) have suggested. The prototype effect found in *fago* could then be accounted for (1) by the notion, already elaborated, that one of the most fundamental culturally constituted goals is to take care of others, and (2) by that part of the cultural model in which attachment to others is seen as under threat of loss.

We can now go on to expand on the relationship between the emotion of *fago* and good behavior. We will do this by considering some of the ways in which this emotion is at the core of the cultural definition of maturity on Ifaluk.

Fago as Maturity, Nurturance as Power

The ability to experience *fago* is seen as one of the central characteristics of the mature person. The paramount importance of the concept of *fago* to Ifaluk life and culture is reflected in the fact that it is perhaps the ultimate quality of good people and competent adults. God, chiefs, parents, and elders all maintain the position and respect they command through their exercise of this emotion. The relative equality of status that women enjoy in many domains on Ifaluk is in part because they are seen as able to feel and act on this emotion at least as much as men, and thus can be defined as equally mature.

Ethnopsychological ideas about the development of *fago* over the life cycle support the association between this emotion and maturity. The ability to *fago* is dependent on the acquisition of mature language skills and of social intelligence (*repiy*), more generally. It is said that children first feel the emotion only after the age of about seven, which is, as we have seen, the age by which they have acquired social intelligence. As one woman told me, "When children understand the meaning of talk, then they know how to *fago*." Conversely, I several times heard people say that a deaf ten-year-old boy did not *fago* people because he could not hear or understand speech. Individual differences are recognized in the extent to which children learn to *fago*—differences which result from variation in their levels of social intelligence. The child who is socially intelligent will *fago,* but, in Ilefagochang's words, "Others don't 'think/feel' [*nunuwan*][13] and so *fago* only a little bit." A child must be thought-full if he or she is to be able to *fago*. *Fago* is an emotion whose full flowering requires the understanding that is attained only through social discourse, and the understanding that constitutes the emotion is dependent on more generic abilities to understand the social world. This emotion is, in effect, treated as a form of intelligence—an intelligence which is more valued by the Ifaluk than virtually any other kind.

Given its association with maturity, the concept of *fago* is commonly used to praise those whose behavior is exemplary in certain kinds of ways. Individuals will be praised by saying of them, "She [or he] is good. She [has] *fago* for people." While any individual can receive acclaim for their especially nurturing or compassionate behavior, the chiefs, benevolent spirits, and the Catholic priest who sometimes visits the island are frequently spoken of as ones who *fago* in great measure. These chiefs, spirits, and priests are distinguished by the fact that their intelligence (*repiy*) is expressed in the form of *fago* or caring for others. The chiefs, who are said to "take care of" the people of the island, do this by protecting them through regulation of such things as potentially aggressive outsiders, the lawbreakers among them, and overfishing of the lagoon. The good spirits of individual ancestors are also said to *fago* people, and particularly their descendents. The *fago* of the spirit of a dead mother for her sick adult child often results in the spirit sending a recipe for the necessary medicinal cure. In contrast to the *fago* of humans, however, the spirits' *fago* may result in some harm to the object of that emotion. This sometimes occurs when the spirit, out of *fago* and longing for the living relative, causes death so that they may be reunited in the spirit realm. The priest is also seen as a person of much *fago,* concerned particularly for the emotional well-being of his parishioners. People often mention that the priest helps them to recover from negative emotions of all kinds, advising them to calm down from their *song* and comforting them in the face of the death of their kin. In this, the priest acts in a parallel fashion to the Catholic God (*got*), who is also said to *fago* all people. The prayers of both priest and parishioners, however, are said to be used to calm God and make him *fago* the people. This belief (as well as perhaps its weakness) was illustrated by one woman's complaint, after news of a nearby typhoon reached Ifaluk, that no one was praying to God to *fago* them and make the typhoon swerve away from the atoll.

The chiefs, spirits, priest, and God, as well as other individuals, *fago because* they are mature or intelligent. One index of that *fago* is their nurturance of those who are in need of their care. A secondary index of *fago* is their calm, well-behaved (*maluwelu*) demeanor. As we have already noted, the calm person can be said by inference to exhibit *fago,* because in being gentle, he or she protects others from the fright and discomfort that they would feel in the face of aggression or other social disruptiveness.

In a sense, it is not only maturity but also *power* which is defined on Ifaluk as the ability to nurture others. Power resides particularly in those who have the mental, social, and physical resources to help others. Thus, the higher one's position is in the social hierarchy on Ifaluk, the more frequent and compelling are the contexts in which one is called on to *fago* and to "take care of" (*gamwelar*) others.

The hierarchy of power that exists in the islands between Yap and Truk is also phrased in terms of the ability and duty of the higher-ranked islands to take care of the lower ranked. At one point in 1978, news reached the island that the education bureaucracy in Yap was planning to build a junior high school on Woleai for the outer islanders. On hearing this, an elder man, Gatachimang, said that he was afraid (*metagu*) that the Woleaians would hit the students if given the responsibility for such a school, "because they are not used to taking care of others." Gatachimang's listeners would probably share his conclusion that Woleaians (who otherwise have no reputation for violence) might be capable of such behavior based on their knowledge that the atoll of Woleai is ranked lower than Ulithi, which is the current site of the high school for outer islanders. Although island ethnotheory does not hold that low rank, in and of itself, induces one to violence, rank does bring experience in nurturing, and in the Ifaluk view, inexperience might lead to the roughness which would go against the essence of what it means to take care of others.

A similarly instructive story reached Ifaluk from Woleai in 1978. Plans had also been announced by the Trust Territory government for an airstrip to be built on Woleai. Although the chiefs had given their approval to the project, many people on Woleai were apparently concerned that they could not afford to lose such a relatively substantial portion of their 1.7-square-mile atoll, particularly as the projected strip would cut through a large section of taro gardens. After this announcement, Woleai's high school students took it upon themselves to write a letter to the Trust Territory's High Commissioner saying that they did not want the airport on Woleai. Their rationale was phrased in terms of the associations we have been discussing among nurturance, maturity, and power. Their island, the students informed the commissioner, is the largest atoll in the area and so plays an important role in sending food to other atolls when a typhoon has damaged their food supply. If the airport cuts into Woleai's taro patch, they would not be able "to send their [the other islanders'] food."

Although the motivation for nurturing is portrayed by the Ifaluk as both mature and altruistic, it can also be seen that the ability to *fago* and care for the needy allows for and legitimates control over the needy person. People who are without kin are pitiable not only because they are lonely or because they have fewer land and labor resources; such people are also to be pitied or even scorned because they do not take care of others. In being denied the opportunity of caring for others, they are unable to control others, and in being unable to do so, they cannot command respect, which has both socioemotional and more tangible rewards.

This was illustrated by a conflict which erupted in one household where an extremely unpopular older man with a reputation for hot temper, Yasechaul, erupted in shouting at his niece and nephew. The cause for his fit of pique was, according to others, his "bad-heartedness" or jealousy over the fact that his younger relatives were not giving him cigarettes. If he had been another person, Yasechaul would have been within his rights to expect others in his household to share such a scarce resource with him. A sister's children in particular will be generous with their mother's brothers out of respect for them. Yasechaul was unusual, however, in both his hyperirritability and his chosen pattern of postmarital residence. While this household was that of his biological mother, his wife was a woman of Woleai, and he ought to have had his primary residence there.[14]

In later discussions of the conflict, people remarked on Yasechaul's hot temper (*sigsig*), selfishness (*farog*), and bad-heartedness (*lalongau*). But most remarkable for those who recounted the story was the statement he was reported to have made during his tirade: "I am," he told his niece and nephew, "the chief of this household." Ilefagochang expressed her astonishment to her sister at a neighboring household, "He is not the head of [that household]. He doesn't get food for them. He doesn't climb for breadfruit or coconut." She went on to describe the role of several of the other adult men of that household in collecting those foods and concluded that "Yasechaul cannot take care of the people of [that household]." The vehemence with which this man was denounced reflects both the value attached to the calm characteristics that he lacked and the centrality of nurturance to the Ifaluk definition of power. It is these two components of maturity—gentleness and nurturance—that contribute to the configuration and the importance of the concept of *fago* to everyday life on the atoll.

It is perhaps only in a society in which autonomous action to ensure individual survival is neither socially encouraged nor ecologically or economically feasible that nurturance will become central to the definition of power. For it may only be in that context that caring for others creates the greatest dependency in the recipient and control in the caregiver.[15]

The relatively powerful position of women on Ifaluk is generated through their ownership of garden lands and control of their products and through their positions as the heads of matrilocal households. But the strength of women is also reinforced by the cultural ideology surrounding the concept of *fago*—an ideology which defines their provision of food and their care of children as indices of both their maturity and their superordinate social position. Western ethnotheory tends, in contrast, to emphasize the softness or even the weakness of the person who nurtures. The nurturant person may be seen as morally noteworthy, but caring for others is an activity that tends to place one further down rather than up in sociopolitical ranking. Mothers, women more generally, and those who are engaged in personal-service occupations—each category of which is culturally defined as nurturant—have lower status than fathers, men, and non-service jobs. The explicit idiom for power is force rather than compassion.

The ways people on Ifaluk use the word *fago* to understand the situations they encounter both reflect the objective conditions of life on the atoll and reconstruct them, that is, make them meaningful in particular kinds of ways. We will now look at these two facets of the problem of the relationship between emotion and culture, first, by contrasting the ways loss is made meaningful on Ifaluk with the concepts used by Americans to make sense of that phenomenon, and second, by speculating on some possible relations between the atoll ecology and social structure and the concept of *fago*.

Fago, Compassion, Love, and Sadness: A Comparison of two Emotional Meaning Systems

The ethnographic understanding of the emotional worlds of other people is accomplished primarily by comparison with the emotional world into which the ethnographer is socialized. The communication of that understanding is usually to an audience of the ethnographer's cultural background and in its language. In the course of fieldwork, I came to think of *fago* partially in terms of the American-English emotion concepts of compassion, love, and sadness. An exploration of the meaning of those three concepts can highlight the fact that *fago* is adequately translated by no one of the three. More important, it can elucidate the similarities and differences between the meaning systems that have grown up around the facts of need and loss in these two societies.

In explicating the cultural meanings of love, compassion, and sadness, I cannot give here what would be ideal, which is the fuller and necessary ethnographnic context of use of the words in everyday life. I also cannot explore the question of the variation in subcultural uses and meanings of the three words in this society, nor is this the place to explore the voluminous literature on the history and social contexts of love in the West. What I will do is to draw on taped conversations about the emotions I have had with working and middle-class New Yorkers, my own native speaker's intuitions, and philosophical, anthropological, and social-psychological writing on the nature of the three emotions.

In what ways is "love" an illuminating translation for *fago* and in what ways misleading or distorting? The Ifaluk ideas expressed in the use of *fago* share some characteristics with love. Each represents perhaps the most highly valued emotion in its culture (although happiness may rival love for many Americans as the most important emotional quality in life). Love and *fago* each empower, as we will see, and so play a role in structuring care and responsibility for others. Each term also can be used to praise another. What is striking about much academic and nonacademic discussion of love, however, is a frequent focus on romantic love as its prototypic form. Although the concept of love is used to talk about both erotic, sexualized, or romantic love and "brotherly" love, [16] romantic love is primary to the more general concept's meaning. It is common belief among Americans that people love their spouses "more than" anyone else (Quinn 1987). As we have seen, *fago* is rarely used to talk about sexual relationships, and this is not merely because taboos surround discourse about the latter. Rather, another set of terms is used to talk about the emotions common to "boyfriends" and "girlfriends," including *chegas* (self-confidence, romantic pride), *baiu* (romantic love/happiness), and *magiuf* (self-confidence, happiness). These emotions are similar to happiness/excitement (*ker*) because, like the latter, they are often seen as dangerous, socially disruptive emotions (see chap. 6).

Averill (1985) describes the central components of love in American understandings as idealization of the other, suddenness of onset, physiological arousal, and commitment to the other. [17] Thus, both love and *fago* can be used to make positive evaluations of other people, but although *fago* can be used to express admiration for the *maluwelu* person, the emotion word is much less often used to elevate or idealize the other. *Fago* may in fact involve an assessment of the other person as weak or incapable of providing for the self. Love, on the other hand, *necessarily* involves admiration for its object. In other words, evaluation of the other as exemplary is central to the appropriate use of the word love and not in the use of *fago*.

In whatever form it takes, love occurs in the context of a pervasive individualistic and egalitarian ethos. Love between spouses, friends, and even parents and children is often presented as the coming together of autonomous and equal partners. As Averill notes, the idealization of the other that is central to love "requires that the target be recognized as a unique and worthy individual in his or her own right, and this requires, in turn, an individuation of the self" (1985:101).

Even the notion of brotherly love makes use of a kinship metaphor suggesting the egalitarian and reciprocal relations of siblings rather than the potential hierarchy of different generations. Said one of the American women I interviewed, "[Love] is a lot of sacrifice, a lot of work, a lot of giving, but it has to be something that's very free, freely given instead of you're forced to it."

While *fago* is occasionally, like love (and particularly romantic love), an emotion which posits an equality of status between the subject and the object, it is much more often an assessment of inequality of ability and resources and status between the two. This contrast is evident in the fact that the most central exemplar for love is probably the romantic commitment between wife and husband, while the prototype for *fago* is the relationship that a parent has with a child, or the chief with commoners. The primary object of love is the desired and idealized other, and that of *fago* is the needful other. To speak of love is primarily to talk about enduring positive feelings; to speak of *fago* is much more often to talk about the other's neediness, the other's pitiableness.

Both emotions entail the desire to see the other person's needs satisfied, although those needs are culturally defined in somewhat different ways. Americans focus primarily on the explicit goal of "making the other happy,"[18] while the Ifaluk focus on the needs for health, food, and kinship, needs whose fulfillment is not spoken of as having the primary goal of creating happiness. Both are emotions of strength in that the person who experiences them is empowered; that is, each sees him- or herself as capable of fulfilling the other's need. The concept of *fago* is often used to stress this to a degree that exceeds that accomplished by the concept of love, which, particularly in its romantic form, may involve a somewhat disempowering admiration or a focus on feeling rather than acting. On the other hand, love is seen as a more unequivocally pleasant, even happy, emotion. Both emotions can motivate nurturance, although this desire is more fundamental to the meaning of *fago*.

"Compassion" is also appropriate as a partial translation for *fago* because each of these two terms is used to make an evaluation that the other is suffering misfortune.[19] Compassion and *fago* both entail the desire to aid or comfort the person so perceived. Although both emotions usually require a general assessment that the victim is blameless for his or her problem, each draws on a different surrounding cultural mythology, in Solomon's terms. In any emotional judgment in the West, there is potentially an important residue of "that medieval conception of misfortune . . . that insists on seeing all misfortune as deserved" (Solomon 1977:344). Nonetheless, *fago* can be described in the same terms as compassion because each "promotes the experience of equality, even when accompanied by an acknowledgment of actual social inequality. . . . [Each] forbids regarding social inequality as establishing human inequality" (Blum 1980:512).

Compassion and *fago* are oriented toward action; each, I have noted, can be used to proclaim a desire to help. Nonetheless, compassion appears to be viewed by many as a feeling that does not necessarily have much to do with helping others. Compassion was defined for me by a number of Americans as a feeling more than a practice. Said one woman, compassion is "where you're able to feel something for somebody, to have a little heart . . . to be compassionate you really have to want to let people know you and you want to know the people." For an older man, it is "listening and really trying to understand another person's viewpoint and relating to them." For another person, "compassion is where you feel sorry for someone and you can almost put yourself in their position." And for yet another, it is "putting yourself in the other person's place. What would you do in any event this [bad] thing happened to you? How would you handle the situation? Can you adjust to a situation like that?" More unusual were comments such as the following two given by a man and a woman: "Compassion has something to do with being aware of somebody else's needs, and trying to help them." "Compassion is care for your fellow human being and the first thing I think of is . . . elderly neighbors and elderly relatives, and I feel very sad I can't spend more time with them . . . to break up their boredom and show that I care. To think about them is one thing, to do something about 'em is another."

Cultural definitions of what constitutes appropriate help surely also differ. For example, the American emphasis on respecting the autonomy of others and on portraying the self as independent and self-supporting can result in a narrowing of the number of contexts in which compassion occurs and includes helping behaviors. The action orientation of *fago* and compassion can be described as an optimistic one; *fago,* like compassion, "often involves resisting regarding situations as absolutely irremediable" (Blum 1980:515). Even here, however, there are potential differences in the degree to which optimism or empowerment can be carried given cultural beliefs about the degree to which it is possible for people to understand and help each other effectively.

While the task of translation is to illuminate what similarity exists in the use contexts of terms in any two languages, it is also important to give a sense of how frequently the contexts actually occur or are perceived as occurring in each of two societies. *Fago* and compassion, while sharing important elements of pragmatic meaning, are nonetheless radically different in the frequency of their use; *fago,* as we saw, is central to everyday discourse on Ifaluk, while "compassion" and even the nearly synonymous but more colloquial "feel sorry for" are in relatively less frequent use in the U.S. middle class.

Finally, there is "sadness." When the Ifaluk spoke to each other about *fago,* I was led to compare what they meant to "sadness" not only because the most central situation in which each of the terms arises is the same (death) but also because their assessment of death is similar to ours. It is seen as a grievous loss, and as a loss which can leave the living weakened. When the Ifaluk talk about the way their *fago* at the death or travel of kin leaves them "unable" (*ta mwel*), they parallel the sad person's "impotent" (Solomon 1976:360) self-description. Both emotions are used to identify a loss without attributing responsibility to anyone for it. Both the sadness and the *fago* that are spoken of in death can be *about* the loss rather than *for* the lost object. But the emphasis in sadness, unlike in *fago,* is more often on the implications of the loss for the self (deRivera 1984). A central component of the concept of sadness is the sense of having been rejected by others and of having failed oneself (Izard 1977). This is consistent with several descriptions of sadness given me by the previously mentioned group of Americans, as when one woman said that her sadness often involves her "remember[ing bad] things that people have done to me, things that people have said. . . . I remember something terrible somebody said to me." On the other hand, the lack of control that creates sadness was emphasized by others: "Sadness is [when] there's anything that's out of your hands, something that you can't change, whether it's illness or death or something that you see happening in the news." The absence of these emphases—on responsibility and control—in the notion of *fago* is importantly related to the way the self is defined and developed on the atoll, an idea we will explore more fully in a moment.

The relationships among sadness, lowered self-esteem (as a result of the generalization of one's feelings of impotence), and depression are not replicated in the theory and practices relating to *fago.* People do not critique themselves in the course of understanding events by aid of the concept of *fago.* Although one person spoke to me about the sense of wanting to die when *fago* is strong after another's death, I never heard suicides or suicide attempts described as having been motivated by *fago.* *Fago* cannot be used to talk about a sense of general

148

hopelessness or global loss, as sadness can. Although the action scenario that accompanies *fago* can be very similar to that entailed by sadness, including crying, passive sitting, and loss of appetite, the meaning of those behaviors is somewhat different. Overall, *fago* connotes or propels activity much more than does sadness, which most American emotion analysts have classified as a passive emotion (e.g., Dahl 1979).

This treatment of the relationships among the concepts of *fago*, compassion, love, and sadness has only touched on the basic outlines of the conceptual structure of these emotion words. It does indicate, however, that translation of *fago* with but one of those terms would give an inadequate sense of the pragmatic value of that word in Ifaluk discourse. Let us turn now to an examination of the broader context from which *fago* takes its meaning, which includes the material and social-structural world of the atoll.

Emotional Meaning and Material Conditions on a Coral Atoll

It has long been recognized that each of the world's languages can say certain things particularly well. This observation has been extended to include the notion that the "specialization" emerges as each speech community comes to address itself to the unique constellation of ecological and social conditions under which it lives. Although experience "does not in itself dictate the terms by which the world is understood" (Gergen 1985:266), language, and consciousness more generally, is formed at least in part for the task of organizing social responses to the problems presented by particular environments. The structure of the language of emotion can be viewed in this same light. While emotion concepts are more typically portrayed as emerging from an internal world of sensations and thoughts, they can be seen instead as having been constructed in the same environmental crucible as the language of such things as ritual, land tenure, or ethnicity. More specifically, emotion concepts are constructed in part by reference to the culturally influenced observation of the objective conditions of life in a particular place—of the frequency of death, of the nature and suddenness of dangers and losses, of the number and kinds of exchanges between individuals. Each emotion concept also exists in dialectical relationship with a set of social practices, both shaping and being shaped by them.

The meaning and practice of *fago* can be related to Ifaluk's precarious and bounded atoll environment as well as to features of its social structure, including the institution of adoption and the competing principles of status ranking and resource egalitarianism.[20] Let us examine each of these aspects in turn. Although people in every society face the threat of death, and often in such catastrophic forms as earthquake or famine, Ifaluk and the other atolls of the Western Carolines stand out as especially vulnerable in this regard. The typhoons which strike the island are both regular in occurrence, with a typhoon of some size striking the general area virtually every year, and potentially devastating to the population. They may also wreak long-term havoc on the staple crop by inundating the taro gardens with salt water. The behavior of typhoons and the distances between atolls may also result in one atoll's being decimated while others in the area are unscathed. The solutions that have been developed in response may also include a strengthening of the institution of chieftainship, which serves to organize the population's response to the emergency. More intangibly, the threat of typhoons also appears to give atoll residents a heightened sense both of the fragility of life and of the way in which their fate is a collective one;[21] when typhoons threaten, people begin to talk to each other about the eventuality that "we all will die together." The emotion of *fago* is adapted to these conditions in a variety of ways—by articulating a notion of collective responsibility, by motivating the food sharing and the kind treatment of visitors which allow for post-typhoon survival, and by legitimizing the chiefs as individuals whose *fago* for commoners helps to ensure the well-being of the island.

Consider as well how the bounded nature and high population density of the island and the highly public nature of much of people's behavior set the stage for emotional meaning. In the first instance, these two factors combine to give people extensive opportunities of observing the suffering of others—the condition which is central to the experience of *fago*. When people become ill or are hungry, their misfortune can be viewed by their neighbors. These opportunities come to entail a moral responsibility in part with the aid of the ideas expressed through *fago*, which enjoins visits to the sick and attention to the potential hunger of others.

It is not only the observability of suffering but also the actual incidence and causes of neediness which influence these aspects of emotional meaning. As we noted earlier, the cultural emphasis on *fago* on Ifaluk contrasts with the more peripheral place of the notion of compassion in the United States, where not only are morbidity and mortality rates lower but hunger and other forms of distress also are less visible, given a nucleated family structure and the value attached to privacy. Although the mass media's entry into and presentation of these otherwise hidden misfortunes (including historical and cross-cultural suffering) represent a potential counterforce, the ideological construction of the meaning of this suffering often includes the notion that the victim is responsible for his or her misfortune, an orientation which is antithetical to the emotion of *fago* or compassion.

Second, the boundedness of the atoll has meant that Ifaluk's citizens have been able to observe, until quite recently, the limits and extent of their social system and the sources of support within it. Contrast this with the situation in large-scale peasant or industrial societies, where unseen actors may be posited as the agents responsible for helping others. Research in the United States has indicated that helping behavior is diminished when a person can assume that someone else can or should help the sufferer or victim (e.g., Darley and Latané 1968). The concept of *fago* encodes the responsibility which each person has to respond to others' pain.

The centrality of a notion like compassion to the Ifaluk cultural system may indicate something about the strength of the ties that exist among people on the atoll. The extensiveness and intensiveness of those ties are in part the result of some features of an island environment. The small size of the atoll means that land and population are limited. Under these conditions of scarcity, land may come to be without laborers or laborers without land. People on Ifaluk, as well as in other island areas of the Pacific, have attempted to ensure their access to land by propagating social institutions that increase their ability to make use of the largest possible number of social affiliations (Silverman 1978). The high degree of potential biological interrelatedness on the island is transformed into extensive and intensive social relatedness. This, in turn, contributes to the stress on the emotions of connection with others, such as *fago,* and to the particular meaning that it has.

The number, strength, and cross-cutting nature of social ties on Ifaluk are evident in a number of aspects of island social structure. In the first instance, individuals live intimately with a relatively large number of others. Extended-family living arrangements result in an average of 13 people sleeping together in one-room thatched homes. Social ties are numerous and strong given the widespread practice of adoption, which creates important social ties between the child and a large number of classificatory parents and siblings. Adoption in fact acts to give most individuals a kinship relation with a significant proportion of the total population of the atoll.[22] In addition, communal work and consumption patterns involve each household in frequent exchanges with a large number of others. The sense of linkage between individuals and households is also strengthened by communal ownership of canoes and, in a sense, of children, who, as several people told me, "belong to everyone." Finally, the ties that link atoll residents do not remain fixed within single descent lines; the principle of matrilineal descent is cross-cut by the rights that children can maintain in their father's lands, while clan siblingship unites distinct matrilines.

The emotion of *fago* seems particularly adapted to the problem of ensuring sharing and cooperation both between and within households. On the ideological level, the emotion concept provides a kind of leveling mechanism. By articulating the idea that need in others is one of the central problems of everyday life, and by positing that nurturance "naturally" accompanies the emotion, it encourages noticing and responding to that need. *Fago* thereby forms a central part of the motivational system which supports cooperation, encouraging the food and labor sharing that helps to maintain the relative egalitarianism of wealth on the atoll. The redistribution of wealth that occurs (however circumscribed by kinship lines) finds its central ideological support in the notion that people *fago* each other. The relative absence of the political-economic fact of alienation corresponds to the absence of the emotion of alienation. *Fago* represents the emotional and ideological product of a society in which it is the rare individual who is separated either from others or from access to land.

On the other hand, *fago* also mirrors, in conceptual microcosm, the problem of power in a society which is at once ranked and egalitarian in structure. These two competing tendencies make the individual exercise of power a complex and difficult maneuver.[23] While rank provides both status and some tangible prerogatives, one must not be seen as focusing attention on those advantages (hence, the concern with the problem of the show-off or braggart discussed above). The character of the emotion of *fago,* and its positive evaluation, provides an avenue for the exercise of power. It does this by sanctioning the display of resources and abilities in the act of helping others. *Fago* is an emotion whose exercise can be consistent both with equality and autonomy and with rank and control.

A people's most basic assumptions about the nature of the self can be seen as the ideological products of particular social structures and political economies. The multiplicity of social ties on Ifaluk runs parallel to what we have already noted is an ethnopsychology in which the self is constructed as a fundamentally interpersonal rather than individualistic one. Both social structure and ethnopsychology work together to create the sense in people that they are more like each other than not and that each can understand (and therefore *fago* and effectively help) the other. The institution of adoption in particular encourages both child and adult to identify with a larger group of others, to see a larger number of individuals as vitally interested in one's well-being, and to view their interests as overlapping one's own. The adoptive parent serves as a model of intensive nurturance beyond the nuclear family, while public discourse about the institution alerts others to the fact that it is the compassionate adopter (rather than the self-sacrificing biological parent) who is the "hero" of any particular adoption story.[24] Here, as elsewhere in Ifaluk culture, the ideal person is portrayed as one who cares for others, who has *fago*. Children and adults may also receive and generalize from the message which Levy posits is sent in all Oceanic adoption, which is that "relationships between parents and children are fragile and conditional" (1973:485). The dual message—that nurturance is expected from and for many of one's consociates and that relationships that were primary may be "lost" to a secondary place—can be spoken about with the "sadly compassionate" notion of *fago*. Adoption is, then, both a training ground for the emotion of *fago* and a cultural site for its utilization.

The conceptual structure of *fago*—in particular the similarity it implicitly draws between need and loss—is related to the interpersonal structure of the Ifaluk self. The contrast with middle-class American emotional lives is instructive. We noted earlier that "sadness" is used to talk about both psychological and physical separation from others as well as personal failure. This is consistent with the American definition of the person in terms of individual potentials and needs. *Fago*, on the other hand, links the pain of separation with the distress of seeing others in need. The other's pain can be more truly one's own when the self is culturally constructed as it is on Ifaluk. While several emotion researchers have noted that loss represents one of the universal conditions of human life (e.g., Plutchik 1980), and therefore certainly has cross-cultural utility as a concept, the cultural emphasis on the links among loss, interpersonal connection, and others' needs on Ifaluk contrasts with the middle-class American link between loss and personal failure.

The Ifaluk make emotional sense of the conditions of life on a coral atoll and are motivated to thrive under them in part through the concept of *fago*. A host of cultural practices, and the institutions that are formed through them, articulate with both the ideas and the behaviors embedded in *fago*. Food sharing, adoption, the treatment of visitors, relations between brothers and sisters, forms of and attitudes toward authority, and the system of health care are all examples of central features of everyday life that take their importance and character in part from the ideological charter provided by the concept of *fago*. *Fago* is central to the way people understand their relationship to others. That understanding includes the sense that the suffering of others is of vital concern, that attachment to others entails active nurturance more than self-contained feelings, that love is explicitly an emotion of power, and that love is heavily tinged with pathos because love's object is weak and because love often equals loss.

CHAPTER SIX
Morality, Domination, and the Emotion of "Justifiable Anger"

As I listened to the Ifaluk discuss with each other the events of everyday life, I was consistently struck by the strong overtones of moral judgment in those conversations. A group of people who sit talking as they grate coconut agree that a neighbor "is bad" because she has started a false rumor about another woman in the village. The husband of another woman is described as bad because he never works, preferring simply to lie about the house. The boisterous style of a young boy is criticized, as are his parents for failing to instruct him in the principles of good behavior. The constant evaluation of the world in moral terms occurs in preference or contrast to the other possibilities for judging an event, which might involve a focus on its aesthetics, its success or failure in achieving the goals of the actors involved, or its power to shape the course of future events. What is most striking about this daily moral judgment on Ifaluk is that it frequently is expressed in the idiom of emotion words.

One of the primary concepts that people on Ifaluk use to express their moral judgment is the concept of *song,* or "justifiable anger." The idea of justifiable anger pervades everyday life on Ifaluk. The term can be heard daily in homes, canoe houses, and taro gardens, in private conversation and in public discussion. In lieu of describing the malicious gossipmonger or the aggressive child as bad, someone will often say "I am [or someone else is] justifiably angry [*song*] at that person." When this emotional term is used, an assessment is

155

being made; the speaker is saying, "Something immoral or taboo has happened here, and it ought not to have happened." As we will see, the moralizing uses to which the concept of *song* is put can also be characterized as ideological in nature. Talk about *song* often reinforces the prerogatives of the more powerful members of Ifaluk society, as it is they who have most appropriated the right to be described, or to describe themselves, as justifiably angry.

Whether the concept of *song* is approached as a moral or an ideological construct, we will also see that the term is not used simply to refer to an event (whether that event is seen as internal or external). The use of the word *song* most frequently involves an attempt on the part of the speaker to portray events *before others* in a particular way. Claims to justifiable anger involve a characterization of the world that must be *negotiated* with the audience for those claims. Involving, as the term justifiable anger does, such weighty matters of right and wrong and of dominance and submission, things could hardly be otherwise.

To understand what people on Ifaluk meant when they said that they or someone they knew was *song,* I did what the reader will do here, which is to move back and forth between my understandings of the concept of anger as it is used in this society and the concept of *song.* The process of approaching an adequate translation of the concept involved an—at times unconscious—process of comparison and contrast between my own emotional world and theirs. What immediately drew the world of anger and the world of *song* together for me as an apt comparison is the sense that each of the two concepts is used to say "I hate what just happened. I want to move toward that thing or person and stop it." Like anger, *song* is considered an unpleasant emotion that is experienced in a situation of perceived injury to the self or to another.

The ways in which the two concepts were not equivalent would also soon strike me. These were many, and they went to the root of the differences in our social experiences, including our experiences of self. Unlike "anger," "justifiable anger" is not used to talk about frustrating events which are simply personally disliked, rather than socially condemned. While the uses to which "anger" is put may often involve the kind of moral appeal that *song* does, the former concept is seen as referring, in the main, to the restraint of individual desire. Moreover, the Ifaluk emphasize, in the concept of *song,* the prosocial aspects of anger. To become justifiably angry is to advance the possibilities for peace and well-being on the island, for it is to

156

identify instances of behavior that threaten the moral order. This view contrasts with the American notion that anger is primarily an anti-social emotion whose only positive functions are primarily intrapsychic.

In this chapter, we will examine both the moral and ideological force of the concept of *song* and the ways in which an understanding of that concept is based, for English speakers, on a contrast with the elaborate web of cultural meaning in which anger is, like *song*, embedded.

Moral Anger and Ifaluk Values

The Ifaluk speak about many types of anger. There is the irritability that often accompanies sickness (*tipmochmoch*), the anger that builds up slowly in the face of a succession of minor but unwanted events (*lingeringer*), the annoyance that occurs when relatives have failed to live up to their obligations (*nguch*), and, finally, there is the frustrated anger that occurs in the face of personal misfortunes and slights which one is helpless to redress (*tang*). But each of these emotions is sharply distinguished from the anger which is a righteous indignation, or justifiable anger (*song*), and it is only this anger which is morally approved. While the other forms of anger are attributed both to the self and to others, the person who experiences them does not gain— and often loses—in moral standing.[1] These amoral forms of anger, if they occur frequently enough, leave one's character open to question or even severe critique. The claim to be justifiably angry, on the other hand, is taken seriously as a moral assertion. By identifying *song* in oneself or in others, the speaker advertises him- or herself as someone with a finely tuned and mature sense of island values.

Each word in a language evokes, for the native speaker, an elaborate "scene" replete with actors, props, and event sequences (Fillmore 1977). The scene that the term *song* paints is one in which (1) there is a rule or value violation, (2) it is pointed out by someone, (3) who simultaneously calls for the condemnation of the act, and (4) the perpetrator reacts in fear to that anger, (5) amending his or her ways. Almost all the hundreds of uses of the term "justifiable anger" that I recorded evoked this scene, making reference to the violation of some aspect of the widely shared Ifaluk value system. By examining the contexts in which justifiable anger is used, therefore, we may draw the outlines of the Ifaluk worldview, as the term marks the existence of those values and serves as an agent for their reproduction.

Chiefly Anger, the Taboo, and the Law

It was an evening after the sun had set, and most men had left the drinking circles where they gather on a regular basis with kin and neighbors to drink the fermented coconut toddy collected from their trees each late afternoon. Some younger men of Mai[2] village, however, had continued to drink into the night and then decided to cross the channel to visit Bwaibwai. Once there, they walked along the village paths speaking in loud voices and occasionally shouting out.

This event was much in discussion the following day. Comment centered on the young men's violation of several standard Ifaluk expectations about how people ought to behave. In their interactions with each other, the Ifaluk value calm, quiet talk, so much so that my first impression of Ifaluk conversation was that of whispered exchanges. Shouting is not only considered a serious disturbance of this otherwise peaceable style but is also seen as intensely frightening. In addition, people commented, these men were from Mai. They had crossed village boundaries in their escapades and, in so doing, threatened intervillage harmony. This is considered potentially more disruptive than misbehavior whose negative consequences reverberate solely within the bounds of one of the four named communities on the island.

Although several people discussed their panicked fright (rus) on hearing the shouting the evening before, most emotional talk centered on the certainty that "the chiefs will be justifiably angry [song]" at the young men. The chiefs, it turned out, were in fact justifiably angry, as evidenced by the fact that they soon met and decided to levy a fine (gariya) of 200 yards of rope on the men. The rope was to be given to the canoe house in Bwaibwai, where the shouting had taken place. This amount of rope, which represents hundreds of hours of work for the men who make it from coconut husk fiber, was a measure of the song of the chiefs.

This episode epitomizes one of the most common ways the concept of justifiable anger is used—a taboo is violated, a traditional law is disobeyed, and people point not directly to the law but to the song of the chiefs. The traditional leaders of Ifaluk, who currently number one woman and three men, each represent the oldest appropriate member of the highest ranked matrilineage of each of four of the island's seven clans. Their responsibilities are conceptualized as those of "taking care of" (gamwela) the island and its people.[3] Their role as moral leaders of the island is evidenced in the periodic islandwide meetings (toi) at which they frequently exhort people to behave

158

properly—to take nothing from the taro gardens of others, to avoid gossip and all "bad talk," and to work hard, particularly at community-level tasks, such as village weeding (see also Burrows and Spiro 1953).

The chiefs are seen as the primary stewards of the island's taboos (*taub*). These taboos forbid traffic in several sacred areas of the island; uttering certain words in mixed company, including particularly a set with sexual connotations; taking the turtle which belongs to the chief of Kovalu clan, or taking marine and other resources out of season, which it is the chiefs' prerogative to declare; walking onto the land of the highest-ranked chief at Welipi (who is the leader of Kovalu clan, and currently is a woman) without good purpose and without deeply waist-bent posture (*gabarog*); women's entering the canoe houses or riding in the large canoes (*waterog*) during fishing trips, or men's entering the birth houses; women's working in the taro gardens during their menstrual periods; and men, women, or children's eating the particular foods that are forbidden to each of them. Although violations of taboos appeared to occur rarely, the idiom of *song* was used to explain the consequences when they did.

On one such occasion, Ifaluk received a rare visit from a private yacht, whose passengers included several European men and a woman. When the boaters asked to be taken for a sail on one of the island's impressive oceangoing canoes, some men agreed to accommodate them. This event, which had occurred several years before I arrived on the island, was still being discussed during my stay.[4] The narrative of the event invariably included, as its central point, the fact that the chiefs were justifiably angry at the local men when they heard that the men had violated the taboo against taking women out (for anything but necessary interisland travel) on the ocean canoes. While it may have been the case that the men who took the Europeans on the canoe had decided that a non-Ifaluk woman's presence would not constitute an instance to which the taboo would apply, the chiefs' justifiable anger served as notice of the leaders' interpretation of the meaning of the taboos in these new social circumstances. The presence or absence of the chiefs' *song* was looked for in other encounters with new social phenomena (such as events at the island school, or new customs or attitudes brought back by young men who had been off the island); the emotional response of the chiefs could be used as an indication of how the rest of the island ought to feel about, and simultaneously morally react to, such social changes.

The emotion of justifiable anger is strongly associated with Ifaluk's chiefs because it is they who stand as the final moral arbiters on the island, and it is *song* that symbolizes the perception of moral transgression. It is the traditional leaders' justifiable anger that marks the violation of those aspects of the moral code seen as most crucial for both the harmony and the survival of the island as a whole. Although their authority is sometimes covertly challenged, the near-universal concern with the *song* of the chiefs is an index both of the legitimacy they enjoy and of the widespread sharing of values, at least on the explicit level, that obtains on Ifaluk. Political and moral leadership are thus here, as in many other social systems, closely linked with emotional leadership. As we will see in a moment, the concept of *song* can also be seen as an element of ideological practices engaged in by the chiefs and others in positions of relative power on Ifaluk to control the behavior of their subordinates and to bolster their claims to moral suzerainty.

Everyday Interaction and the Marking of Value

The chiefs are certainly not the only individuals on Ifaluk who may claim to be justifiably angry. In an important sense, every person on Ifaluk, from the oldest matriarch to the socially emergent toddler, not only can be, but is *expected* to be, *song* at appropriate junctures. As *song* is treated as the essential moral sensibility of a person, the total absence of *song* in an individual could be condemned by others. Let us look now at exactly how this moral sense operates in everyday interaction on Ifaluk.

One of the most frequent contexts in which people spoke about their justifiable anger was when someone failed to live up to his or her obligation to share with others. People are expected to share everything from their cigarettes, food, and labor to their children. These expectations are reinforced by the daily sharing that does occur. A woman who smoked a cigarette by herself without sending it on complete rounds among the others with whom she was chatting or working would be considered deeply thoughtless at best and stingy at worst; a family eating outdoors and within sight of a village path is expected to call out "Come and eat!" to anyone, kin or relative stranger, who passes by; a group of five people sitting down to eat after an unlucky day of fishing will break the few ounces of their single reef fish into five parts; certain household tasks, such as special food preparation, taro-garden weeding, or the periodic rethatching of a roof will be done with the contribution of the extrahousehold labor of up to forty or fifty people; and, finally, the adoption of children from their living parents after about the age of three is valued as a sign of generosity in both adopter and adoptee and has resulted in an adoption rate of 40% for all children over the age of five. Both the sharing behavior that occurs every day and the daily conflicts over such cooperation are an index of the extent to which sharing is an entrenched aspect of people's value orientation on the island. Another index is the fact that the person whose behavior earns him or her the label of "stingy" (*farog*) is perhaps the most disliked type of person on Ifaluk, with the sole exception of the hot-tempered (*sigsig*) individual.

What can be termed "typhoon stories" are frequently told on Ifaluk, and their telling overflows with messages about most of the central emotions and values that occupy people on the island, including particularly the value of sharing. People tell of the entire village's gathering together to eat whatever food can be caught or salvaged after the storm's devastation. The stories draw an image of one coconut being split open by the chief and divided into miniscule but equal portions for the survivors. They also tell of the punishment meted out by the chiefs, again as a measure of their *song*, for those caught eating alone (and hence not sharing what food they have found)—a circle is drawn in the earth out in the direct sunlight, and the culprit is made to sit there for an extended period, a sanction that is notably harsh in comparison with those for other infractions of law and morality.

The anticipation of the justifiable anger of others is often the explicit motivation for sharing.[5] The consumption of pork and of sea turtle, which are relatively scarce and highly valued resources, is surrounded by careful attention to equity in the distribution of portions to neighbors and relatives.[6] A representative of each of the families that is to receive a basket of turtle or pork pieces is usually asked to assist in its preparation. Accordingly, I was sent one afternoon to help in the cooking of a large pig belonging to Lemangemar, the clan sister of Tamalekar (the man who was my adoptive father). As we sat around the work area, it was clear that there were many more hands than tasks that required them. Most of those invited were implicitly there in order that each family might directly observe the equitability of the division (*gamaku*) of the food, thereby preventing *song* at Lemangemar's household. After small baskets were woven and set out, and as her daughter dropped the fatty pieces into each, Lemangemar supervised by calling out, "Put more pork in that basket, or the people of [that household to whom the basket belongs] will be justifiably angry." The daily anticipation of the justifiable anger of others is a fundamental regulator of interpersonal relationships and a basic factor in the maintenance of the value of sharing.

What happens when the value of sharing is contravened? Justifiable anger is declared, usually by the party or parties most directly injured by the failure to share. In some cases, an entire village may be justifiably angry. In one such case, the women of two households attempted to circumvent the mandate that each household bring its traditional and clearly identified allotment of food (in this case, one bowl of taro or pot of breadfruit) to communal feasts or to households where there is a serious illness or recent death. These women came to one village feast with a single pot of food they had collected and cooked together and so brought less than the amount expected. As soon as the feast was over and the women in question had left, people declared their justifiable anger and reviewed the offenders' misbehavior. As is often the case in emotion attribution on Ifaluk, people spoke in the first person plural: "We are *song*," one woman said, "because those women did not bring their allotment [*tub*] of food. Those people are bad."

What was also typical about this incident was that confrontation between the angry parties and the offenders was avoided. Gossip rather than head-to-head discussion is the usual means by which someone's justifiable anger is communicated to another, and this indirect communication is crucial for the prevention of future violations. The damage that gossip can do to one's standing in the eyes of others is damage done by the accusation of wrongdoing implicit in the voicing of *song*.

Each time a person declares "I am *song*" is a gambit or bid in an effort to install a particular interpretation of events as the definition of that situation to be accepted by others. In the above case, as in many others, the opening bid is accepted and the force of public opinion sides with the person who first asserts that the situation is one of rule violation and hence one of justifiable anger. In other instances, however, the violation of cultural norms is either ambiguous or contested by others, and a more extended negotiation process must occur. This negotiation occurs over the aptness of, or justification for, someone's justifiable anger, in other words, over the meaning to be assigned to an event. The process of negotiation may take only a few moments, or it may continue over the course of many months, as we will see.

Social Change and the Reconstruction of Emotional Meaning and Value

Common to many of the cases of extended negotiation over the ascription of justifiable anger is the involvement of relatively newly introduced cultural elements. Attitudes toward particular social changes, and regulation of them, are constantly in process of formulation. On Ifaluk, these changes include a sudden influx of cash as a direct result of the American colonial administration's favoring of direct government subsidies. This cash, moreover, has entered the island economy in a highly inequitable way; whereas cash was once primarily acquired through each household's ability to prepare and sell small quantities of copra, most money is now brought to the island through the small number of individuals who receive government salaries, including the teachers and health aides. Unlike Ifaluk's primary valuables, such as taro, fish, and canoes, cash is both readily hidden and hoarded, and people have not yet decided how its sharing ought to be handled. Emotional ambiguity and conflict are the result. Values and social relations in flux thus mean emotions in flux—emotions in process of cultural *reconstruction.*

Take the case of a young woman and her husband, whose government job gave him a salary and often kept him near his assignment on Yap. When the woman became pregnant, it was decided that she would give birth in the hospital on Yap,[7] and she was accompanied on her ship journey from Ifaluk by her mother's sister and the latter's husband, who had business (which provided him with some cash) on Yap. During their several months stay, the elder man made several requests of the young husband for cash for cigarettes and food items. After a point, the requests were ignored, and both parties privately declared their justifiable anger. The young man and woman appealed to the idea that the elder couple had much cash of their own and, hence, should have used that rather than asking for the others' money. In explaining their *song,* the older couple spoke of how they had taken care of the young woman through her travels and birth and of their *gashigshig* (state of being indebted to by others; literally, tiredness) on account of the young woman.

To some extent, each party to the conflict had appealed to a principle of proper behavior to which other Ifaluk subscribe. On the one hand, this includes the idea that one should not ask for something one already has in abundance, and, on the other, the expectation that there be reciprocity in relations with others such that one party to an exchange should not feel exploited or "tired." Were cash not involved (nor, perhaps, the changes in attitude in the younger men whose deference to authority is tempered by their new power in the outside world), the issue might have been clear. The younger couple would have been expected to share any apparent abundance with the elder, and the elder would have had sole claim to justifiable anger were such sharing not to take place.

A more dramatic example of the destruction of emotional meaning that has accompanied the social changes of the most recent colonial period was provided by the return of a "prodigal son" to the island. I had heard Tamalekar speak often of his sister's son, Palemai, who had gone to school in Oregon many years before and not returned. Quite suddenly, however, Palemai appeared as a passenger on the field ship that connects the island with Yap. His family was overjoyed to see him alive and to think that he might have returned to stay. Their joy was quickly tempered by consternation, however, as Palemai, who had arrived drunk, proceeded to sing boisterously—as he careened between his relatives' homes—the *bwarug* (love songs) that should never be sung in the company of both men and women. Between his arrival and departure with the ship a day later, he remained very drunk and displayed the kinds of boastful and disrespectful behaviors which cause justifiable anger in others, behaviors I had never observed in such profusion in one person at one time. In talking with others, he declared that he needed to return to school to get a degree and that he would return and get a "high" (important, top-ranking) job which would greatly help Ifaluk. The frequent repetition of these assertions occurred in the face of the very high value placed on modesty and self-effacement.

In the evening, Palemai came to visit Tamalekar, whom, as his mother's brother, he owed the greatest respect. Tamalekar, though nonplussed by his nephew's behavior, began to talk quietly to him in the style that is used when someone is attempting to *garepiy* (instruct, cause to become intelligent) his or her social subordinate. Rather than taking the usual quiet listening stance that is expected in these contexts, however, Palemai would periodically interrupt him by breaking into love songs. To Tamalekar's query about why he had stayed away from the island for so long, he responded with the taunt, "You [Tamalekar] are the one who gave me permission to go to school." Palemai went so far at one point as to slap his uncle on the back "playfully," a move that is only appropriate between peers and then only when they are drinking together.[8]

Tamalekar's pain at his nephew's disrespect, or more accurately his "craziness," was palpable, and as the night wore on, he looked more and more only at the ground in front of him, his shoulders slumping. The tears that he began to shed marked his confusion, his inability to become justifiably angry (or perhaps to feel anything with a name and an accompanying and effective behavioral script) in the face of inexplicably affronting behavior in a man whom he loved and who ought to respect him. Palemai's horrendous response to his awkward position between two worlds was certainly idiosyncratic, but it was set up by the historical changes of the American colonial period. And so long as an individual's emotional experience in its fullest sense is a social achievement, reached only through some basic agreement between people on the terms in which life's problematic moments are to be defined, such dramatic social disjunctures can only result in emotional ambiguity at best and emotional chaos at worst.

R. Rosaldo (1984:186) points out that people often emotionally "muddle through" traumatic life events—that each affecting event, such as a death, is in some way a unique experience for which cultural scripts cannot completely prepare people, and that each emotional experience reflects the particularities of individual lives. Tamalekar's "dark night" with his nephew reveals one source—historical social change—of both the rich diversity and the ambiguity of emotional experience in the midst of what is nonetheless clear, culturally shared affective meaning.

The Place of Justifiable Anger in Moral Socialization

The explicitly moral purposes to which the concept of justifiable anger is put gives it a particularly important role in the socialization of children. The prominent place of the "ought" in all aspects of Ifaluk everyday life is replicated in their approach to children and contrasts dramatically with the view of socialization as a form of reprehensible coercion that occurs in several more radically egalitarian societies, such as the Ilongot of the Philippines (M. Rosaldo 1980) and the Semai (Dentan 1978:96–97) of Malaysia. People told me on many different occasions that a parent *must* at times become justifiably angry with his or her child, "or the child will not know the difference between right and wrong." All the most undesirable behaviors that a child or an adult can display—laziness, loudness, disrespect, disobedience, or boldness—are explained as the result of the parents' failure to be justifiably angry when those behaviors were first exhibited by the child. The adult's justifiable anger is seen as telling the child that a value has been contravened. In one sense, *song* is seen as a clear and natural signal to the child about the forms of value and the characteristics of bad behavior.[9]

The way children learn the uses of *song* was illustrated by the following episode involving a flower wreath. I was sitting in my one-room thatched house on a limp June afternoon in 1978, writing in a field notebook on what I had seen and heard earlier that day. Tachimangemar, the five-year-old son in my adoptive Ifaluk family, saun-

165

tered in. The two of us had had some difficulty adjusting to each
other. In Tachimangemar's eyes, I was no doubt somewhat unpredictable. I found the boy's behavior regressive, even obnoxious. Although it was typical of the style of many island children between
the ages of two and five, it was all the more difficult for me to deal
with when contrasted with the soft-spoken cooperativeness of nearly
all children over the age of six. Children of Tachimangemar's years
are considered by adults to be too old for solicitousness and not yet
old enough to have developed the social intelligence (*repiy*) that pre-
vents unsocialized behavior (including particularly temper tantrums
and showing off).

I was feeling charitably inclined as he entered on this particular
afternoon, however. Noticing that he wore a flower wreath on his
head of the sort that women often affectionately weave for their kin,
I asked, with what I meant as a pleasant show of interest, whether
the wreath were his. He replied, "Ilefagomar [his mother] is not *song*
[justifiably angry]," puffed out his chest, and strode out into the coral-
covered yard. Earlier in my stay on the island, this response would
have mystified and perhaps depressed me. After six months on Ifaluk,
however, I could make some sense of it. It had taken me those six
months to develop the required cultural competence such that Tachimangemar could communicate a relatively obvious point easily to
me. I remained alien enough, and committed enough to another way
of seeing children, anger, and authority, to need to be *reminded* of the
obvious, and to find the terms he used striking, both then and now,
some years later.

Tachimangemar had drawn several inferences from my question,
including the idea that I believed the wreath to belong to someone
else. I also understood that, in stating that his mother was not *song*,
he was telling me that he had done nothing wrong in wearing the
wreath, that only Ilefagomar and not I had the authority to make
moral judgment of his behavior, and that he likely would continue
to wear the wreath as long as he pleased. Tachimangemar's statement
takes much of its sense and rhetorical force from the fact that the
Ifaluk elaborate and emphasize a distinction between moral and immoral anger and from the articulation of the concept of moral anger
with the atoll's social hierarchy. It also indexed his knowledge that
his mother would have communicated her justifiable anger to him
had he been doing something wrong in wearing the headpiece.

Time and again, children were reminded—most often by children a bit older than themselves—that some adult would be justifiably
angry if they continued to misbehave or failed to do something they

ought to have done. A girl tells her younger sibling to stop being uncooperative with the teacher at school, or their father will be *song*. A boy who uses a taboo word is warned by his older brother that his parents will be justifiably angry. Sent on an errand by our "mother," the teenage foster daughter of my household and I go to the taro garden to gather leaves for soup. In response to my question about how many taro leaves to collect, she tells me, "Ilefagomar didn't say how much to take, but we'll fill up the basket so she will not be *song*."

The role of *song* in the generation of valued behavior is thought to stem from the fact that justifiable anger causes fear (*metagu*) in the person at whom it is directed. Thus, *song* would not have its effect on the moral life of the community were fear not to be evoked by it. In this regard, the concept of *ker* (happiness/excitement) plays what is, from an American perspective, a paradoxical role. Happiness/excitement is an emotion people see as pleasant but amoral. It is often, in fact, *immoral* because someone who is happy/excited is more likely to be unafraid of other people. While this lack of fear may lead them to laugh and talk with people, it may also make them misbehave or walk around showing off or "acting like a big shot" (*gabos fetal*). As happiness/excitement (*ker*) dispels the individual's fearfulness, it disturbs the normal functioning of *song,* and with it, the moral compass of this society. Here, as elsewhere, the relationships among emotions in local thought are crucial to defining the meaning of each.

Whereas American approaches to child rearing and emotion elevate happiness to an important position, setting it out as an absolute necessity for the good or healthy child (and adult), the Ifaluk view happiness/excitement as something that must be carefully monitored and sometimes halted in children. Taking the former cultural perspective in my approach to Ifaluk children, I watched one day with an amused smile as a five-year-old girl danced and made silly faces for me as I sat outside her house. A woman with me at the time noticed my grin and said, "Don't smile at her—she'll think that you're not *song*." The reasoning process behind this woman's statement to me entailed some of the most central tenets of Ifaluk emotion theory, which are outlined, in schematic form, in figure 1. If I looked justifiably angry at the young girl, she would become afraid (*metagu*), lose her happiness/excitement, and then sit properly and quietly.[10] In this case, the woman did not wait for *ker* to produce misbehavior but anticipated it.

The concept of justifiable anger marks the boundary between acceptable and unacceptable behavior, for both child and adult. Learn-

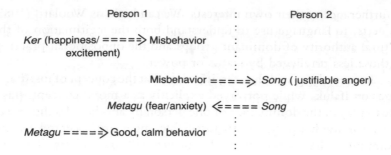

Figure 1. Ifaluk Propositions about the Relationships among Justifiable Anger, Fear, and Happiness/Excitement

ing to become attuned to both declarations and nonverbal demonstrations of that emotion is crucial to acquiring an Ifaluk soul and a favored place in society.

Domination and the Ideological Role of the Concept of Justifiable Anger

The moral ideas that prevail in any particular time and place come into being in the context of the configuration of power relationships existing in that society. In case after case, it has been observed that the unequal distribution of power in society carries with it the risk that the ideas of the dominant sectors will take precedence over other possible perspectives and, moreover, that those ideas will be presented as the ideas of the entire group and as natural rather than contrived or self-interested ideas. The power of some members of society to reinforce their prerogatives will include the power to "sell" their ideas and their morality to the rest of the group.

By some definitions, the "ideological" is a process of consciousness-in-use which is in a constant state of production and reproduction through the actions of individuals (e.g., Therborn 1980). The ideological is, therefore, not simply a rigid structure of domination but is the arena of thought and practice in which groups and individuals struggle to assert control or to avoid subordination (e.g., Corrigan and Willis 1980; Myers 1982; Taussig 1980; Woolard 1985). We can thus expect to find in cultural meaning systems—including those aspects which can be termed emotional—both the outline of relations of dominance as well as the occasional appropriation or alteration of those meanings by the subordinate members of society in furtherance of their own interests. We can look, as Woolard (1985) suggests, to language use to understand both the legitimation of the cultural authority of dominant groups and the oppositional practices of those less privileged by status or power.

In everything said thus far, it is clear that the concept of justifiable anger on Ifaluk, while portrayed explicitly as a moral concept, has a role to play in the domination of one person by another. To the extent that an individual's claims to justifiable anger are accepted by the community, that person exerts his or her will over others. The fear that should result from justifiable anger stops others in the pursuit of their immediate goals; justifiable anger thereby controls them. In addition, the aura of moral superiority that inheres in the notion of justifiable anger makes the concept a symbol of legitimate power which can further bolster the position of the person who claims to experience the emotion. The claim to moral sense and rectitude which the justifiably angry make is also, then, a claim to power and a crucial part of the ideological process.

While the Ifaluk do not distinguish natural emotion from other personal processes construed as more cultural, they too "naturalize" dominance moves when they portray them in the idiom of justifiable anger. The idea of justifiable anger does not draw on a biological charter so much as on the sense that emotions, in many of their forms, are homogeneous across individuals, moral, rational, inevitable, and uncontestable, and so more independent than in the Western views of personality, of a motive to control, or of a partisan or idiosyncratic political position. In the Ifaluk representation of emotion as morality and of the chief's exercise of power as simultaneously an emotional and moral response, the chief's individual will becomes community will. In local terms, *tip-* becomes *nunuwan* (see chap. 4). The interests of chiefs and chiefly lineages and the relations between chiefs and commoners become less rather than more questionable when expressed in the idiom of *song*.

As may already be apparent, the social hierarchy on Ifaluk is sharply outlined by the source of most assertions of justifiable anger and by the direction in which that anger usually flows. It is much more often the case that persons of higher rank or status are justifiably angry toward those of lower station than the reverse. The chiefs are justifiably angry at community members, adults are justifiably angry at children, older women are justifiably angry at younger women, and brothers are justifiably angry at their younger sisters. The direction in which justifiable anger flows is predominately *down* the social scale.

Resistance to the structure of domination also occurs every day on Ifaluk, and the concept of *song* is used in attempts to alter that balance of power. Teenage women sometimes resist their elders' attempts to marry them off, women attempt to push back the boundaries of the work men expect them to do, and people malign the actions of the Yapese, and through them, the whole colonial system. In each of these types of instances, the idea of justifiable anger is marshaled as a source of legitimacy and a method for condemnation of the system as it exists.

The sites at which the regular exercise of power and power struggles occur on Ifaluk are revealed by the use of the term justifiable anger. If we look carefully at the cases in which *song* is used, we observe the network of power relations on the island and gain insight into political processes. Daily negotiations over who is justifiably angry and over the proper reasons for that anger lie at the heart of the politics of everyday life.

We can begin with the one most important area in which power relations are, however, *non*negotiable. No one, in my observation, ever openly declared her justifiable anger at the chiefs in their capacity as traditional leaders. While their edicts and laws are not always obeyed, their judgment is not explicitly called into question. When the chiefs speak at all-island assemblies (*toi*), their words are seen as having a fundamental weight. The secure place of the chiefs at the head of the Ifaluk social structure is both evidenced and further ensured by the failure of their subjects to claim justifiable anger at them.

The relationship between a brother and sister forms a primary "building block" of Carolinean social structure (Marshall 1981). Although brothers will marry into another household, exchanges with their sisters will continue throughout their lifetimes and constitute the most important source of interhousehold exchange. Sisters send their brothers the fruit of their gardens and adopt their children. Brothers exhibit great interest in their sisters' children, taking the ultimate responsibility for their proper upbringing and protection. The emotional tone of the relationship between brothers and sisters is often one of extraordinary affection (see chap. 5), but it is also one in which the authority to make decisions about each other's lives rests much more heavily with the brother than the sister. Although this authority is generally only fully exercised by a man who is older than his sister, it forms a fundamental source of power in Ifaluk society.

An important index of how solid the authority of men over their sisters is can be found in the way women are at pains to avoid the justifiable anger of their brothers. A woman who has done something improper or about whom a piece of gossip is started will as often worry out loud that "my brother will be *song* [justifiably angry]" as she will worry about the anger of her parents or of other elders. These concerns are realistic ones; some of the most dramatic demonstrations of *song* were in fact carried out or threatened by brothers of women who had violated some code of conduct. In one such instance, a young woman got on the interisland steamer with her husband to go to their Woleai household without asking permission of her Ifaluk classificatory brothers. When they heard that she had left, they were justifiably angry and threatened, in a traditional gesture of extreme anger, to burn down her house.[11]

The relations between the generations on Ifaluk generally run smoothly. This is particularly true when one looks at generations of women, whose continuous coresidence from birth to death creates strong and deep bonds between them.[12] The household hierarchy is clear, with the eldest women making the most fundamental decisions and delegating work and authority to the middle-aged women, who in turn direct teenage and younger girls in work. Elder women decide how some of the most basic forms of household wealth are to be disposed of. It is they who decide the occasions for giving away the lavalavas woven by women in the household, who direct the sending of pots of taro and breadfruit to other households, who primarily decide when children are to be sent out as temporary help to another household or when more permanent adoptions are to occur, and who play what is sometimes a major role in arranging marriages for the sons and daughters of the household. And it is these powerful women who become justifiably angry if their charges in the household disobey their instructions, fail to contribute to household production, or behave so as to become the object of well-founded gossip in the village.

Younger women more often than not anticipate the justifiable anger of their elders in deciding how to behave. The fear that properly results from the anticipation of *song* usually acts to create obedient and deferential younger women. Young women, and particularly unmarried women in their teens and twenties, however, sometimes fly directly in the face of the expressed wishes of the older women of their household or wider kinship group. While the justifiable anger of older women is ensured by this defiance, it is also occasionally the case that the younger will attempt to ignore that anger by failing to become fearful (*metagu*) or will even declare their own justifiable anger.

One such case was that of Lesepemang. A sixteen-year-old girl, she was being temporarily fostered by Ilefagomar, the woman who headed the household in which I lived. She had been sent from her household primarily to help Ilefagomar through the later stages of a pregnancy, birth, and confinement. While she was living in the household, a marriage was arranged between her and a young man from another island who was staying on Ifaluk. She did not want to marry, however, fearing the loss of her freedom and the increased likelihood of pregnancy. Her protest of this arranged marriage took many forms. She would be told to prepare a meal for her husband by one of the older women but would either silently refuse, giggle, or take an inordinately long time in bringing him food. When no one but I was with her and her new husband, she would tease and "speak badly" (or brusquely and impolitely) to him. The protest soon escalated into a general refusal to perform any and all assigned tasks except under heavy pressure.

The adults around Lesepemang explained her behavior as due to the fact that she, like all new spouses, was "ashamed and embarrassed" (*ma*). In the attempt to change her attitude and behavior, she was frequently lectured (*garepiy*), with one older woman expressing a common theme in telling her, "What woman isn't ashamed and embarrassed [*ma*] around her new husband? But we [women] listen to our mothers and so take care of that man." In private conversations with me and other young women, however, Lesepemang portrayed herself, not as ashamed and embarrassed (*ma*), but as justifiably angry (*song*) at her family (and particularly her mother's brothers) for making her marry. In negotiating over the emotion term to be used, Lesepemang was not only denying the older women's definition of the situation but was also saying that this was *not* a normal or usual marriage (one that produces *ma*) but rather was one that should not have occurred (one that produces *song*). Her choice of emotion terminology constituted a strategy of using this fundamental concept in the Ifaluk ideological system against that system.

A final and central arena in which justifiable anger plays an ideological role is that of gender relations. With the important exception of their roles as brothers, mother's brothers, or chiefs, men did not declare justifiable anger at women appreciably more often than did women at men. This is consistent with the fact that the classes of women and men are not seen as sharply distinguishable on the basis of their moral sense. The reasons for justifiable anger did differ in men and women, however, and reflect the expectations held of each gender. The women, for example, frequently voice justifiable anger at men for failing to show up in great numbers or to put out much effort at the weekly (and theoretically male and female) village weeding sessions. Women also say they are justifiably angry when men become drunk and fail to fulfill their household obligations. Men's justifiable anger at women is generated by what they see as a female propensity to gossip. Men also sometimes become justifiably angry when they are hungry and the women of their household have not prepared food.

The context of women's use of the concept of justifiable anger reveals the nature of what they expect from men. Take the example of Lemalesep, a woman in her late thirties, who answered my question about when she had recently been justifiably angry in the following way:

> I was *song* when they were reroofing the canoe house last week and [my husband] got drunk and didn't tell me beforehand [that he was going to drink]. [My adoptive son] came and told me. We had no more food [prepared at the household] and I had planned to give my husband our baby [to take care of so that I could make food]. I was really furious [*sig*] and ran away to my relative's house. Then he went over there to me, and I was also still *song*. I didn't want him to come over there.

Lemalesep appeals here to the expectation that a woman with a small baby ought to be aided by other members of the household, including the husband, and most especially when she has an important task to perform, such as food making. Her statement also draws on the common assumption that a man's drinking may be cause for justifiable anger when it results in irresponsible or uncooperative behavior. A woman in fact is seen as reasonable if she tells her husband to stop drinking after she has had a baby, so that he will be better able to help tend the infant in the evenings.

While men dominate women as brothers and mother's brothers and as the main holders of traditional office, they are not clearly dominant over women in their capacities as wives or as females in general. The ideological struggle on the field of justifiable anger reflects this relative gender balance. We have seen that only one party to a conflict may appropriately characterize itself as justifiably angry because only one general value system is accepted in most cases, and thus only one party is absolutely in the right. While negotiation over the right to use the concept of *song* is absent or rare when one individual is significantly more highly ranked than the other, it is much more likely the more equally ranked two parties to a conflict are. In relations between men and women, and particularly between husbands and wives, there are frequent struggles over the use of the emotion term to describe the self and the situation.

The accusations and counteraccusations between men and women are not generally taken as seriously as are the other cases of justifiable anger that we have been looking at so far. Several women told me, for example, that the men are always justifiably angry at the women when the interisland steamer comes, because the women do not make food. But, they said, the women do not listen to the men and just continue in their happiness/excitement (*ker*), visiting with the new arrivals and gathering the news from other atolls.

This brief tour through some of the configurations of power in Ifaluk society has demonstrated that the concept of justifiable anger can be seen as more than the central moral construct of this people, reflecting and constraining their structures of value. *Song* is also an important signifying practice in the pursuit of power and legitimacy. It is a powerful symbol of both dominance and morality, and the appropriation of the right to use the concept can constitute both an ideological ploy and a subversive move. The uttering of the word *song* in everyday life rises like a red flag, marking the form of, and fissures in, Ifaluk sociopolitical structures.

The Scene that Constitutes Justifiable Anger

Thus far, we have been looking at the contexts in which the concept of *song* is used or the events that precipitate or are structured by it. This constitutes, however, only a part of the more elaborate "scene" that is evoked for the Ifaluk listener by the concept of justifiable anger. Equally important are the scripts entailed for subsequent action. Central to these scripts are strategies for communicating one's view of the situation (as violating accepted community values) and for doing this as indirectly and nonviolently as possible. The scene that follows justifiable anger involves, first and foremost, moral condemnation of one person by another. This condemnation is accomplished through one or several of the following maneuvers, including a refusal to speak or, more dramatically, eat with the offending party; dropping the markers of polite and "calm" speech; running away from the household or refusing to eat at all; facial expressions associated with disapproval, including pouting or a "locked" mouth, "lit-up" or "lantern" eyes; gestures, particularly brusque movements; declarations of *song* and the reasons for it to one's kin and neighbors; throwing or hitting material objects; and in some cases, a fast or the threat of suicide or other personal harm. In discussions with each other, people commonly look for such behavioral cues in speculating about the emotional position of an individual. When people were asked explicitly by me what the indicators of justifiable anger are, they mentioned most of the above factors, as well as the idea that the justifiably angry person sometimes "thinks of swatting" the person at whom he or she is *song*.

The expected scenario continues beyond this immediate communication of emotional position. The target of the justifiable anger is subsequently expected to become *metagu* (fearful/anxious), as we have already noted. This occurs when word reaches him or her through the gossip network that the other is justifiably angry. It is sometimes expected that there will be a later *paluwen,* or payback, for the offense that caused the justifiable anger. Thus, in a case that I have already had occasion to mention, Ilefagomar was not invited to the birth hut of another woman when she ought to have been. She later "paid back" this woman by not calling her to her own labor and birth celebration several months later. An apology, the payment of a fine, or the more informal sending of valued objects to the justifiably angry person or family is also expected to occur on some occasions. It is said that the objects that are sent, such as cloth or tobacco, cause the recipients to become *ker* (happy/excited) and so forget their justifiable anger.

Another important aspect of the scene that is implicit in the concept of justifiable anger is the performance of a kind of semiformal "emotional counseling" by someone close to the angry person. Individuals are said to vary in their abilities to assist those who are justifiably angry, but there are some who take special pains and pride in their abilities in this regard. These people, who might be characterized as "emotional advisers," are said to be those who are not hot tempered and who do not allow themselves also to be provoked into a parallel justifiable anger by the angry person's account of the event.

The most important thing that a person can do to help the justifiably angry person is to calm down the other by speaking gently to her or him. This style of speech involves marked politeness and low volume. A solution to the problem which began the episode may be suggested; if, for example, a theft has occurred, the adviser might offer to go to the household of the thief and ask for the return of the object (although it is likely that such a promise will not be carried out in order to avoid the confrontation it would possibly involve). More commonly, however, the justifiably angry person will be advised to "forget it." This counsel comes not from the assumption that the justifiable anger is not just but rather from the sense that the offending person was at fault in the matter and is not reasonable. This inference is drawn by the listener from the adviser's frequent statements that the person at whom the justifiable anger is directed is in fact "crazy and confused" (*bush y saumawal*).

When someone is justifiably angry, people often anticipate and fear the possibility of aggression against the violator of cultural values; on the other hand, it is expected that those who are justifiably angry will *not* physically aggress against another. And in fact, interpersonal violence is virtually nonexistent on the island. The dual expectation of both violence and reflective self-control is evident in the kinds of advice that are typically given to those who are justifiably angry, as in the following, which represents a reconstruction of the stylized speech that the counselor will make to a justifiably angry person, in this case a man:

> Sweetheart, you shouldn't fight because you are a man. If you fight, people will laugh at you. Throw out your 'thoughts/feelings' about that person [at whom you are angry] because she [or he] is crazy and confused. We men divide our heads [separate the good from the bad] and then throw out the bad. We don't 'think/feel' so much so we won't be sick. You should *fago* [feel compassion/love/sadness for] me and follow my 'thoughts/feelings' and not be *song*. If you fight, your sister's children will be 'panicked/frightened' [*rus*].

Although the two expectations—of violence and of the lack of it—may appear contradictory, this approach to the angry person can instead be interpreted as the means by which the Ifaluk remind themselves of the possibility of violence while fully expecting that it will be prevented by the individual's maturity (including mature masculinity) and by feelings of *fago* (compassion/love/sadness) for others, of *ma* (shame/embarrassment) over the prospect of being violent before others, and of *metagu* (fear/anxiety) of the person who arrives to calm one down.[13]

These emotional or interactional strategies, or scripts, are learned by the Ifaluk in the course of growing up. The theory of justifiable anger and the social course it follows is, however, a script which is creatively used rather than mechanically followed in the pursuit of various goals. The concept of *song* is particularly useful for organizing the control of social deviance and for protecting one's interests as they are damaged by such deviance. Simultaneously, the scripts promote the reproduction of the gentle interpersonal relations that characterize the island. The various scripts that are encoded in the concept of justifiable anger are also guides for predicting and interpreting the behavior of others.

Anger, *Song,* Personal Restraint, and Moral Judgment

We necessarily compare the emotional lives of others to our own in attempting to understand the former; in translating between two emotion vocabularies and worlds of emotional interaction, I draw on the reader's tacit understanding of the semantic and pragmatic dimensions of American-English emotion words. Let us look, then, at the emotion concept of anger which has been implicitly invoked as the comparison point for all that has been said about the Ifaluk experience of *song.*

If the emotions are fundamentally social facts whose understanding requires an exploration of the totality of culture and social life, a truly adequate comparison of the concepts of anger and *song* would require descriptions of the full range of social structural and cultural belief features of both American and Ifaluk society—a task that is clearly impossible within the constraints of this chapter. The task of comparison is made yet more difficult by the lack of existing ethnographic studies of American emotional life to parallel the kind of material presented about the Ifaluk.[14] We can proceed, however, on the basis both of known general features of American middle-class social life and of some interview, questionnaire, and linguistic research (e.g., Averill 1979; Lakoff and Kövecses 1987; Tavris 1982) conducted on commonsense, cultural understandings of anger held by some English speakers.

Anger is an American-English emotion concept used to talk about feelings generated when a person is offended, injured, or restrained in such a way as to prevent his or her acting as he or she would like. In the most common view, anger is seen as a response to personal restraint or frustration. We become angry when we are frustrated by our inability to pursue our goals, generally because someone or something stands in the way. The psychologist Izard expresses this more general cultural view when he defines anger as an emotion that occurs when a person "is either physically or psychologically restrained from doing what one intensely desires to do. The restraint may be in terms of physical barriers, rules and regulations, or one's own incapability" (Izard 1977:329–30). According to another such definition, anger results from any interference with one's pursuit of a goal (McKellar, cited in Averill 1979). This cultural definition of anger as restraint or obstacle has organized much experimental work examining the emotion in American psychology. Anger was experimentally induced in the infant subjects of one study, for example, by holding down their arms while a desirable object was held in front of them (Stenberg, Campos, and Emde 1985).

But there is more to the concept of anger than the notion of restraint and personal frustration. Averill (1979) and Tavris (1982) present evidence that injured rights constitute central causes of anger (cf. Solomon 1978). In a questionnaire study, Averill (1979) asked a middle-class sample to examine a recent experience of anger and to describe it in terms of whether or not the instigation to anger was justified or not. The majority of respondents indicated that their anger was the result of an unjustified or negligent act on the part of another.[15] The concept of anger clearly is used in moral judgement, as is *song,* although the relationship between the questionnaire responses and more naturally observed reasoning about anger and its instigation is uncertain. In any case, the distinction between these possible subsidiary senses of anger, that is, between anger which is a response to personal restraint and anger which is a response to a moral violation by another, is lexically coded by the Ifaluk and not by Americans and so aids the former in thinking in those ways.

Moreover, it appears that for many Americans personal restraint represents a violation of the moral principle of individual freedom. American cultural logic makes personal frustration and a sense of unjustifiable injury nearly synonymous. Many Americans believe, at some level, that they have a right to what they desire (at least to the extent that their efforts and abilities are used in the pursuit of those desires). As a result, frustration *is* injustice or unjustifiable injury, especially when its causes are construed as external. The American usage of "anger" expresses our sense of individuals' rights and how extensive they are.[16] The Ifaluk uses of *song* express a sense of the claims of social norms to universal adherence and a view of the individual not as a nexus of rights but as a component of relationships. In perhaps too simple outline, offenses threaten relationships on Ifaluk, rights in the United States.

Both anger and *song,* then, involve a very general proposition that something offensive has happened, and so mark the existence of cultural values (even though the Ifaluk are much more explicit about the moral component of anger). The cultural definition of what an offense is differs in the two cases, however, as a result of differing values. Anger arises in the pursuit of the values of fair play, competitiveness, and individualism in the United States (Tavris 1982), while communalism, nonaggression, resource sharing, and respect within a system of status ranking are the concerns that animate *song* on Ifaluk. To respond sensibly and correctly to offense in each of the two societies requires that one learn a number of things, including (1) what counts as an offense. On Ifaluk, it is cause for *song* if someone smokes next to you without passing the cigarette to you. In many sectors of the U.S. upper-middle class, anger is considered an acceptable response to others' smoking in one's immediate vicinity. (2) What values underlie the sense of offense. An Ifaluk person's smoking in the corner offends because she or he fails to share, while an American in the corner with a cigarette violates the value placed on not infringing on the rights of others. (3) What entity is potentially offended. *Song,* we have seen, is often portrayed as the response of a group (of chiefs, elders, or all mature island residents) to an offense, while anger is more often the response of an individuated self to a violation of individual rights or of values construed as personal and not shared.

The scene that is expected to follow anger reflects some of these general notions. Lakoff and Kövecses (1987) identify the American conceptualization of anger's sequence as the following:

offending event → anger → attempt at control
→ loss of control → act of retribution.

A "hydraulic model" is behind parts of this sequence, in which anger unexpressed can build up over time to explode eventually in a violent episode. Lakoff and Kövecses (1987) have identified this and other aspects of the ethnotheoretical model of anger that are evident in metaphors used to describe the emotion. Anger builds up over time ("His pent-up anger *welled up* inside him"); it puts pressure on the "container" of the body ("I could barely *contain* my rage"); and, eventually, the anger can explode from the person ("I *blew my stack,*" or "She *erupted* in anger"). Although anger often is seen as socially useless or even antisocial, this hydraulic model may lead those who hold it to the somewhat contradictory idea that the emotion must be "expressed" or "channeled" in small doses in order to prevent its explosion in the form of aggressive behavior. Tavris (1982) has pointed in particular to the way in which this model encourages the expression of anger rather than its suppression. Averill notes that "anger is interpreted as a passion so that an individual need not be held responsible for behavior (interpersonal aggression) which is generally condemned by society, but which is also encouraged under certain circumstances" (1979:26).

The use of this implicit hydraulic model for understanding anger and aggression has set up several kinds of dilemmas for those observing those peoples, in the Pacific and elsewhere, who have been characterized as nonviolent. In the first instance, it follows from the tenets of the above theory that these nonviolent people are most likely not angry, at least on the surface. But the question remains, "Where does their anger go?" Because they must inevitably become angry, what channeling mechanisms, if any, prevent them from "exploding"? This tension can be seen in, for example, J. Briggs's account— *Never in Anger* (1970)—of her encounter with the Utku people of northern Canada. In attempting to understand Utku gentleness, Briggs expends some effort in searching people's faces and gestures, looking for the tics of repressed anger boiling to the surface.

To become angry is, given the injunction to control it, often experienced by Americans as a source of subsequent shame, however justified the resort to anger may have seemed to the individual at the time of its occurrence. The fact that anger is generally viewed as a relatively immature and disvalued response on the part of those who "indulge" in it contributes in part to reciprocal anger in the other. A person's anger may be seen as constituting an affront or injury to another. The shame that can be attached to episodes of anger, along with the emphasis on individual responsibility for the emotions, may also contribute to the low level of cultural elaboration of recipes for coping with others who are angry and to the large number of strategies for coping with one's own anger (e.g., "counting to ten," going for a walk, etc.). Although many of the facial and behavioral indicators of *song* are also indicators of anger, there is no parallel in American culture as elaborate as the counseling scenario that exists on Ifaluk.

Anger is seen, however, like most of the other emotions, as something which a mature person ideally can or should transcend. Several factors contribute to the generally negative evaluation of anger. The view of anger as dispensable arises first from the general cultural theory of emotion which portrays much emotion as chaotic or irrational. Second, anger is often seen as an antisocial emotion because it can involve protest against restraints that are social ("rules and regulations," in Izard's above definition). Ambivalence about the legitimacy or validity of these social rules, however, is common, given, among other factors, the prevalence of an individualistic ethos in the United States. Anger against restraint is then valued to the extent that it is the proud protest of an individual against a larger system. Third, anger is painted in a yet more negative light by the strong association posited between anger and aggression.

In sum, we have seen how the Ifaluk emphasize the distinction between justifiable anger and an emotional response to purely personal frustration. The Ifaluk emphasis, in both theory and practice, on the *prosocial* aspects of anger contrasts with the middle-class American notion that anger often tears relationships and societies apart. Lakoff and Kövecses (1987) also note that righteous indignation is a non-prototypic or peripheral sense of anger. Although both *song* and anger, in the general sense, are considered unpleasant emotions to experience, the Ifaluk see that experience as a morally obligatory one for mature persons. Although anger is thought to be something that can produce fear in others in some circumstances, it is equally likely that reciprocal anger will occur; on Ifaluk, *song* is thought almost always to produce fear. The reasons for the production of fear are also differentially construed in the two cultures; anger is fearsome primarily because of the correlation posited between angerlike emotions and harmful aggression, while the Ifaluk see *song* as fear inducing for the additional but primary reason that it implicitly contains a moral condemnation of its target.[17]

Conclusion

The similarities between anger and *song* result from the universal fact that ideal and real worlds diverge and that intrasocietal conflict occurs. Both concepts are used to make sense of, if not manage, that moral discrepancy and interpersonal conflict. What differs is each people's interpretation of what both ideal and real worlds are like and of how vigorously, how collectively, how verbally or nonverbally, and so forth one addresses the problem or offense. The differences between anger and *song* have everything to do with the problem of how one copes with the problem of interpersonal offense in two kinds of social systems—one a small, relatively homogeneous, face-to-face society where concern with reputation makes gossip an effective sanction across the community, and the other a large heterogeneous society without agreement on a large number of social norms but with extensive formal, legal, and penal institutions that deal with offenses. *Song* enters Ifaluk discourse as a daily regulator of interpersonal relations. Through it a constant reissuing and renegotiating of law, custom, and etiquette go on. A cultural definition of anger as moral signal or as justifiable indignation clearly functions as a form of social control. It may atrophy both where consensus on values breaks up and where formal and abstract legal codes develop and make emotional/moral discourse less central to public discourse.

The concept of justifiable anger plays both a moral and an ideological role in Ifaluk everyday life.[18] The person who declares *song* is making, on the one hand, a moral assertion, a statement about how things ought to be. The concept is used to mark the violation of the values people subscribe to, including the expectation that others will be cooperative, nonaggressive, respectful, and will share resources. As the primary concept in moral discourse, *song* links the person's sensibilities with the wider obligatory order, and thereby mediates between the two.

Justifiable anger is also an ideological practice, that is, linked with the exercise of power. The more powerful factions in Ifaluk society—the chiefs, the brothers, the older women of a household—make more extensive use of the concept, and their legitimacy and influence are enhanced. The more powerful are continually reinvested, through their manipulation of justifiable anger, with the moral superiority which is at once the source and the manifestation of their power. Power is also subverted and appropriated, however, through this same concept when it is used in protest by the less powerful. The use of the term *song* in everyday discourse, then, both reinforces and undermines domination and authority. Having moral and ideological force, justifiable anger maintains a vital position at the center of Ifaluk social life.

CHAPTER SEVEN
The Cultural Construction of Danger

Fear is often seen as one of the simplest and most natural emotions, and so is placed at the end of a continuum whose other pole is occupied by guilt and shame, the cultural and moral emotions par excellence (e.g., Levy and Rosaldo 1983). This perspective may reflect the defensible notion that the sense of danger which is at the core of the emotion of fear is more immediately central to the survival of the organism than any other kind of problem (including, e.g., loss or interpersonal conflict).[1] It can be claimed, however, that culture has no less relevance for fear than it does for guilt, and this claim is supported by the evidence that societies vary in the degree to which they perceive danger in their everyday encounters and in where precisely they see that danger (see Howell 1981; Robarchek 1979; Scruton 1986; Taussig 1984). Its cultural importance is also evident in the fact that fear often plays a role in local moral systems, particularly when taboo behaviors are defined as dangerous. These differences in cultural views of danger have important implications for understanding what risks people in fact take (Douglas and Wildavsky 1982) and for the amount of stress with which they live. In this chapter, we will look at how the Ifaluk have come to understand danger in their world.

The universal problem of danger or threat does not appear to have been solved biologically by the development in humans of a large number of innate elicitors of a fearful emotional response (Campos et al. 1978). The dominance of the ethological model for fear, however, has meant an emphasis on the parallels between the fear and flight of an antelope encountering a predator and fear in humans. This obscures the symbolic nature of danger for humans, for whom threats from predator and accident pale next to those of lost access to a food supply due to social conflict or change, or those of environmental catastrophe or illness whose causes are not immediately apparent (e.g., Scruton 1986). To perceive and understand such dangers require both learning and complex information processing that go far beyond instinct. As a result, the cultural transmission of a sense of where danger lies becomes all the more important in protecting the individual from threats both tangible and intangible. This process takes place both in the socialization of the vulnerable infant and child and in the adult. In the latter case, for example, the military socialization of young men often involves an attempt to eliminate or reconceptualize the nature of danger. To equate human fear with animal fear is akin to equating the English or Woleaian language with bird songs.[2]

After examining the various forms in which danger is constructed on Ifaluk, we will also note the existence of some intracultural variation in the perception of threat. Differences in vulnerability in this (or any) society and the ambiguity of emotional meaning contribute to this variation. We will also note how people use the rhetoric of fear to present themselves as moral, that is, as adhering to Ifaluk notions of the good and proper.

The Nature of Danger

A day does not go by on Ifaluk in which someone does not talk about her or his sense of danger. People frequently and dramatically tell each other stories about brushes with danger, as when the older and highly ranked man Gatachimang told me about the time several years earlier that a group of men from Puluwat, an atoll far to the east, arrived by canoe on Ifaluk. They cut an aggressive and wide swath through the island, and people scattered; eventually, they made their way to his house, where, he recounted, they loudly demanded whiskey or toddy. He was extremely afraid, he said, as he told them in a small voice that he had none, and he imitated the cowering and fearful posture he took then in the course of his storytelling. What struck me then, and now, is not only how threatened by the Puluwatese Gatachimang felt himself to be but also that as an older and high-ranking man he felt no need to present himself before me and others as fearless. Here and at many other turns I was made aware of how central both violence and strangeness are to the Ifaluk sense of danger as well as of how fearfulness is considered moral. A person who declares her or his fear—either *rus* (panic/fright/surprise) or *metagu* (fear/anxiety)—can be seen as saying to others, "I am harmless, and because I am harmless, I am a good person and worthy of your respect." By looking at what people see as threatening and hence to be avoided, we get, by implication, a sense of their view of the good life.

What the Ifaluk define as dangerous situations include an encounter with unfamiliar people, spirits, physical injury and death (including the threat of typhoons), the prospect of interpersonal violence, the possibility that one will incur the justifiable anger of another, and any sudden and unexpected event. The fact that people can expect to find themselves in one of these situations daily means that everyday life on the atoll has a fearful tone. To characterize the Ifaluk as "fearful," of course, is to contrast their sense of danger with my own, and, in many situations, the Ifaluk saw danger where I saw none. This was so because I lacked either knowledge and experience, for example, of harmful animals on the reef, or (what I would characterize as) belief, for instance, in the existence of spirits or in the possibility that I might be hit by a village neighbor. As we will see, there were exceptions, equally illuminating of cultural differences, in which I emphasized danger more strongly than my neighbors.

One episode will illustrate the experiences that underlie this account of Ifaluk fear. When I first arrived on Ifaluk, Tamalekar—the man who had adopted me—asked me whether I wanted to put my sleeping mat in the main residence with the rest of the family or in a separate building within the household compound. While this question struck me as merely considerate at the time, I later realized that it also entailed a subtle act of cultural and emotion translation on Tamalekar's part. Like most other Ifaluk, he would not have asked such a question of a clan sister visiting from another atoll, with whom he would likely have shared a common and deep-seated assumption that people who are alone are afraid. After years of first-hand experience with a succession of Peace Corps volunteers who had lived in a neighboring village, however, Tamalekar had observed that Americans' emotional lives were exotic. In particular, he had noticed that they often slept alone, presumably without fear. In even considering the possibility of a separate residence for me, Tamalekar had translated, where I initially could not, between the two emotional worlds of the Ifaluk and the American.

After some days of anxious reflection on my two options and their conflicting possibilities of isolation and privacy, intimacy and claustrophobia, I expressed a preference for a separate house, and Tamalekar attempted to accommodate me without abandoning island good sense. A cook house about twenty yards from the main residence was selected for conversion into my home, and Ilefagochang—my mother's sister—and other relatives wove new thatch walls for it. They then moved the house from its original position to the new postholes they had dug at a distance just feet from the main house. In shifting the houseposts, Tamalekar retained his commitment to a particular view of the nature of fear, solitude, my need for protection, and appropriate residence patterns, even while he accommodated my exotic emotional world or, in other words, my deviant approach to social relations.

People on the atoll use a variety of terms to talk about danger. The most common are *metagu* (fear/anxiety) and *rus* (panic/fright/surprise), with the former being used more often to talk about on-going or anticipated threat, as in the statement "I am afraid of spirits" (*Gang i metagu yalus*), or "I am afraid that my brother will hit me." *Rus,* on the other hand, is used to talk about the immediate encounter with danger, as in the statement "I was panicked when I saw the spirit" (*Gang i ya rus etoa i weri yalus we*), or "I am panicked whenever I hear airplanes go by overhead."[3] Although each term can be used to talk about the same set of threats, differences in the usual object of each emotion can be discerned in counts of use contexts of the two terms. Most important, *metagu* is much more often used to talk about the response to strange situations and to another's justifiable anger, while *rus* is more often used to talk about events which are seen as posing an immediate physical threat to oneself or another, such as meeting either a drunk on the path or a shark while spearfishing, or realizing that one's child is about to die.

The two emotions are also conceptualized as similar in creating flight or avoidance reactions in those who experience them. People may run away from the dangerous object in each case, but *rus* is often described as freezing its victims in their tracks or causing them to run about in a confused and crazy way. One woman described the response people have to *rus* as taking one of the three following forms:

> Some people [who are *rus*] don't speak, even if we talk to them. [Others] become crazy and confused. I would ask what you are *rus* about. You would say something else [irrelevant]. Our eyes are not clear because of the *rus*. People sitting far away may have seen that *rus* thing

and even though I was closer to it, I won't know or understand about it because I'm *rus*. My insides are random. Other people are still smart in their heads even though they are *rus*. People who are *rus* run around . . . and their eyes aren't the same. They hold themselves [wrapping their arms around themselves as if cold] and sometimes their voices shake. . . . We shake inside. Our legs tremble as we walk, and we think we'll fall.

The "panicked" (*rus*) person thus sometimes has trouble focusing on a course of action or understanding what has happened. The common inability to talk or walk takes the form, in extremis, of unconsciousness. The panicked person's face is distinguished by blank or unclear eyes, paleness, or a "squinty" appearance. A common gesture indicative of the emotion, to which the woman above makes allusion, is holding the forearms firmly to the chest, with the upper arms tight against the sides of the body. In sharp contrast to most other emotions, *rus* is talked about in often graphic physiological terms. People describe *rus* as having distinct internal feelings associated with it, particularly shaking in the region just under the breastbone. It is as if, people said, something comes up from one's gut into the chest, stopping there suddenly. One person described it as like "something is moving up inside the gut, like something inside is alive and is crawling up." *Rus* is an emotion of paralyzing intensity, and one which can lead in the worst cases to sickness or death.

The emotion of fear/anxiety (*metagu*) is, by contrast, a less dramatic emotion. Although it also involves an assessment of danger and of the need for avoidance, *metagu* is described as involving ideas more than bodily changes. The frightened person often ruminates anxiously on the dangers, poring over possible consequences. Loss of appetite is common in association with this emotion (as with many others). Stress is placed on what the person does to avoid the object of his or her fear, such as not going out alone at night, getting a sleeping companion, or staying out of the water or canoes.

Let us look now at some of the most common forms that danger takes for people on Ifaluk.

The Stranger

Of the many events that came to constitute for me the meaning of the Ifaluk concepts of fear, one is now a kind of snapshot. I observe two teenage boys from behind as they stand at a short distance from the edge of a large number of sitting people who have gathered for the island's grammar school graduation. I overhear them as, holding hands, they whisper to each other in planning how they will make their way to the other side of the crowd. Their somewhat anxious discussions have to take into account the need to avoid the many dangers represented by the group—of relatives owed respectful avoidance, of eyes that might catch sight of or imagine dirt on their legs or loincloths, of high-ranking individuals whose anger might be incurred by walking too close, of kin who might call to them to come and share food, thereby requiring difficult decisions whether or not to accept, and then how much to eat of a small bowl of prepared bananas.

People often speak of being afraid/anxious (*metagu*) when they for some reason have to venture into or past relatively unfamiliar households. This occurs even though most adults know virtually every other adult on the island, often in great biographical depth. It can in fact be considered an axiom of Ifaluk ethnopsychology that people are naturally afraid (*metagu*) of people they are not used to (*yeori*), although it is only total strangers (and particularly those who are expected to be violent) who inspire panic (*rus*). What is feared is particularly that one will become an object of attention or, worse, ridicule. Gossip, even overtly uncritical, is seen as a threat, as it brings unwanted attention. The gaze of others is often seen as critical, and that criticism holds the danger of harming one's public and self-image.[4] This fear of the gaze of others is often phrased as a fear of shame or embarrassment (*ma*). Men who are called on to speak in public may avoid doing so out of either fear (*metagu*) or shame (*ma*). People who are called to in a gesture of solidarity or generosity to come and eat will often refuse out of fear.

One of the most fundamental contradictions in the Ifaluk sociocultural system involves the perception of others as both nurturing and dangerous, a conflict that parallels the distinction between *fago* (compassion/love/sadness) and *metagu* (fear/anxiety). There is at least partial incompatibility in this sense of the danger of others with the requirements for cooperation and sharing. Both the fear of anger and the fear of others' attention act to fragment social life to some extent, as neighbor avoids neighbor. This conflict of principles is most dramatically evident in food sharing between households. Although offering food is said to reduce feelings of fear/anxiety in the recipient, such an attempt to create intimacy is often unsuccessful. The many passersby on a path who will be called to come and eat at a household almost invariably refuse. Although *metagu* is not always involved in those refusals, people usually must balance their hunger with the danger that they sense inheres in accepting the offer. Such dangers include the possibility that you will be taking food from others' mouths, that is, that the call was simply polite, and the involvement of one's own household in obligations to reciprocate that may not be welcome or feasible. The neighbor who calls to you to come and eat may choose to regard a refusal as a rejection of a call to an exchange relationship, as a sign that the person has a commendable concern to preserve the other's food supply, or as the valued timidity which means the person can also be expected to be gentle and well behaved. While fear/anxiety is seen as the foundation for good behavior because it leads to a calm personality and indicates a healthy concern for the possible anger of others, this same emotion can prevent social intercourse and sharing, even between close relatives.

The fear of others is both heightened and allayed by the institutions of marriage and adoption, which provide for much movement between households. When a man marries into another household or a child enters through adoption, great attention is paid to the likelihood that the new member will be afraid/anxious in his new home. This was the case when I first came to live with my adoptive family as well as when, many months later, a young man married into the household. We were each frequently told, "You should not be *metagu*. You should not be *metagu* to ask us for anything you want." A lack of *metagu* and a corresponding readiness to accept offers of food is considered to be a positive sign of intimacy and mutuality. On several occasions, I was told, or overheard people talking about, how bad it was for a person to be afraid to eat. A separate term (*gafoiufish*) is in fact used to talk about the fear of eating. It is even possible to say that kinship—defined positively on Ifaluk as the sharing of food—is conversely construed as the absence of a sense of danger, an absence of fear. Feelings of *metagu* frequently, however, persist, especially where the system of rank and authority in the household act to reinforce it through the role of authority in distributing justifiable anger. These emotional conflicts have many parallels and some genesis in the contradictions of Ifaluk's social structure; this includes particularly the contradiction sometimes engendered by the combination of a ranked social system and a general egalitarianism of wealth and frequent exchange. Where the other is defined as at once dangerous (by virtue of being more powerful) and safe or even weak (by virtue of sharing), the emotional tone of everyday interaction will show that tension.

A related context in which *metagu* is used is cross-gender relationships. The many taboos and practices which segregate the sexes create the same unfamiliar relationship between them that characterizes intervillage and interhousehold relations generally. People of both sexes claim that women are *metagu* of and thus avoid men. This belief about the emotional perceptions of women reinforces gender segregation. Both men and women speak of their own fear/anxiety in the face of the unfamiliar and of the possibility that they will feel ashamed or embarrassed (*ma*) on crossing those boundaries. Men say they are afraid/anxious (*metagu*) of asking for a woman in marriage lest they be rejected and suffer shame or embarrassment. Women, on the other hand, often say they are afraid/anxious of groups of men and avoid them because they would be ashamed or embarrassed and would become the object of men's justifiable anger for breaking the taboos that regulate much public cross-gender contact.

Foreigners inspire some of the most dramatic declarations of all types of fear, as in Gatachimang's description of the aggressive Puluwatese. The earlier colonial period and particularly World War II have certainly had a hand in creating this view of outsiders. The war may have been evoked, for example, on the day that Ilesepeneuf, an older woman, came running toward the school building as a Navy plane flew low overhead. "I am panicked [*rus*]," she said breathlessly as she approached me and began laughing as she explained that she thought it was the Germans who rumor had it were coming to visit the atoll (although the gossip was that they were to arrive by yacht). Despite her laughter, Ilesepeneuf did expect danger; "If the plane comes over again," she said later in the conversation, "I will run down to [the household of my relatives]."

In another such case, I was in my house on an afternoon when the interisland ship sat off the reef. Ilefagomar called me in a panicked voice to come quickly into the big house (presumably as some kind of protection for her) when she saw a man approaching who she thought to be Korean. Later she said she had been panicked and told the story of one of several Korean fishing boats which had stopped at the island over the past several years. Sailors from the ship had caused great fright by peeking into houses, causing some people to flee to their neighbors. The Koreans also apparently grabbed at and chased women. The Yapese are feared as sorcerers, and people sometimes spoke of their fear of being poisoned when they visit Yap. While people never spoke to me of fear of Americans, it is probably unlikely that they would do so in my presence. Other ethnic groups who were spoken of as particularly fear-inspiring include "New Guinea" people and Belauans. What makes most of these people dangerous in the Ifaluk view is their violence: Belauans murder, New Guineans cannibalize, and Puluwatese fight.

Fear of the strange is, of course, not unique to Ifaluk. The perception of the unfamiliar as dangerous is certainly much heightened among atoll residents in comparison with middle-class Americans, however, for whom either sociability or indifference might be seen as the more usual, as well as the more mature, responses to encountering new people.[5] The "thinness" of the cultural elaboration of the idea of fear of the strange in the United States has its corollary in the positive value attached to fearlessness. While potentially drawing from and helping provide for the needed mobility of the work force, these American perspectives may have contributed to the notable lack of discussion of this emotional understanding in the fieldwork literature. Fieldwork represents, for the anthropologist, a situation that is strange in several ways. The anthropological denial of danger and hence fear is common and powerful, however, and this is so despite the fact that it might be expected that fieldwork provides more opportunities than does the home context for the construction of a sense of threat. By attempting to learn how to behave acceptably in new terms, the anthropologist increases the dangers of social failure and criticism. By taking on the new and relatively ill-defined task of conducting research, he or she also encounters these same dangers. Added to this is the likelihood of being ill-informed about the kinds of physical threats present in the new environment. And finally, residual racial and ethnic stereotyping may be present, setting up at least an initial sense of the other as threatening.

Spirits

It struck both Melford Spiro during his 1947–48 fieldwork and me thirty years later that people perceive the spirits, or *yalus,* as one of the central dangers in their lives. Spiro argued that the existence of the belief in spirits (*alus,* in his account) can be explained by the manifest and latent psychological functions that belief serves. After describing the ways the spirits were viewed and their dangers discussed by the Ifaluk during my stay, I contrast Spiro's psychodynamic explanation of the emotional meaning of spirits with the ethnopsychological approach to that issue taken here. In particular, I argue that Spiro's account, while similar to my own at several points, has the disadvantage of turning the fear of spirits from a moral and discursive process into a mechanical outcome of psychological processes and makes use of the limiting dualism in which a natural set of emotions (aggressive feelings and anxiety) confronts a set of cultural prohibitions against violence.

Although the spirits who inhabit Ifaluk may be either benevolent or malevolent, they can represent a real threat to life and limb. While the good spirit may bring medicinal recipes for an ill relative, the greatest danger is presented by others, who can bring both illness and death. In either case, people speak of being both *metagu* and *rus* in the face of either the spirits' power or their harmful intentions. Something of the nature of the danger that the spirits pose for people can be gleaned from the following story that Ilefagomar told one evening, (perhaps coincidentally) several days after a teenage boy's accidental death.[6] Her children, obviously familiar with the legend, made fearful sounds ("eeeee!") but encouraging smiles as she began it.

There was a woman, she recounted, who had no sisters or husband and but one son. The son married matrilocally into another village and had several children, but he failed ever to come back to see his mother, to check whether she was sick or not. One day she became ill and later died with no one attending her. The spirit that she became went to her son's house at night and found everyone there but the son, who was fishing. She gouged out the eyes of her daughter-in-law and of all the children but one, a boy who pretended he was dead. The spirit then propped the wife's lifeless body against the interior wall of the house and placed banana-fiber thread in her hand and a thread-cutting shell between her lips [where women typically hold the tool while making thread]. Then, sitting by the door and looking out at the moon, the *yalus* sang and waited for it to set and for the son to return. The fisherman son eventually came ashore and approached the homestead. As he did, the surviving child darted out of the house, calling to the father to flee. Father and son ran down to the canoe house, the spirit in pursuit, and warned the people there. Together they beat the spirit, who climbed around the ceiling of the canoe house trying to escape the blows, and killed her.

This tale implies a host of dangers—of obligations to relatives unfulfilled, of shifting residence at marriage, of households temporarily without adult men, of death, and perhaps even of mothers themselves. All these dangers and more coalesce in the spirits, who are encountered by people, not only in legends, but in everyday contexts. They are especially prevalent at night and in the wooded interior of the island, and people will avoid going out unaccompanied in those situations for fear of meeting one while alone. Children both younger and older who find themselves alone at night, even at a few yards distance from their home and relatives, will often run screaming into the house. Adult women and men can be seen running out of the bush on occasion, having had a brush with a spirit. Being alone, even during the day and in the household area, is avoided whenever possible. Although being alone is also considered boring and lonely, it is perhaps above all seen as threatening because of the possibility of spirit encounter. This contributes to making the solitary person a relatively uncommon sight.

Terrifying omens and dreams are often caused by spirits. Dreams of both adults and children are frequently visited by spirits, with people describing in the morning how they were awakened in the night by their *rus*. In these dreams, people are chased and frightened by spirits, or disaster befalls a member of their family. These latter dreams are sometimes seen as portents from the spirits and may leave people *rus* for some period afterward. *Rus*-causing omens are also sometimes sent. Walking to the beach with a teenage girl one night, I held the flashlight that guided our way when a bird suddenly flew into the light and dropped to the ground. The girl brought the bird back to the house for her family to identify. Upon hearing her mother give the bird's name, she burst into tears, thinking, it turned out erroneously, that the species was a bad omen for the household. Describing her *rus* to her mother, she said that she was panicked and shaking and that the feelings "had rushed toward me".[7]

Spirits come up in conversation, particularly during illness and in the aftermath of death. In serious illness, both speculation and divination are directed toward trying to ascertain what spirit caused the threat and to finding a cure. The spirit realm may thus represent both the danger of sickness and its elimination. The danger that death represents is intensified by the belief that spirits are especially active at that time. Toward the end of the daylong funeral of Tomas, described in chapter 5, people (including myself) heard a wailing go up from what turned out to be an empty household near the funeral site. This wailing was interpreted as a visit from the spirit of a deceased woman of that household who had come to express her compassion/love/sadness (*fago*) for the family members in their loss. The spirit continued to visit the area for some time after the death, inspiring a sense of danger in people despite her benevolent intentions. The danger of other deaths is more intense, however, as when the teenage boy mentioned earlier died in a fall from a tree. Accidental death and suicide leave the deceased a particularly malicious spirit, and the entire island spent the next several weeks speaking frequently of spirit sightings and of their *rus* and *metagu*. Death represents danger in many ways, not the least of which is the possibility that more deaths will follow, a possibility that people on Ifaluk at least partially attribute to the machinations of spirits.

Spirit possession also occurs on the atoll, and regardless of the spirit's intentions, can cause *rus* in those around the possessed person. In one such case, an older woman, Lafiletotil, became possessed, and at a time when her household was afflicted with a sick child and had been visited regularly by a benevolent spirit who brought medicine. Lafiletotil began speaking rapidly and incomprehensibly, inspiring *rus* in those around her. One young woman, Latil, told me later that in her *rus,* she saw colors in front of her eyes, her head spun, and she could hear nothing going on around her. When she began to shake, some people gave her medicine and she returned to her normal state. She was unsure, she said, whether this medicine was spirit medicine (*taffeyalyalus*) or *rus* medicine (*taffeyalrus*), indicating that her problem might be attributed to either the spirits or the emotion of panic itself.

When Spiro encountered the Ifaluk running out of the bush in fright after having encountered a spirit, he asked why a seemingly irrational belief that causes such fear and anxiety is maintained. His answer is complex but includes the central notion that the belief in malevolent spirits allows the Ifaluk to express aggression which is otherwise prohibited. Aggressive drives, Spiro argues (following Freud), are present in the Ifaluk and "like other imperious drives, demand expression. If they are not permitted expression, they are deflected from their original goal and are either inverted or displaced" (1952:498–99). The spirits become a socially acceptable channel for the expression of hostile feelings.[8] In addition, Spiro argues that Ifaluk child-rearing practices create much anxiety, whose true cause adults have repressed knowledge of. By creating dangerous spirits, the Ifaluk are able to attach their free-floating anxiety to an object and so manipulate and control it better. While the latter argument is certainly weakened by the fact that there are multiple other dangers (such as illness, typhoons, and foreigners) to which the generalized anxiety might affix itself, the former bears discussion. Spiro argues that while the Ifaluk appear to express fear of the dangers of the spirits, they are really afraid of the dangers of their own aggressive impulses and the danger that those impulses will destroy their community.

The argument I make here is, in very broadest outline, similar. Talk of spirits and their violence (like talk of the potential violence of drunks, Koreans, and others) serves psychosocial functions. In both analyses, island ecology makes intracommunity violence not unthinkable but more threatening to survival, and the talk of spirits aids in avoiding it. In both, the spirits present a forum in which dangers are rehearsed and manipulated. In both analyses, the dynamics of the links between anger and fear in Ifaluk lives are crucial.

The psychodynamic account of Ifaluk spirit belief, however, has several fundamental difficulties from the ethnopsychological perspective taken here. First, rather than conceptualize talk of spirits as a transformed expression of internal life, there are advantages to viewing it as moral discourse concerned with defining—simultaneously for self and for others—the problem of violence. A mechanical model of affect generation, psychic manipulation, and discharge has all the disadvantages that Solomon (1976) and others have identified; although he may overstate, Solomon laments that "psychology becomes urology" when we follow Freud in seeing emotions as "demanding" expression, thereby excluding choice and responsibility from the domain of emotions. The person becomes not an agent but a passive reactor to internal emotional forces. Solomon substitutes for hydraulics an existentialist language of choice and authenticity, although this too draws on local Western concerns with sincerity and individual autonomy. The ethnopsychological approach, while having its own Western cultural correlates (see chap. 8), uses metaphors of conversation and social project or construction which allow us to model the place of things like spirit belief in Ifaluk lives as open-ended, emergent social practices. Like talk in general, they are not simply indexical of an inner life but pragmatically embedded in a constantly changing and diverse set of social practices, including those termed moral. The ethnopsychological approach is to privilege (note, not to substitute) indigenous meanings over external ones, in part with the assumption that consciousness transforms reality rather than overlays it. Spiro's analysis ignores what the Ifaluk find primary in their understanding of the world, which is the distinction between anger as an "insistence on ideals" (Solomon 1976) and anger as the emotional correlate of aggression.[9]

The links that Spiro makes between anger (or hostility—he treats them as synonymous) and fear are internal; the Ifaluk primarily fear their own violence, not others', in his view. The links that the Ifaluk make between the two in both explicit and implicit ethnopsychology are in fact more specific and more socially embedded. The danger of spirits, in their view, is their violence, their lack of *fago* (compassion/love/sadness). As Spiro also remarked, the spirits personify danger, give it a face. By so doing, they allow for more complex explanation and rehearsal of danger and community response to it. The drama of the spirits on Ifaluk communicates that the anger of others, whether spirit or human, should produce fear, not angry counterattack. This, the drama says, is our path to safety, at least for now, at least here.

The Threat of Physical Injury or Death

Impending injury, serious illness, or death are some of the most common situations in which people talk about *rus* (and, to a lesser extent, *metagu*). The nature of this danger varies from the catastrophic and communal to the more mundane and personal, from hearing about an approaching typhoon on the radio to contending with fish bones as one eats in the dark. Much of it emerges from the special dangers of coral atoll life, particularly the sea and its weather and the occupational hazards of fishing and climbing extremely tall trees for coconut and breadfruit. The reality of these threats is reflected in mortality figures which show men at much higher risk than women for accidental death from drowning or falls from trees (there were two such deaths in the two-year period 1978–79). Recent cases of maternal death in childbirth are relatively few but the real possibility is partially behind women's expressed fear of childbearing.

The typhoons, which we have already seen are a crucial force in Ifaluk emotional life, are central to the sense of danger as well. Typhoon stories include accounts of who was and was not panicked (*rus*), when they first became panicked, and what they did. People spoke frequently of the 1975 typhoon, of how the water rose and the children went to play by the shore, few adults taking the problem seriously. What struck me about these descriptions of the self and others in crisis is how often people stressed that their sense of danger was essentially concern for the safety of others. Ilefagomar told me several times how her father "was not panicked [*rus*]" during the typhoon, but rather was worried/conflicted (*waires*); he stayed awake through the night, walking around to monitor the water level, to check on the stability of house posts, and to pray at the church, even as the water swirled around his knees. Several other women described their own panic as due to thinking that their children would die in the storm.

Illness also obviously represents danger, and *rus* is the more common term used to talk about it. Danger is perceived especially when children and infants are sick, reflecting the fact that mortality rates are highest in the youngest age brackets. A fever or rash in a child produces strong and immediate emotion in parents, a reaction which initially stood for me in striking contrast to the somewhat more casual attitude in the United States. My own failure to become *rus* over the fever of a two-year-old boy in my household reflected my lack of experience both with parenthood and with the prevalent and rapidly progressive and fatal disease of meningitis, of which high fever is one symptom. People often recount in vivid detail the past illnesses of their children or other relatives, stressing not only their compassionate behavior (see chap. 5) but also their panic as they anticipate death.

In general, the infant is perceived as a tremendously vulnerable creature whose fragility is almost synonymous with death, and declarations of *metagu* are common when people talk about how they see and deal with babies. Many people, especially teenage girls, would spontaneously talk about the fear/anxiety (*metagu*) they feel in the presence or handling of infants. Midwives are frequently remarked upon laudably as able to overcome the feelings of *rus* and *metagu* at birth. It was, then, not entirely remarkable that we heard panicked shouting one day from the neighboring household with a month-old infant. The mother and father, who were alone with their child at the time, had looked at the sleeping infant and suddenly became *rus*, thinking that he had died. Their shouting brought other nearby household members—with similar expectations of infant death—running.

Societies, as well as the adults within any society, vary in the extent to which threat is perceived in the environment or in particular events. People on Ifaluk often communicate their sense of danger and attempt to convince others of its reality. In the process, it is possible to observe how the emotional meaning of events is socially established through continual attempts at emotional socialization of one person by another. An example of this involved a storm that occurred during my stay. The full force of a typhoon strikes Ifaluk relatively infrequently, but the winter season of high winds usually brings several storms, carefully radio-monitored, in the region. For many, however, the threat presented by radio reports is not real, and they are either ignored or listened to as one might to the telling of a frightening but quasifictional legend. People came frequently in one such instance to ask about the reports on my radio of a distant but approaching typhoon. While some declared themselves to be panicked (*rus*) that the storm would reach Ifaluk and kill them all, others seemed more excited than frightened. One afternoon, as several of us sat waiting for further news, Yarofailuch, a man in his forties, entered the house. When he heard that the typhoon was getting closer to Ifaluk, a small grin crossed his face. A younger woman in the house saw him and said, in angry tones, "Look at him making *pitifas* [a small smile]," and went on to complain that no one was going to church to pray so that the typhoon would swerve away from the atoll. Thus, people try to reorient emotionally those who fail to demonstrate the appropriate sense of danger. This example illustrates not only that emotional negotiation takes place but that what is at stake with fear is often the mobilization of others for mutual protection against the perceived threat.

An ethic of bravery (*berag*) and endurance (*timwegil*) exists on Ifaluk alongside the emphasis on threat and fear. Endurance is seen as the good and necessary effort which is needed to continue working through disgust, weariness, or pain. While endurance is required in both genders, bravery is a quality seen as particularly appropriate for men and for seafaring. This perhaps is not surprising, given that the life threats that men's work involve must not immobilize them if fish and coconuts are to be brought into the household. Men often talk, however, about their *rus* and *metagu* in the face of sharks, sudden storms, and strong currents. What is notable about the value placed on bravery is that it is not associated with interpersonal confrontation. The man who conquers fear in the face of the threat of another's aggression is *not* brave, but either foolish, or more likely, simply "bad."

Interpersonal Violence

One of the most common contexts in which people speak of their sense of danger is in relation to the possibility that they will be hit or that others will physically fight. Despite the fact that violence is rare, people see it as a real and fearsome possibility. *Metagu* and especially *rus* are constantly spoken of when men are drunk, for fear that they will fight. Walking along the island paths with other women and seeing a man approach from the other direction, I would sometimes be pulled off the path, to somewhat frantic explanations that the man was drunk and might hit us unless we fled. Shouting, although rare, is often interpreted by distant listeners as indicating that two men are fighting, as it was one particular afternoon as Lesepemang and I sat grating coconut. To my suggestion that we go see what was happening, she replied, "We don't run toward shouting, because men could be fighting." Young people who have misbehaved in some way often anticipate the justifiable anger of their relatives by saying, "Now they will hit me," or expressing fear that their property will be destroyed in retaliation.

Although men can be panicked over the prospect or reality of violence, it is most often women who speak about their *rus* in such situations. Men are portrayed by both genders as the protectors of women and children when violence threatens, and in households which are temporarily without men there will be much discussion of panic.

Women in such households say that they fear that drunk men will come in the evening in combative moods. They will therefore make some effort to get more people to sleep in their houses, or to be invited to stay with others. In both genders, however, the proper response to violence is flight or deflection rather than counterattack.

Hot-tempered people similarly inspire fear because people anticipate aggressive behavior from them.[10] Both the drunk and the hot-tempered persons are said to lack *metagu*. An absence of *metagu* is at the root of antisocial behaviors of all sorts, including harsh words and violence. As we saw in Gatachimang's narrative about the violent Puluwatese, then, declarations of *rus* or *metagu* tell others that you are not aggressive, that you are harmless. You thereby negotiate both your moral status as a gentle person and the legitimation of your own compliance or subordination.

The horror that the idea of violence evokes for the Ifaluk was evident in their discussions of the rumored aggressive tendencies of Americans and some other groups. Several people checked with me to see if the stories they had heard about the existence of murder in the United States were in fact true. When I confirmed them, one man imagined out loud, as many did, the terror he would feel if he found himself in America: "If I had to travel from one place to another," he said, "I would get in the car and drive and drive and never stop until I arrived, even if I could not sleep or eat for four days." Gatachimang, who had been on the island of Yap during its aerial bombardment in World War II, continued to tell and retell the story of his bottomless terror as the explosions went off around him. Similarly, one of the most riveting and stressful experiences for people in the postwar period has been their exposure to the violence in Western movies that have been brought to the island by U.S. Navy vessels stopping on "goodwill" tours. People frequently talk about their panic on seeing people shot and beaten in those movies and relate how some individuals were terrified for days afterwards. In a few such cases, the person became ill, and in many others, refused to see movies that arrived in later years. In their discussions of the aggression of others and the rehearsal of their fear of it, the Ifaluk replay and reinforce the scenario which has contributed to keeping them relatively safe from violence, at least through the recent past,[11] and this is the scenario in which they cringe or run terrified from the prospect of violence. In these rehearsals, they remind themselves and each other of the horrible consequences of violence which is casually accepted.

This conception of danger contrasted with my own sense of security among neighbors whom I construed as gentle. This was reversed on one occasion, however, when I awoke suddenly in the middle of the night to see a man entering my doorless house. The danger I saw in that instant led me to scream out, using unreflectively the sense I had brought from home that strange men entering your house at night intend violent harm of any number of kinds. Although I had been on the island long enough to know that sexual rendezvous occurred in this way, with men sneaking at night to silently call the woman out of her house, I had to make sense too quickly of what was happening. As the no doubt nonplussed man fled and my family hurried over to see what the matter was, hilarious laughter greeted my announcement that I had been afraid. Although men may be seen as somewhat frightening in public contexts or when drunk, the night visitor is, if not the antithesis of fear, at least nearly so.[12] Despite the laughter (or perhaps as part of it), my parents were also clearly proud of me and my display of fear. Ilefagomar told the story to many neighbors as, I sensed, proof of my sensibleness and spoke to me over the next day or two with the special politeness that always meant approval to me.

The Justifiable Anger of Others

One of the most significant dangers in everyday life is the possibility of incurring the justifiable wrath of another. Given the frequency with which justifiable anger occurs, it is not a negligible source of daily fear. That sense of danger is illustrated by the following incident. Gossip was circulating that Lauchepou, a young woman, had been drinking. Having heard the talk, Lauchepou anticipated that her brother would hear, believe, and thus be justifiably angry. She later told me how she had been afraid/anxious (*metagu*) and then, seeing him approaching her on the path, had walked far out of her way to avoid him. People also speak of being *rus* that another will be justifiably angry. In one such case, a woman described to a group of women how she had badgered her husband about his failure to keep his sisters from misbehaving. However, she said, she became panicked (after some reflection) that her teasing would make her husband justifiably angry.

We have already noted that the concept of justifiable anger outlines what is considered unacceptable behavior and pragmatically indexes the rank of the speaker who declares him- or herself angry. We have also noted that justifiable anger is thought to be (and in actuality is) necessarily followed by fear in the person who is the object of that anger. The danger that justifiable anger represents is multifaceted, however, being composed not just of moral disapproval by one's compatriots but of the myriad problems of subordination to any other. Inseparable, then, are the dangers of justifiable anger, of the violence which in theory may follow, and of rank, both lineage and gender based.

Rank, taboo, and cross-gender interactions are dangerous because each context involves the potential for justifiable anger. Young people often express fear of their elders, even when their justifiable anger is not immediately at issue, as when Gasugulibung, a young man in his twenties, asked me to go to a high-ranked household (to which I was adoptively related) to get a book that he had lent them because, he said, he was afraid (*metagu*) to go there. On another occasion, I heard Tamalekar tell his sister's son about the time he had been on a canoe, lost at sea. He had been asked to steer for a while but was *metagu* that one of the older men would be angry with him. Although he might also have feared doing a poor job, Tamalekar emphasized the men's age and superordinate rank. Women also commonly express fear of men, an index of the dangers of violating the various taboos that separate the sexes as well as of the authority and even the violence of men. Women sometimes announce themselves to be afraid when near large groups of men. They also attempt to shame any deviant who acts as if she were not, as several women did in one case by describing a particular woman as crazy because "she is not afraid of men."

To the Ifaluk way of thinking, fear is what keeps people good. The person who fears the justifiable anger of others is one who carefully watches her own behavior's "social wake," always attentive to the risk of rocking another's boat. In many contexts, declarations of fear can be seen as attempts to negotiate the meaning of behavior that has disturbed others. To be fearful is to acknowledge the justifiable anger of others and thus the illegitimacy of what one has done. This interpretation illuminates what was said by Lesepemang, the young girl whose marriage protest has already been described. It had been several days since the marriage, and Lesepemang's young husband came into the house and sat next to her. When she completely ignored him, he fled out the door in shame (*ma*), people later agreed. While at first she laughed somewhat manically, Lesepemang later said that she was afraid that her parents would hear what had happened and would be angry (*sig*) at her. She declared in that way her allegiance, however belated and partial it really was, to the principles of obedience to the elders who wanted her to marry and behave nurturantly and politely to her husband. *Metagu* negotiates, on innumerable other occasions, the moral status of the individual by announcing her adherence to local codes of conduct, even as they have just been violated.

The relationship between fear and the control of behavior finds its antithesis in the opposition which we saw exists between fear and happiness/excitement. People who are happy/excited can cause trouble because that emotion causes them to forget to be afraid. I was several times admonished to inspire some fear in those who were seen as my subordinates (i.e., children and teenagers) as a way of socializing them to better behavior. In one such case, a young adolescent girl, Lelam, who was related to the people in the household in which I stayed, had been coming by frequently to ask me for cigarettes. While I had always complied with these requests, my adoptive parents one day remonstrated with me not to give her cigarettes if she asked and, in fact, to scold her if she took them without asking, something they suspected she had been doing. Both the suspicion of theft and her boldness in asking me for things caused my parents concern (although they may have also been worried about the drain on the tobacco supply of the household). They also believed that my failure to recognize and respond angrily to her misbehavior was due not to my ignorance but to fear of Lelam. "You must not be 'afraid/anxious' [*metagu*] [of Lelam]," my mother told me, "or she will be happy/excited [*ker*]." It was thus primarily the absence of justifiable anger which would delight Lelam by allowing her the inference that there was no danger in continuing to get tobacco from me.

The Unexpected

When something happens suddenly or unexpectedly, people often breathlessly say that they are panicked (*rus*), and this is the case even when the sudden event is anticipated and there is no immediate physical danger perceived. (*Metagu* is not used in such contexts). This aspect of the meaning of *rus* was brought home to me most forcefully when Gatachimang talked about a man on another atoll who, after falling victim to leprosy, had his toes and fingers amputated. On first hearing the news, he was *rus*, he said, as he did not expect that to happen. On another occasion, Ilefagomar and I were sitting in the house while her husband, Tamalekar, began to put a stick away for safekeeping up in the rafters. Although no one was in danger of being struck by it as he worked, Ilefagomar said that she was *rus* thinking "that the stick would fall." Sudden noises made by falling coconuts or people also create *rus*.

Culturally, the most significant form of the unexpected is found in other people's behavior. We have seen that the stranger, the drunk, and other people in general pose a threat primarily because they are sometimes expected to act violently. Not only violence, however, but any unpredictable behavior is cause for declarations of *rus*. The ideal personality trait of calmness (*maluwelu*) is defined in part by its predictability and by its antithesis to creating *rus* in others. The mother of one five-year-old boy who was making the transition from the craziness of early childhood reprimanded her son for a string of immature behaviors. She admonished him by saying "people are panicked from you because one day you are smart [*repiy*] and the next day you are crazy [*bush*] and saying bad things to them." That a five-year-old boy causes *rus* in others is not because he is potentially violent but rather because he is unpredictable.

The avoidance of sudden stimuli begins with the newborn. Infants are seen as particularly susceptible to *rus,* and adults describe several of their practices as protecting the child from the emotion. These include gentle handling and attempts to eliminate quick movements or loud noises around the child. The sleeping infant is laid on its side with a wadded cloth arranged against its chest in an effort to mitigate the shaking that would accompany *rus*. When the occasional plane is first heard approaching the island, women with young children will rush to their mats or cradles to hold them and prevent their *rus*.

There is thus no term, like the English "surprise," which is used exclusively to talk about the unexpected. The concept of surprise is used to talk about the evaluatively neutral perception of suddenness. The surprise may be good (as in the surprise party or being "pleasantly surprised"), or bad (as in the formulaic "I don't like surprises"). *Rus* is not viewed as pleasant, even in less problematic or serious cases. Suddenness in anything is viewed as unpleasant.

Variation in the Perception of Threat

We have already noted individual variation in the perception of threat in particular situations. In addition, some people are identified as *garusrus,* or always panicked. Their disposition was explained to me in a variety of ways. Some people said the "always panicked" are so because they are also calm (*maluwelu*) in character, and as a result are constantly alert to the possibility that others will be offended by what they do. Others explained that *garusrus* people come from households where men speak quietly and are not hot tempered when drunk. Conversely, people from houses where drunk men shout and move brusquely are not *garusrus* because they are accustomed to such shocking behavior. Several spoke of *garusrus* as being generated by "thinking too much about frightening things." Another person stated that a traumatic experience can make someone *garusrus;* a person who has seen a man's body broken after a fatal fall from a tree may become easily panicked, reacting strongly when he or she sees other injuries. Old people, babies, and confined women were also identified as more often *garusrus*. And finally, one woman described the easily panicked as people who are not smart (*repiy*). This is in some potential contradiction, it should be noted, with the notion that the valued, intelligent trait of calmness may also be associated with it.[13]

Gender differences are also believed to exist in the susceptibility to *rus* experiences. Women are identified (more or less emphatically by different individuals) as more likely to be panicked (*rus*) and hence *garusrus*. This is sometimes explained by the fact that it is men who fight. Some people claimed that men may have "stronger" or more intense panic, while others would agree with one woman's statement that "men are only *garusrus* if they are needy and not strong and so cannot hold [in self-defense] someone who might kill them." In any case, women, it is agreed, recover from panic more readily, while men are more likely to succumb to a "*rus* sickness" as a result. The many actual recent cases of *rus* sickness were overwhelmingly in men and boys. They include the case of one man who became ill after finding his son dead at the bottom of a coconut tree, and the boy whose *rus* sickness was diagnosed as caused by his "thinking too much" about a boil he had developed. Parents are more concerned with *rus* in their sons than in their daughters, and mothers are said to tell their sons that they should not be panicked in order to avoid sickness. While this evokes the conventional advice for the grieving, in this case it is not unexpressed but rather excessive emotion which causes illness. The symptoms of the *rus* sickness include nausea, vomiting, and diarrhea, as well as fever, headaches, and numbness inside, and a *rus* medicine (*taffeyalrus*) will be given to its victims.

Although there is general concern about the threat of *rus* to men, on a number of occasions people laughed about the actions of men who were panicked. What seemed to elicit the laughter (and, by inference, the sense of incongruity, inappropriateness, or quaintness) in several of these cases was the men's expression either of affection for their wives or of fear for their own lives. In a case of the former type, a man whose wife was staying on the island of Elato became a source of amusement during a threatened typhoon when he said that he was panicked and wanted to die together with his wife on the other atoll.

Finally, it is important to emphasize that people on Ifaluk do not see threat in every ambiguous situation, nor do they invariably see it even in stimuli often associated with danger, such as shouting. A dramatic example of the effects of individual perception on the emotional meaning of events is provided by the afternoon when a cyclone was sighted close outside the reef. A great shouting went up from those who saw it, but the older man I was with at the time relatively calmly directed me to shelter under the canoe house. His adult daughter, whose children were in another village, ran crying past us in their direction, explaining later that she was panicked. Other people also described their understanding of the shouting after the incident. A large group of women who were attending the feasting at a birth hut, and who for that reason may have had eating on their minds, said they had been *ker* (happy/excited), thinking that the shouting meant that a school of tuna had been sighted in the lagoon. One man with an especially avid interest in Western manufactured goods was also happy and excited thinking, as he said, that the inter-island ship (and presumably its cargo) had arrived. While one young boy declared himself panicked because he assumed that some men had started to fight, another, teenage boy, a visitor from a distant atoll, thought a canoe had sailed in over a taboo reef, perhaps reflecting his outsider's concern with inadvertent violations of custom and taboo. And the anthropologist, perhaps projecting the fears of loss that accompany distance from home, initially took the shouting as announcement of the death of someone on the island. This illustrates that not only individual disposition but also the person's immediate situation help to frame and lead the interpretation of events, particularly in the initial or ambiguous stages of the event's development.

The Things That Are Done with Fear

One of the most important ways in which emotional meaning and cultural meaning are intertwined is in constructing both a sense of danger and a scenario for how protection is achieved. Cultural conceptions of fear then mobilize or fail to mobilize a society against its own vision of threat and according to its own image of appropriate action. For the Ifaluk, the latter most often means flight, although the ethic of bravery is selectively used to warrant necessary confrontation with threat, as in sea travel and tree climbing for food. In focusing on typhoons, the critical gaze of neighbors, and the other factors just examined, the Ifaluk ignore other potential dangers. Currently downplayed are the dangers of such things as a changing diet, as sugar and baby bottles become available, and of dependence on American typhoon relief supplies, which can have the effect of eroding traditional interisland support networks (Marshall 1979).[14]

The rhetoric of fear is used to make statements about the speaker's morality no less than the language of *song* (justifiable anger) and *fago* (compassion/love/sadness). In claiming to perceive danger of various kinds in everyday life, people can be seen as striving to present themselves as good in the various ways that this is defined on the atoll. People make use of the cultural meanings surrounding *rus* and *metagu* to declare themselves harmless ("Violence frightens me"), conformist ("Others' justifiable anger frightens me"), or desirous of the company of others ("Being alone frightens me"). They also use those notions to explain their reluctance to go beyond the household or to confront others with uncomfortable requests. The sometimes odious tasks of visiting others to solicit something or of placing oneself in the presence of higher rank can actually be negotiated by use of this emotion idiom because the person who can most convincingly demonstrate fearfulness may be excused from certain kinds of social encounters or of work.

The language of fear also serves the indexical function of pointing to ambiguity without being called on to resolve it. The rich ambiguity of fear consists in the fact that it often refers to the unknown—to the area beyond death, the future fluctuations of wind and weather, the puzzling contradictions of rank and egalitarianism and what people make of encounters with others. Not all that is unclear is dangerous, in the Ifaluk view, but much of it is.

The rehearsal of the scenario of danger begins in parent-child interactions in which a special spirit, the *tarita* (Lutz 1983), is called to frighten children. It is particularly when a child has misbehaved that a woman of the household will slip away and return to the edge of the yard area disguised in cloths in impersonation of this bush-dwelling spirit. There she will motion the child toward her, all the while making eating gestures, thereby evoking the image of the *tarita* as an eater of children. At this, the child usually leaps in panic into the arms of the nearest adult who, after calling the *tarita* to "come get this child who has misbehaved," often ends up holding the child in amused approval of its reaction. In this and numerous other ways, parents create and recreate the scenario of danger, in parallel and contrast to emotional socialization in other cultures, such as the U.S.

underclass parents whose creation for their children of a scene of challenge and angry defense has been described by Miller (1986).

My reaction on seeing this scene for the first time says something about cultural differences in the handling of the sense of danger. I walked up to one household very early in my stay to find four small children shaking violently as they huddled against an older woman while the *tarita* threatened nearby. The shock and some disgust I experienced followed on my native inference that the deliberate use of fear has no place in socialization and that the motive for *tarita* impersonation could only be aggressive. In developing the sense of fear, however, Ifaluk parents act morally to create the desired citizen, for whom nonconformity and misbehavior ought to represent danger. Neighbors define the *tarita*-impersonating parent not as cruel but as conscientious and clever. It makes less sense to ask what hostility or other feelings they "really" have than to explore the ways the person and the community of people together construct, over and again, the meaning of the spirits, their socialization practices, and their fear. In marked contrast to the U.S. notion that fear is a necessary but amoral survival instinct at best and a character weakness at worst, the Ifaluk use the emotions of danger in the moral socialization of children, just as they more generally approve of the occurrence of the emotions in adults.[15] The morality of *rus* and *metagu* (although primarily the latter) consists in the fact that both emotions are considered to be at the root of good behavior. People conform to cultural ideals when they are attuned, through these emotions, to the dangers involved in flouting social conventions.

Finally, we have compared the ethnopsychological paradigm used here to describe Ifaluk fears with the psychoanalytic explanation for the prevalence of spirit fears used by Spiro in his important earlier ethnography of the island (Spiro 1952). That analysis of Ifaluk emotional life saw fear of spirits as intense in direct proportion to, and as a result of, the degree to which interpersonal aggression is forbidden. The disadvantage of such a model for attempting to understand Ifaluk lives is not only that it elevates some local, Western assumptions about the innateness of aggression and its hydraulic operation to the status of a universal statement. In addition, this model transforms what the Ifaluk experience as a moral system (particularly the link they see between justifiable anger and fear) into the terms of symptoms and pathology, and translates their moral reflection, choices, and actions exclusively into mechanical principles of affect transformation and discharge. This view of aggression might better be seen, as Shafer has suggested for the psychoanalytic view in general, "as both found and made" (1984:404). By introducing the terms of local self-understanding into the explanation of emotional meaning, the alternative ethnopsychological approach has the advantage of highlighting the ways in which people themselves have often tackled, philosophically and practically, the potential for danger in themselves and in their environment.

CHAPTER EIGHT
Conclusion: Emotional Theories

The preceding chapters have described some of the social scenarios in which emotion talk is embedded on Ifaluk. They have demonstrated the fundamental daily importance of the emotions for negotiating social relationships and for maintaining or questioning the island social order. I have also tried to convey a sense of how emotions and cultural values or morality are related. The evidence presented here can be used to suggest that emotion experience, both in the West and on Ifaluk, is more aptly viewed as the outcome of social relations and their corollary worldviews than as universal psychobiological entities. In conclusion, it will help to review and expand on what has been said about the cultural construction of emotion. In particular, we can detail three of the ways emotions are constructed, which include (1) the construction of emotion by local social and cultural systems, (2) the construction of emotion through the interaction of that local system with the perceptions of foreign observers who use other cultural frames for self and feeling, and (3) the construction of emotion by science.[1]

The First Construction: Local Theories of Emotion

Like all human groups, the Ifaluk have understandings of self and social relationship, emotion categories, and modes of emotional interaction that are, in some ways, historically and culturally unique.

The complex emotional experiences of everyday life, then, are not unmediated psychobiological events; the "first construction" entails their being built out of the raw materials of historically specific social experience, received language categories and speech traditions, and the potentials of the human body. Everyday life on Ifaluk demonstrates how shared ways of thinking and speaking about emotion help order lives and how emotional meaning is a social and cultural achievement. We have seen, first, that cultural views of emotion help construct people's interpretations of their experiences. For many Ifaluk, being alone is taken to be fearsome. For many, a brother's parting feels more painful than a father's. When his long-absent nephew came home to the island with an arrogant and boastful manner, Tamalekar interpreted his behavior, with the help of others, as causing certain emotions and not others, including *song* (justifiable anger). While the physiological aspects of emotional experience have not been considered in this work, it is important to stress again in conclusion that the biological basis of human experience, including that termed emotional, is not denied here. Rather, the point has been to critique essentialism in the understanding of emotion and to explore the relatively neglected ways in which social and cultural forces help to give emotions their observed character.

The idea that emotional experience is culturally constructed is not simply a claim that emotions are universal experiences that take on cultural particularity through variation in the situations that come to elicit them. DeRivera has noted that "it would be incorrect to say that a situation causes an emotion or that an emotion causes a perception of the situation. Rather the person's situation is always interpreted *by* some emotion" (1984:47; emphasis added). While women on Ifaluk typically lavish more affection on their brother's children than do American women, the contrast between the meanings and social articulations of *fago* and those of "love" and "compassion" are at least as crucial as the difference in the objects of emotional attachment. M. Rosaldo calls attention to this when she describes emotions as "embodied" interpretations and notes that "cross-cultural shames must differ easily as much as our notions of shame and guilt, at times . . . providing for the boundaries required to protect a status–occupying *self*, at others . . . shaping a social space wherein a group of would-be equal peers can manage to make claims on one another without evoking anger by violating an interlocutor's autonomy" (1983:149).[2]

Each emotion concept is, as we have seen, an index of a world of cultural premises and of scenarios for social interaction; each is a system of meaning or cluster of ideas which include both verbal, accessible, reflective ideas and implicit practical ones.[3] The discrete emotion concepts, like all concepts (Hutchins 1980), have nested within them a cluster of images or propositions. We recognize the existence of an emotion by the occurrence of a certain limited number of the events that those images or propositions depict. More precisely, emotion-language use involves the perception of the *legitimacy* of the application of a particular emotion concept to what is perceived (however opportunistically) as the occurrence of the culturally defined criteria for an emotion attribution. In each cultural community, there will be one or more "scenes" identified as prototypic or classic or best examples of particular emotions. Thus, on Ifaluk the prototypic scene evoked by the concept of *metagu* (fear/anxiety) might be the encounter with a spirit, a flight from the encounter, and the recounting of that episode to sympathetic others. The prototype of *song* (justifiable anger) would involve a clear transgression by one person, the stern-faced but quiet identification of that violation by another, and the reaction of fear/anxiety (*metagu*) in the transgressor. The prototypic case of "anger" might be one in which a person who is offended or frustrated yells at another, with indefinite specification of the response of others to that anger.

The scenes each emotion concept evokes are most typically *social* scenes involving relations between two or more individuals. The emotions can be seen as sociocultural achievements in the fundamental sense that they characterize and create a relationship between individuals and groups.[4] DeRivera sets out this perspective on emotion, defining it as one in which "the fundamental unit of analysis is not an organism in an environment or a being-in-the-world, but a person-other relationship. . . . Emotions are concerned with adjusting the relationship between person and other, and . . . each emotion ideally functions to maximize the *values* of the relationship" (1984:118). Thus, *song* (justifiable anger) is about a relationship in a state of disrepair and within which an injustice has been identified. A relationship that is asymmetrical in terms of power and fortune and in which caretaking and care-accepting behaviors are likely is one characterized by *fago* (compassion/love/sadness). "Guilt" is used to talk about relationships in which responsibility for wrong-doing is unequally divided, with focus being placed on the shared sense by both parties that one of them is primarily responsible.

Emotion is surely also experienced in response to overtly nonsocial events. On Ifaluk, one can speak of *fago* (compassion/love/sadness) for a small pig, or of *rus* (panic/fright) in the face of an approaching typhoon. In most of these cases, however, it can be argued that the social world plays a significant part. *Fago* for a piglet may be modeled on previous and more significant human social relations, for example, and the experience of *rus* before typhoon threats is, as we saw, publicly dramatized and socially reinforced. When the Ifaluk speak of *miseig* (enjoying) a cool breeze or of *niyabut* (disgust) over having to walk along a muddy path, these responses are nonetheless still not aptly portrayed as reflections on a feeling so much as statements about a perceived relation between self and world. Emotions are social not only by virtue of being generated by living in a world with multiple others whose desires, for example, conflict with one's own. Their existence and meaning are also negotiated, ignored, or validated by people in social relationships. A woman becomes angry with her husband or neighbor because she is involved or has a relationship with that person; in addition she becomes angry through negotiation with that other person over the meaning of preceding events and of that relationship. Numerous cases have been presented of the ways social relations are culturally interpreted and of how the emotions that are structured by and within those relationships reflect that fact. A woman can become *song* (justifiably angry) with her husband on Ifaluk for failing to take their toddler with him to his tasks at the canoe house. The cultural definition of gender roles and obligations provides the frame with which to interpret and evaluate the social "facts."

The tendency to look at emotions in isolation from the social field has led to an emphasis on emotions as singular events situated within the individual rather than on emotional exchanges between individuals.[5] Anger, for example, is examined as a response to a particular set of circumstances, but the equally important emotional response of others to that anger (and that emotion's subsequent transformation) is generally ignored (but see Schieffelin 1976). The importance of these culturally constructed exchanges was exemplified in the Ifaluk elaboration of a reaction of *metagu* (fear/anxiety) to the *song* (justifiable anger) of others, or the reaction of *song* or *bosu* (excitement/jealousy) to others' *ker* (happiness/excitement). Ifaluk cultural logic elucidates how each emotion presupposes the other in the above pairs. These exchanges, which are more or less culturally stereotyped, are socially achieved scenarios, and they are culturally interpreted and learned. This view of emotions more adequately reflects the emotional flow of everyday social interaction, underlining as it does that the emotions can serve as the medium of all exchange or conflict.

The cultural definition of emotions also constructs people's sense of how they ought to or must behave and in that way help to structure people's social behavior. The force of emotion (Rosaldo 1984) is to a great extent the sense of moral or pragmatic compulsion, the sense that one must do what the emotion "says" one will do. We saw that each of the three emotions of *song, fago,* and *metagu* has fundamentally to do with moral obligations and moral ideals. The good person displays emotion in the proper time and place—*song* when taboos are violated, *fago* when poverty or illness strikes another, *metagu* when in the midst of a group of elders. Conversely, particular moral ideas take what force they have from the commitment people learn to feel to them. The notion that violence is bad would be an empty norm were it not that people on Ifaluk in fact feel intense horror or panic when the prospect of aggression arises. Although emotions bear important relation to what Hochschild has termed "emotion rules" (1979) or cultural norms, they are first, in a sense, about values and commitments felt.

The tandem development of emotional and moral maturity on Ifaluk was evident in several of the common scenarios recounted. When young children are encouraged to fear the unfamiliar villager approaching their home compounds, it is a preliminary to the later moral lesson that only bad and immodest people "walk around" and are not afraid of others. When a two-year-old is told to *fago* his brother and split a banana in two to share, morality and emotions show themselves as forming a single unit. While there are often occasions when disjunction occurs between individual desire and social morality, the interpretation of the experience of being "at odds" is also culturally constructed (Abu-Lughod 1986).[6] For example, a common refrain in Ifaluk love songs has a woman speak to her lover of her lack of concern with the gossip that swirls around their affair. "My insides," she sings, "fart at them all." Contempt for those who gossip is a cultural theme that is called on to express the personal value of a romantic relationship in the face of social condemnation.

Finally, we have seen that social structure, social relations, and the material conditions of life on this coral atoll both order and are ordered by local theories of emotion. These conditions create the concrete situations that people encounter and need to interpret, often with the aid of emotion concepts. The material conditions include such things as the islanders' limited land, vulnerability to catastrophic typhoons, relatively high infant-mortality rate, and the density of population. Some of the features of island social structure whose relationship with emotional understandings has been outlined include the centrality of the brother–sister relationship, gender relations more generally, the distinction between chief and commoner and the hierarchy of rank, cooperative labor institutions, and historical changes in the basis of authority and generational relations when young men increasingly take on wage labor and new status as, for example, school teachers and health aides. Resource egalitarianism and cooperativeness, embedded in a hierarchical social structure, create the context for emotional interpretation. That interpretation includes recognizing the necessity of avoiding confrontation with more powerful others, whose legitimacy can go unquestioned when all are fed. The emotional perspective of the less "needy"—be they the chiefs, the female elders of a high-ranking lineage, the father of a child, or the healthy in the presence of the ill—is one that, in its focus on compassion and justifiable anger, acknowledges the practices of sharing and of dominance or responsibility over others that most highly ranked people engage in daily.

The configuration of and emphasis on the emotion of *fago* was described as in part a cultural response to the problem of the atoll's ecological fragility and land limits. The concept of *fago* also gains its cultural significance and moral force from its legitimation of the social organizational principle of hierarchy. The socioeconomic links that bind the people of Ifaluk to each other are strong and clearly observable. In this context, the absence of alienation as structural fact or experience has its corollary in the emphasis on an emotion which codes the connection to, and responsibility for, the other's well-being. *Song* (justifiable anger) was shown to mark and support (or occasionally subvert) the prevailing distribution of power. In addition, the conflicts that *song* articulates are recognized by the Ifaluk within the constraints of a clearly organized hierarchy of power. Conflict also occurs in the context of a high degree of consensus on the desirability of resolving conflict and on what constitutes a "good" resolution of the conflict. Finally, the physical dangers of living on a half-square-mile of low-lying land in a typhoon belt were seen reflected in the meaning of *metagu* and *rus,* as were the social dangers of confronting, alienating or being judged by others when relatively few escapes from or options to living one's entire life with the same small group of others exist.

The task for future comparative work on the relation between emotions and culture is to specify further how these aspects of social life are given emotional meaning or, in other words, to examine how the political, economic, social, and ecological conditions of life for particular people provide the impetus and framing for the emotional consciousness that develops among them, as Abu-Lughod (1986), Lindholm (1982), Myers (1979), and M. Rosaldo (1983, 1984) have begun to do. The variety of ethnopsychological systems that have developed are evidence both of the broad interpretive freedom that humans have to construct emotional meaning and of the constraints those conditions place on it.

The Second Construction: Foreign Observers and Their Emotional Theories

Cross-cultural encounters involve at least some degree of erroneous or distorting reconstruction of the feelings, motives, and meanings of the behavior of others. I came to Ifaluk with a variant of the everyday and implicit emotional theories of my culture, class, and gender, wanting to know, for example, how islanders "really felt," and assuming that their emotional lives were essentially private matters, that fear and anger were things to be "conquered" and love to be publicly avowed, and that emotions were valuable things to have. My portrait of Ifaluk lives, like all foreign renditions of other's emotions, is constructed in part in the image of those Western cultural assumptions and what they led me to expect or want to see. Although anthropologists have often found or construed the field experience as a route to some awareness of or even liberation from received Western cultural categories and beliefs, it is difficult, perhaps impossible, to imagine a way of talking outside those received categories and still making sense to oneself or to others.

When the people of my household laughed at my fear over a night visitor (chap. 7), what jarred me was their "failure" to observe danger where I had seen it. And when I had earlier determined to sleep in a separate hut in the household compound, my "failure" to interpret solitude as fearsome set me apart from them as different (although how fundamentally I do not know). What is at issue in the many differences between us in emotional interpretations is not simply variation in our personal or interior lives. Implicated are differences in the actors who populate our worlds (rapists, in the above instance, for me, and spirits, for them), the sense of how intimately selves relate to the others around them, and many other social facts.

Foreigners do not use their own emotional paradigms to understand others in a direct and simple application of the theory to cases seen in bird's-eye fashion. They are in fact most likely living in some kind of relationship to those others, whether as seller to

215

buyer, as boss to laborer, as tourist to local sight, or, in the present case, as anthropologist to informant or guest to host. If emotions are defined as phenomena that are fundamentally *about* social relationships, then the relationship that the foreigner establishes with others (1) necessarily has an emotional quality and (2) limits the understanding of others' emotions because the relationships are more limited than those which locals can have with each other.

The tension between alienation and belonging that has been identified by many observers as a central theme in American culture takes on special contours and vigor under the conditions of anthropological fieldwork. In the field, the tension arises from the experience of being an outsider and the drive for acceptance as a "real" person into a local nexus of people and feelings. Bourdieu has noted that ethnographers necessarily remain outsiders, "excluded from the real play of social activities by the fact that [we have] no place . . . in the system observed" (1977:1). The estrangement of the field-worker is then "elevated," according to Bourdieu, and portrayed not as an imposed exclusion but as the ethnographer's freely made choice to follow the canons of scientific method that call for detachment in the name of objectivity. Scientific method, in other words, idealizes the practical alienation of the anthropologist.

The somewhat bizarre position of fieldwork may have a fundamental influence, then, on both the second and the third (or social scientific) construction of emotion. The ethnographer's or other foreigner's position may tend to pull us toward one of the two extremes of viewing emotions as either fundamentally universal or culturally particular and exotic. In the former, the other's emotions are indistinguishable from my own because I have not had to shift emotional perspectives, the bird's-eye view of objectivism often being indistinguishable from a nonindigenous cultural view; in the latter, they are ultimately strange because my relations with local people are estranged ones, thereby preventing me from imagining the other's emotional position. These two positions are rejected by R. Rosaldo when he notes that "the modest truism that any human groups must have certain things in common can appear to fly in the face of a once-healthy methodological caution that warns against the reckless attribution of one's own categories and experiences to members of another culture. Such warnings against facile notions of universal human nature can be carried too far and harden into the equally pernicious doctrine that, my own group aside, everything human is alien to me" (1984:188).

Rosaldo has taken Bourdieu's reflections on the position of the ethnographer and noted that "most anthropologists write about [the emotions of] death as if they were positioned as uninvolved spectators who have no lived experience that could provide knowledge about the cultural force of emotions" (Rosaldo 1984:193). A more adequate view of the emotional lives of people in other societies, in his view, is one built out of a wider range of personal experiences with emotional import (and introspection on them).[7] While we can, as Rosaldo suggests, draw on our own emotional experiences to understand others', emotion is about deep commitments to particular other persons and to seeing events in certain ways. The external viewpoint, which our status as outsiders and the objectivist epistemology of science promote, places us in a position in the local social system that works against the development of a shared emotional perspective on events, that is, against the development of deep commitment to, for example, a mother. And while Ilongot and Ifaluk and American mothers share certain fundamental characteristics, they are also distinctive in their social positions, in their behavior, and in their thinking about the issues of nurturance or production or power. Understanding the other's emotional position requires a recognition of the generic relationships that, in an important way, constitute the emotion (such as a father's losing a son). It also requires whatever understanding can be achieved of the particular, situated, historical positions of persons.

Like most outsiders, I modeled my developing relationships with people on the island on earlier home relations. With my adoptive father, Tamalekar, I took aspects of the emotional position I already had experienced with my biological father and understood how other people on Ifaluk felt about their fathers in those terms. This kind of modeling permits us to "create" a shared emotional understanding with the other. Nonetheless, like most ethnographers, I did not share with my Ifaluk hosts a commitment to permanent membership, a common fate, and a shared nonrelativistic and permanent moral interpretation of events. The ethnographer's position in the field would often seem to prevent the full development of the central condition necessary for emotional understanding, which is a shared social position and, hence, a shared moral and emotional point of view.

The second construction is often mediated by language. Although cross-cultural accounts have been presented traditionally as natural rather than cultural events (i.e., as scientific discoveries rather than historical products), they have made use of concepts taken wholesale from the lay emotion language of the West. Thus, when the

Japanese are described as a "shame" culture, this draws on an elaborate Western cultural meaning system surrounding notions of the person, of "emotion" generally, and of "shame" more particularly. In subtle ways, therefore, the non-West has been constructed in the emotional image of the West—as emotionally almost indistinguishable from the West (e.g., Ekman, Friesen, and Ellsworth 1972), as emotionally opposite to the West (e.g., Benedict 1967), or as emotionally deficient in terms of Western notions of emotional normality (e.g., Goldschmidt 1975; Leff 1981). Let us look briefly at each of these types of emotional construction in turn.

Ekman's studies, which focus on the facial expression of emotion, claim to have identified pancultural elements in the presumably universal emotions of happiness, sadness, anger, fear, surprise, and disgust. If one uses these categories as the basis for investigation, however, and ignores the problem of translating between these emotion categories and those of the other cultures studied, the latter are necessarily constructed in a Western image because the cultural assumptions about personhood and about the range of emotion-related situations are implicitly imported into the analysis with those Western categories. Our attention is drawn to the ways the anger or the sadness of the Fore of New Guinea is "the same as" that of Westerners.

Benedict, whose research predates Ekman's, wrote in the context of the highly motivated attempt of the American public to understand the Japanese during and after World War II. Her description of the emotional lives of the Japanese is sympathetic and relativistic; Japanese behavior is made explicable by Benedict's exploration of the worldview that gives certain feelings their local cultural sense. Nonetheless, Benedict's rendering of the Japanese is organized around the questions of how and why the Japanese are emotionally "not like us," as when she says, "The arc of life in Japan is plotted in opposite fashion to that in the United States. It is a great shallow U-curve with maximum freedom and indulgence allowed to babies and to the old . . . In the United States we stand this curve upside down" (1967:253–54).

The importation into the field of Western ethnotheories about emotional functioning has resulted, in studies such as Goldschmidt's and Leff's, in explicit judgments being made about the emotional ill health or abnormality of the people of other cultures. Goldschmidt, for example, describes the Sebei as having a "low affect level," and consequently as having a "lack of empathy towards those who are suffering," a "lack of involvement . . . with one another in all relationships," "inconsistent values," and "little commitment to tradition"; mothers are "emotionally blank" and "absent" in relations with their children (1975:157–58, 162). All these things are bad, it goes without saying, from the perspective of the Western ideas of the emotional norms from which they deviate. Leff, a cross-cultural psychiatrist, makes a similar judgment using implicit Western standards in commenting that "In traditional societies, where relationships are more or less stereotyped, emotions remain unexplored and undifferentiated" (1981:72).

In sum, by unself-consciously using the category of emotion and the categories of discrete emotions that have been constructed in the West, elaborate implicit theories about the nature of the self and of emotion have been drawn into the analysis simultaneously, there to reconstruct the emotional lives of members of other cultures.

The Third Construction: Culture and Ideology in Academic Emotion Theory

The second and third constructions of emotional experience seen in anthropological writing on the emotions of other, non-Western peoples are closely related. In going to Ifaluk, I went with the emotional theories both of a young woman from the American middle class and of a (fledgling) Western social scientist. Those two sets of assumptions are very similar, as I have tried to show and as others have demonstrated for diverse domains (Buss 1979; Gergen 1973; LeVine 1980; Said 1979; Sampson 1981). All emotional theories (including those of the Ifaluk, the one advanced here, and those claiming objective status or objectivist goals) reflect some prevailing cultural assumptions about self, society, and epistemology. In addition, all theories (of emotion or other phenomena) are emotional in the sense that their construction is driven by interests, values, and commitments. Chapter 2 discusses some of those I have been able to discern in my own work; many more remain to be analyzed (see note 9). For example, the deconstructive turn of this manuscript can be taken as bearing some relation to the cultural changes that Jameson (1984) has identified as accompanying the shift from classical to late capitalism. The cultural movements he identifies as postmodern include "the waning of affect" which follows from the rejection of various types of depth models of human experience. These models rely on the distinctions between appearance and essence, between signifying language and signified thing, and between latent and manifest meanings (e.g., as required by the concept of repression). Postmodernism critiques the presupposition of "a whole metaphysics of the inside and the outside, of the wordless pain within the monad and the moment in which, often cathartically, that 'emotion' is then projected out and externalized, as gesture or cry, as desperate communication and the outward dramatization of inward feeling" (1984:61). In so doing, a constructionist treatment of emotions, in its most extreme or developed form, can give emotions a feel of "flatness" which is, as Jameson suggests, both a "symptom" and a sign of the sociocultural milieu from which it emerges. Its value relative to the other models critiqued here implicitly and explicitly, however, remains.

Social-science theories of emotion differ from lay emotional theories in as many ways as they resemble them, the most important being their goals. One of the goals of normal social science is structured by what Habermas (1971) has identified as the "technical interest" (cf. Geuss 1981). The technical interest is a prominent force in the construction of what passes as knowledge (specifically, equating it with precision) and is concerned primarily with the prediction and control of the environment and behavior. As the prestige and practical achievements of the scientific study of nature grew, those who would study social life strove to prove themselves capable of capturing the essence of social and personal life. The increasingly technical definition of rationality led to a similar technical emphasis in social-science views and treatments of the person and of emotion (Hochschild 1975; Sampson 1981). Emotion came to be virtually synonymous with that which could be physically measured such as facial muscle movements or galvanic skin response. Emotions also tend to be portrayed as discrete or separate entities as a result of the need to measure.[8] They also came to be implicitly evaluated by social scientists in terms of their approximation to (or rather failure to approximate) the technically defined ideal of the person as cognitive problem solver. This has made social-scientific thinking about emotions even more concerned than is everyday thought with portraying emotions either as an inferior form of mental process because vague, imprecise, and unpredictable (e.g., Lévi-Strauss 1963) or as amenable to the same kinds of control as cognition (e.g., Beck 1971). A special paradox is presented by this technical reconstruction of the concept of emotion, which was, as we saw, hitherto closely identified with all that opposes both the mechanistic and the rational.

Twentieth-century anthropologists have generally striven to eliminate or replace their own cultural assumptions through confrontation with other cultures (Comaroff 1978; Leacock and Nash 1977; Taussig 1980). Despite this trend, there has been little explicit recognition of the cultural basis of theorizing about emotions (but see M. Rosaldo 1984). That an explicitly cultural perspective on emotions has not been taken until very recently is owing in part to the "naturalness" with which emotion is imbued in Western thought. In his analysis of devil beliefs in South America, Taussig notes, as did Marx before him, that the character of social relations under capitalism intensifies the widespread tendency of people to experience, as "elemental and immutable things," phenomena which are in fact social products. "This blindness to the social basis of essential categories makes a social reading of supposedly natural things deeply perplexing" (Taussig 1980:4), and so presents particular problems for a cultural reading of the categories of emotion. For, in this society, emotion is seen not only as more natural than cultural but also as irreducibly natural in its essence.

The acultural treatment of emotion theories is also correlated with the rise within anthropology of the universalist perspective (Shweder and Bourne 1982), which emphasizes the commonalities in human experience. This approach only succeeds, however, in pushing the cultural perspective of the anthropologist "underground, into the subconscious," with the result that anthropologists then simply "project their intuitive understanding, based on Judeo-Christian precepts, onto a presumed universal structural framework of human thought" (Leacock and Nash 1977:642).

The theories of emotion currently dominant in social science tend to reflect (and hence tacitly reproduce and sanction) a particular ideology of self, gender, and social relations. They reinforce the idea that "higher" forms of rationality are technical, nonemotional, and nonmoral. This is seen not only in those theories that maintain the radical split between the essence of cognition and that of emotion but also in those theories that strive to "elevate" emotion by linking it to its superior mental cousin—two strategies related, as just noted, to the "technical interest" of social science.

In addition, the widespread assumption within social science that the studies of Ekman and his colleagues (Ekman 1977; Ekman, Friesen, and Ellsworth 1972) have proved the universality of emotions bears some examination. The claim to universality for any human psychological, social, or cultural phenomenon can imply its legitimation, its immutability, or its origin in law-bound material processes. It may also imply the existence of a single human community that, having some universal form or goal, *ought* to be subject to a set of general or universal moral imperatives. If emotions, patriarchy, aggressive impulses, or the family are universal, a powerful charter is provided for the continued existence of those phenomena as they currently exist or as they are defined by social science. While this is not always the case, such implicit and "nonscientific" agendas often structure the scientific search for universals in human life (Fausto-Sterling 1986; Geertz 1984; Lewontin, Rose, and Kamin 1984).[9]

This is not to say that social science plays a major ideological role in this regard when compared with other social institutions, such as television news; it is not to say that there is a one-way structuring influence from social science to everyday thought (chap. 3 demonstrates the dialectical relationship between academic and everyday thought about emotion); and it is not a claim that the present work is exempt from the cultural influences identified. It *is* to suggest that social-scientific thought about emotion is fundamentally based in a Western cultural discourse that articulates with and sometimes partially opposes relations of power and, hence, is ideological.[10] It is to suggest that, as expert or authoritative discourse, academic thought about emotion has real and perceptible influences on the way its proponents, their students, and the culture as a whole thinks about the issues of self and social life that are studied (e.g., Linde 1987).

Current Western theories of human nature and emotion, both academic and lay, articulate with alienation in its various forms. A number of observers (e.g., Heller 1979; Ollman 1976) have linked the alienation of people from the products of their labor under modern industrial capitalism to the separation of the person into a public, rational, market self and a private, expressive, intimate self. The former "thinks," while the latter "feels." This is the alienation of the self from itself, of thought and perception from passion, and to a large extent of both thinking and feeling from valuing and from acting on those values. Ollman has identified the general process as one in which "What occurs in the real world [the alienation of humans from their work activities, products, and contemporaries] is reflected in people's minds: essential elements of what it means to be a man [*sic*] are grasped as independent and, in some cases, all powerful entities, whose links with him appear other than what they really are. . . . Alienation is the splintering of human nature into a number of misbegotten parts" (1976:135). The Western perspective on emotion exemplifies this process. Scheper-Hughes and Lock (1987) suggest another aspect when they identify "body alienation" as the lost sense of the body (and, we can add, of emotions) as integrally connected to other aspects of the self—mental and social—common in advanced industrial society. One source, they hypothesize, is "the symbolic equation of humans and machines, originating in our industrial modes and relations of production and in the commodity fetishism of modern life" (1987:17; see also Osherson and AmaraSingham 1981). The distinction between bodily emotions and rational thoughts also finds symbolic parallel in the division and hierarchization of mental and manual labor (1987:17).

Alienation takes a second form in the estrangement of the person from other persons. We can observe this process in several domains. In the first instance, the split of thought from emotion, as we have seen, has been transferred onto the domain of gender, with the result that women and men as classes are alienated from each other. What might be seen as unified and inseparable human capacities are divided and sorted by gender. Second, the alienation of the individual from the social world, which is codified in the ideology of individualism, is mirrored in the way emotion is conceptualized, that is, in the way it is interiorized. Emotion is located within the person; although external events are said to "trigger" affect, these events are rarely examined in any detail. The emotions are the "private property" of the individual. They are often either vilified as a primal residue within the person or glorified as signs of individual personality or uniqueness. The study of emotion is most firmly associated with the social-science discipline (psychology) that is the ideological "center" for the study of the individual (Sampson 1981). Any attempt to change emotional experience is necessarily focused, then, on the individual as a relatively autonomous unit (although the rise of family therapy presents a limited exception to this generalization, as it involves the inclusion of a minimal social unit as the emotional system to be treated). Depressive sadness, anger, and guilt are each examples of emotions whose "treatment" is focused on changing individual views of the world or, sometimes, individual biology through drug therapies. Other cultural systems that cannot be characterized as having an ideology of individualism, such as that of the Ifaluk, also obviously talk about the emotions as located to some degree "inside" the person. It is clear that emotion words are everywhere used to talk about the relationship between the self and the world. What is culturally variable, however, is the extent to which the focus in emotion concepts is on the self or on the world which creates emotion, and on how autonomously that self is defined. The portrait of the anomic emotion, arising within the individual (however much an environmental event is portrayed as a root cause) and ending there, may or may not characterize emotional life in twentieth-century America. It serves poorly, however, as a model for socioemotional relations in all cultures.

These forms of alienation are accompanied by a new episte-mology in which the apparent is no longer the really real (Errington 1984). The apparent is construed as public and social, while the real and the seat of "personal identity move[s] inward to the subjective self. . . . In the modern industrial West, it is the private realm of home, family, and love where individuals are most likely to seek, express, and experience their real selves . . . to understand what another person really is requires a penetration of the public presen-tation of the self to probe at a largely hidden subjectivity" (Errington 1984:185–86). The prominent concern in social science with locating emotion beyond the social self—distinguishing between what people really feel and what they express publicly—reflects both the ideolog-ical and the objective conditions of life in the contemporary West. The contradiction prompted by the split between the public and the private is nowhere more evident than in the simultaneous underval-uation of emotion (as antithetical to market values) and its overval-uation (as the source of personal identity and the really real).

As noted in chapter 3, the current conceptualization of emotion and thought places morality in a difficult position. When emotion is seen as both involuntarily motivational and irrational, and when cog-nition is seen as the source of rationality but not of action, value and the strong will to act are separated from cool calculation and max-imization. The connection between this split and the ideological cor-relates of alienation is also clear. Thought provides access to facts; emotion, to subjective desire, and value is left to link itself with whichever of the two is most expedient at any given moment. The distinction between facts and values sunders the world in a way di-rectly analogous to the way in which the emotion/thought distinction does. Ollman describes the former distinction as "founded on the belief that it is possible to conceive of one without the other. Given a particular fact, the argument runs, one may without contradiction attach any value to it" (1976:45). This perspective, however, consti-tutes a "self-deception". "Rather than being logically independent of what is, any choice—as well as the idea that one has a choice—is linked by innumerable threads to the real world, including the life, class interests, and character of the person acting. Judgements can never be severed, neither practically nor logically, from their contexts and the number of real alternatives which they allow. In this per-spective, what is called the fact-value distinction appears as a form of self-deception, an attempt to deny what has already been done by claiming that it could not have been done or still remains to do" (1976:45–46). Similarly, the notion that emotion involves not choice but impulse and not facts but desires and the notion that value inheres in neither emotional response nor cognitive understanding work together as an ideological system to disguise the value judgment involved in any act of thinking *and* feeling.[11]

Rather than modeling people as either thinking *or* feeling, we might view people as almost always "emotional" in the sense of being committed to "processing information" or understanding the world in certain culturally and personally constructed ways. It becomes possible to model people's participation in cultural forms not simply as coolly enacted habit or as attempts to understand "the truth of the matter," in however cultural a set of terms, but rather as motivated creation (M. Rosaldo 1984). No amount of conceptual reworking will prevent the imposition of assorted contemporary Western ideas about the nature of the person, of rationality, and of morality onto the experience of others. Reflection on what exactly those ideas are, however, can help to mitigate the effect of their use by removing them from exclusive residence in the realm of the natural—and thereby from the requirement that they be used as a standard of human normality—into that of the cultural and historical. The emotional discourse of people like the Ifaluk then more clearly illuminates some of the alternative ways people can become passionately involved in the world.

Epilogue

Ending an ethnography is, like ending fieldwork, sometimes a struggle between the wish to remain and the desire to flee. When I left Ifaluk on a preternaturally bright afternoon in 1978, I knew it would be some time before I returned. I sat on the shore with my family, waiting for the launch to take me to the ship at anchor outside the reef. Tobacco and thread were unloaded, children were carried through the shallow water to waiting arms, then the leaving of a man to paid work on Yap, a family for their kin on Woleai, then my turn. As I "kissed" my mother's hand, leaving tears on it, she shifted slightly (at least it seemed to me then) to keep me from embracing her small boy Yangitelig whom I had quickly grown to love over the previous year. Was she protecting me from the pain of too much parting as I had seen others do for their relatives bent on voyages? Was she pushing me away from a fuller relationship, as I had feared on some other gloomy days? What were we to each other, then—not quite mother and daughter, not simple host and guest, not quite universal sisters or easy friends? Our relationship's novelty was its emotional ambiguity—love frustrated and *fago* partially achieved. The launch that took me to the ship also hauled behind it a huge driftwood log being sent to another atoll, an image it seems to me now of the bounty and burden of what I have taken from Ifaluk. This ethnography is, like most writing projects, abandoned rather than completed because that relational and emotional ambiguity can be endlessly reformulated. It is abandoned in the sense defined by Smith (1983:24) when she says that readers receive a work that is "not so much the achieved consummation of that process" of composition (and also, in this case, of fieldwork) as "a temporary truce among contending forces."

Notes

Chapter Two

1. This kind of approach glosses over the kinds of idiosyncracies involved in my own specific familial and other experiences and thereby in this ethnography. It appears necessary to do this, however, because of both constraints of time and space in this monograph and my sense that these cultural and historical factors supersede the individual in explanatory import.

2. These attitudes are certainly problematic. If all cross-cultural encounters were to be framed as a search for the enactment of particular kinds of values, it might be that neither genuine tolerance nor cross-cultural criticism could result. It is important, however, to distinguish an approach which recognizes explicit motivations behind its "looking" from both ethnocentrism (which judges ignorantly and without reflection or doubt) and an unquestioned universalism (which assumes, rather than explores the possibility of, shared values). It is also clearly possible to defend this approach from the charges of nihilism to which a thoroughgoing cultural relativism is prone (Rabinow 1983).

3. The ethnographic record is, of course, not "photographic" but is the product of the cultural framework of the previous ethnographers of a society.

4. See Alkire (1965, 1978) for a description of the ecology of coral atolls, and Tracey, Abbott, and Arnow (1961) on Ifaluk's particular atoll environment.

5. The force as well as the salt content of the water kills the plants. A typhoon's inundation of the taro gardens can have other effects, as Marshall notes: "Wave damage can also eradicate the intricate boundaries marking individually owned taro plots, an action equivalent to loss of land registration files in the United States" (1976:35). Also see Marshall (1979) for a description and analysis of the often deleterious effects of the typhoon relief sent to affected islands by the American administration since the war.

6. Burrows and Spiro's (1953) middle-aged informants in 1947 remembered six typhoons, only one of which involved rising water and the deaths of some persons.

7. These visits were also motivated by the situations which ostensibly instigated them, such as the illness of a relative on Elato.

8. Carolinean navigators apparently did not set out intentionally from their home islands for the Philippines. The western landings were made by canoes which had lost their bearings on the way to other destinations. Rubinstein notes that these were likely *not* drift voyages, however, but rather were based on the decision to cease searching for the atoll destination and to steer for the Philippines (Rubinstein 1979:327–28). Several men on the island of Fais told Rubinstein that some Carolinean navigators currently know sailing directions to and from the Philippines.

9. The Spanish used both guns and forced relocation in their attempts to control (and to baptize) the Chamorro people. These measures, along with disease, resulted in genocide; the Chamorro population, which had been between 70,000 and 100,000 strong by the estimate of the Spanish missionaries on their arrival in 1668, was reduced to 3,672 by 1710 (Joseph and Murray 1951:10–11).

10. Marshall and Marshall think it likely, on the basis of the historical documents that they examined, that the Chamorros of the Marianas learned the fermentation technique from the Filipinos or the Spanish, or both (1975:443).

11. Although the Interior Department officially took over the administration of the Trust Territory in 1951, the U.S. Navy continued to control Guam and the rest of the Marianas through the 1950s. Guam was closed to outsiders until 1962; given its role as transportation gateway to the rest of the Trust Territory, this Navy policy effectively continued the explicit exclusionary policy of the more immediate postwar period (Gale 1979:86).

12. See McHenry (1975) for details on U.S. intentions and its explicit policy in Micronesia.

13. Ifaluk had, in 1978, a dental aide and two nurses, each of whom was frequently assigned to work on other islands, including Yap. The island also had six teachers and a young man trained in air-conditioning repair, a specialty he would have had to travel at least 500 miles to practice. This exemplifies the results of the U.S. emphasis on training Micronesians for service jobs and government employment, rather than production.

14. These figures are those generated by the U.S. Department of State, as cited in Peoples (1985), and exclude the Northern Marianas. On the effect of U.S. colonial policy on Micronesia, see Peoples (1985), Petersen (1979), Lutz (1984), and Roff and Clark (1984).

15. See Alkire (1965) for a discussion of this office.

16. People bathe in the lagoon when they need to defecate during the day. The association between bobbing in the lagoon and bodily functions accentuated brother-sister avoidance in this case, as sexual or scatalogical reference is strictly enjoined in the presence of cross-sex siblings.

17. On Elato, this respect behavior was followed much more stringently than on Ifaluk, with deeper bends being made from greater distances by women passing their brothers.

18. There is not, of course, unanimity in these matters. I once asked a sailor on the interisland ship what people there think of visiting Americans. He replied with a story about a Belauan man who saw a female Peace Corps volunteer wearing a lavalava (the local women's skirt). The Belauan said to the sailor, "The Americans should come here to teach us, not to imitate us." Some Micronesians, including perhaps some outer islanders, would prefer (at least some kinds of) visitors to differentiate themselves from locals.

19. This has been particularly true in American psychology, which has been the traditional site in the social sciences for the investigation of emotion. That discipline, even more than anthropology, has historically striven to define itself as a "hard" science with "hard" data, such as physical measures provide.

20. Briggs's (1970) study of emotions among the Utku of northern Canada, mentioned earlier, was a crucial source of methodological inspiration for the current one. Both her concern with the Utku concepts of emotion and their phenomenology and her honesty about the interpersonal and interpretive missteps she made were pioneering, although her ethnography remains today a somewhat isolated example of that approach (the exceptions include Dwyer 1982, Dumont 1978, Rabinow 1977, and several of the essays in Golde 1970).

21. Others who have looked at emotion vocabularies include Davitz (1969), Wallace and Carson (1973), and Averill (1975), for American English; Gerber (1975), for Samoan; Myers (1979), for Pintupi; Rosaldo (1980, 1983), for Ilongot; Howell (1981) for Chewong; and Riesman (1977), for the Fulani language.

22. Each of the terms was defined for me by between three and ten persons. Despite the problems associated with the use of quasiexperimental tests, some insights into aspects of Ifaluk emotional understandings were also gained through the use of a card-sorting task utilizing emotion terms (Lutz 1982) and through a ranking task in which children were asked to rank by intensity the several situations which they had described as emotion related in their earlier interviews (Lutz 1985).

Chapter Three

1. It is somewhat misleading to speak of a 2,000-year-long discourse on emotion when in fact that category bears only a family resemblance to the variety of related Greek, Latin, and other concepts which have occupied Western thinkers. Each historical period has also seen the use of a set of related terms to talk about the domain—such as the contemporary set of "feeling," "emotion," "affect," and (somewhat archaic) "passion"—each of which was used in varying and ambiguous ways in virtually all periods (Gardiner, Metcalf, and Beebe-Center 1970).

2. There are other subtle differences in historical and cultural source and connotation among "emotion," "affect," "feeling," and "passion." "Feeling," e.g., tends to be used to talk about internal body sensations more exclusively than do the other terms. "Passion" may be used synonymously with "emotion" but tends more often to refer specifically to love or sexual desire, or to enthusiasm, while "affect" is now rarely heard outside academic discourse.

3. See, e.g., the portrayal of persons in the popular theories of Goffman (1959).

4. The point is borrowed from Averill (1985), who uses the film to make a similar point about the popular view of emotionlessness as dehumanizing.

5. In this regard, there may be a subtle difference in everyday talk between the uses to which the term "emotional" and more specific emotion terms are put. When, e.g., someone is said to be angry, the sensibleness of that feeling is, to some degree, taken for granted. In other words, while anger may be warranted in some cases, emotionality (the personality trait) and emotion behavior (or generic emotion) are not.

6. The roots of the links between emotion and chaos, and the negative evaluation of both, Hillman also notes, are quite ancient ones in Western thought. The Greeks believed that "order, goodness, reason and the upper regions of the body belonged together" (1960:209) and that stability and the absence of emotion were desirable states; "the Church Fathers perfected the model by identifying it with God, Whose perfection would not allow the attributes of disorder, change, corporeality, evil and the irrational" (209).

7. This frequent critique of conceptualizations of emotion is itself a reflection of the intense Western concern with personal (rather than social) responsibility for action, as well as with mental disorder (see White and Marsella 1982).

8. As Toulmin (1979) and others have pointed out, there are two traditions of thought in the West about the nature of cognition; one identifies it as a brain, or physical, function, and the other locates it in the "mind," which is defined as a nonphysical entity.

9. The philosopher Langer's view of emotion strikes us as original precisely because she plays against the view of emotion just described. She

describes human evolution as being marked, not by the development of a cognitively defined rationality, but by "a vast and special evolution of *feeling* in the hominid stock" (1967:xvi; noted also in Levy 1984).

10. This perspective on the relationship between the emotional-qua-the-physical and the mental has a clear parallel with the culturally common view of the relationship between disease and mental processes. The idea that sickness is rooted squarely in the body, and is influenced by the mental only secondarily and less genuinely, is evident in the suspicion Americans hold of those who claim to be sick when no physical cause can be found. The distinction between disease (as underlying physical process) and illness (as the socially elaborated response to and cognitive experience of disease), which is common in the medical anthropological literature, draws on the same belief in "a stable and universal core of biophysical realities" (Comaroff 1983).

11. Sentiment is defined in the dictionary as "an attitude, thought, or judgment prompted by feeling; refined feeling, delicate sensibility, emotional idealism, a romantic or nostalgic feeling verging on sentimentality." Although it is not a term used in everyday talk, these anthropological uses are intended to draw on the notion that it is only thought (including "thought . . . prompted by feeling") that bears the impress of culture, while pure, preconscious emotion does not.

12. In Beck's view, certain types of premises, representations, or silent assumptions held by individuals intervene between an event and depressive feelings and create the possibility for the emotion. Here, cognition is the "creative subject" and affect the "resource," in Strathern's terms. Hochschild, in examining the social organization of emotional expression among airline stewardesses, critiques the process whereby the women's natural feelings are warped by the social pressures exerted by their bosses. Again, natural emotion is molded by the active pressure exerted by social expectations.

13. I am grateful to Jane Collins for this insight.

14. Freeman also talks about emotions in the positive sense which nature can have in his mention of the love which Samoans feel for each other, but this is certainly a minor theme.

15. See Sabini and Silver (1982) for a wonderful exposition of the various ways (they find eight) in which the term "subjective" is commonly used in everyday discourse. If, as Sabini and Silver point out, "notions of subjectivity are individually harmless, but dangerous in a mob" (1982:183), it is important to distinguish these distinct senses for our purposes.

16. American beliefs about the appropriateness of particular emotions to particular situations obviously also enter into the assessments of these public figures. Tears (although not wailing) are expected at funerals but not in political contexts. But a man who did not cry at a funeral, or a woman who cried because her husband was insulted in a political campaign, would be unremarkable, because culturally proper in their emotional behavior.

17. This same dichotomy of the instrumental and the expressive is used not in reference to gender explicitly but to the stance taken to fieldwork

by Schwartz (1986). He suggests that a Western bias toward an instrumental view of personhood has meant that anthropologists may privilege the need to control others over the "experience of spending time together" with informants. He also suggests that one anthropologist, in a published article, "risks losing contact with her feelings about how she was changed by [her own fieldwork] encounter" (Schwartz 1986:176). Schwartz, then, implicitly suggests that the instrumental approach to fieldwork be replaced by its (at least partial) antithesis, the introspective and expressive.

18. Rousseau himself, however, showed a remarkable inability to revise his orthodox understanding of women (as necessarily subordinate and inferior to men) in order to bring it into keeping with his radical reconceptualization of the relations between nature and society (Okin 1979).

19. Gilligan's work has been critiqued by some feminists for a variety of reasons. First, she is seen as replicating the traditional view of woman as "the angel in the house," or the more morally elevated gender. Second, her emphasis on gender differences (rather than similarities) is seen as regressive or as supportive of patriarchy. These critiques distort Gilligan's thesis, it seems to me; she can be read as arguing that the morality of women is currently *undervalued* culturally and as calling for its reintegration into a pangender morality, not for its use as a universal standard. On the second point, she emphasizes that the gender differences are relatively subtle group patterns rather than absolute or individual ones. Gilligan, I, and other feminists, however, enter into rather than transcend (which is impossible) the cultural discourse on gender and emotion even as we emphasize the socially constructed nature of women's "character" and critique the life conditions which patriarchy produces. The argument must also be made, however, that these gender ideologies have an important effect on the experience of self rather than simply being externally imposed and individually opposed notions.

Chapter Four

1. Both of the last two points are relevant to interpreting the meaning of ethnopsychological ideas expressed in ethnographic interviews. Andrew Strathern points out, e.g., that ethnopsychological statements about gender differences made in his interviews with Melpa speakers in New Guinea vary from those made in more public situations where certain rhetorical purposes may be at the forefront (1981:287–89).

2. When I use the terms "person" and "self," my only intent is to distinguish two contrast sets—in the case of "person," between significant social actors (see n. 3) and nonsignificant ones (or nonpersons) and, in the case of "self," among particular perspectives that can be taken by persons. These appear to be categories and definitions which coincide reasonably well with Ifaluk distinctions. I do not intend to distinguish between "cultural" and "psychological" levels of analysis. The term "individual," with its connotations of the natural or precultural (Rorty 1976:315), seems unnecessary

both from a theoretical perspective and from the perspective of Ifaluk ethnopsychological ideas. Where "individual" is used in this chapter, it is synonymous with "particular person."

3. I am restricting the term "actor" here to those figures in the social environment whom the Ifaluk see as significant (i.e., as both salient and sufficiently complex) intentional agents. Animals are therefore excluded. An important exception is the porpoise, whose superanimal abilities have placed it in the category of "spirits."

4. "Autonomy" and "assertion of self" are my own terms.

5. Not all person descriptions are, of course, individualized. Ethnic characterizations do occur, although these are almost invariably descriptions of distant peoples, such as Yapese, Americans, Japanese, and New Guineans. The few statements I have heard that stereotypically grouped island residents nearly all referred to one particular village. People of that village have traditionally been considered of low rank and interactions between them and members of other villages may have been less frequent until quite recently. Thus, in both of these cases, group representations occur when the other is more distant and unknown.

6. The root of this word—*feral*—refers to the center vein of a tree, through which sap rises. A synonym for *niferash,* in less common use, is *nifitigosh,* which is literally "inside our flesh."

7. The term that is translated here as "think" is *mangimeng.* Although the dictionary (Sohn and Tawerilmang 1976) gives its meaning as "to think, remember, consider, ponder, expect," the term is not used in the same contexts as *nunuwan. Mangimeng* connotes somewhat aimless, confused, or ignorant thinking; as one woman told me, "socially intelligent [*repiy*] people don't *mangimeng* a lot."

8. The term *tip*—takes a direct possessive suffix and will be used in its appropriate forms in the text including *tipei* (first-person singular), *tipum* (second-person singular), and *tipash* (first-person plural, inclusive).

9. D'Andrade, in a comparison of Ifaluk and American ethnopsychologies, mistakenly, I believe, reads the Ifaluk as making distinctions as we do between thoughts and feelings. He states that in both the Ifaluk and the Western models, "thoughts, feelings, and desires are distinguished. Feelings are considered a natural response to experience, not under self-control, and also to have the power to move the person toward action" (1987:44). It is of course possible for an Ifaluk individual to learn all that we mean by the distinction between thought and emotion and then to be able to "recognize" distinct experiences, just as it is for an American, such as myself, to reinterpret my own psychosocial experience, after an encounter with Ifaluk ethnopsychology and social practice, as validating the "fact" that the relevant distinction is between emotional thoughts that are idiosyncratic and emotional thoughts that are socially standard (*tip-* and *nunuwan*). This is taken for granted, however; the point here is instead taken to be the description of local ideological practice.

10. Both children and the mentally ill are labeled *bush,* or "incompetent." The incompetent have, according to some informants, "different insides." Depending on both the informant and the incompetent individual in question, it is sometimes said that it is possible to be "socially intelligent inside" but unable to express that understanding in language.

11. There is a strong resemblance between this view of the role of expression and the theory behind the "disentangling" sessions described by White (1985) for the A'ara. In both cases, the goals of verbal expression are seen as psychologically and socially therapeutic. Similarly, the Marquesans (Kirkpatrick 1983) see some mental events which do not lead to action as intrinsically disrupting or disorganizing for the person. Note both the similarity of evaluative terms and the difference in metaphor in the way an American informant answered a question about how a better rather than a worse course of action was selected: "My bad half was held in by my good half" (D'Andrade 1987:136). Control rather than sorting and discarding is emphasized, perhaps paralleling differences in social organization in the two societies (cf. M. Rosaldo 1983)—the one more hierarchical and with more elaborate institutions of social control, and the other less.

12. The English word "lovesick" is in common use by adolescents to describe the experience of loss or absence, particularly when an individual experiences unrequited love or separation from a boyfriend or girlfriend. It is relevant to the argument being advanced here that this, the only English emotion word that has been borrowed, includes an explicit association between emotion and illness.

13. The condition of *gos* is characterized by one or more of the following—a neck and joint rash, white spots on the skin, and a cough. *Gos* can occur, however, without the mother's mental-emotional state being seen as the root of the problem.

14. Emotions are not distinguished by the Ifaluk into those which are environmentally caused and those which are not. An elaborate set of propositions details the situational causes of *all* of the emotions.

15. The belief in contact between individuals after death appears to predate the period of contact with missionaries, according to those with whom I spoke. Burrows and Spiro also report the belief in 1948, before Catholicism reached Ifaluk, although they note that spirits in the afterworld lived, not in the households they occupied at death, but in their clan lands (1953:214).

16. Most people assume they will become good ghosts. Accidental death, then, represents a reverse in expected fortunes.

17. Ward Goodenough, remarks to the symposium, Folk Psychology in Pacific Cultures, at the meetings of the Association for Social Anthropology in Oceania, Hilton Head, South Carolina, March 1982.

18. People are also distinguished on the basis of their gender, clan membership, chiefly status, and life experiences. Although important behavioral inferences about such categories of persons can be drawn by local

observers, a consideration of these groups is beyond the scope of this chapter. See Caughey (1980) for a lucid treatment of the relationship between social and personal identities.

Chapter Five

1. See chap. 4 for a fuller description of the ethnopsychological ideas surrounding these personality trait descriptors.

2. People recognize that this is at least potentially figurative speech. As one older woman told me, "*Ye tewasiy segai.* That is talk, the manner of our insides. We can't see our insides to know if it's true."

3. Burrows and Spiro had the same reaction on observing Ifaluk funerals, which one of them notes, in an excerpt from field notes, were "one of the most depressing sights I have ever seen . . . [the funeral lament] is tragedy itself, penetrating to the very soul" (1953:308).

4. People identify some of the grave goods that they collect as those of specific older relatives, though currently in good health, they must be prepared to bury at a moment's notice. Included along with the lavalavas in these bundles are photographs of deceased relatives, as well as objects which had belonged to them, such as turtle-shell bracelets and earrings and other small purchased items (e.g., rings and combs).

5. This woman went on to describe how she was given the medicine that is prescribed for those suffering from the illness known as *rus*. See chap. 7 for a further description of this emotional illness.

6. "Manner" is the translation of *ununul,* a concept which encompasses a person's typical behavioral style, appearance, and temperament.

7. The sign of affection referred to here is one which is used in parting and with babies. It is in fact "sniffing," rather than kissing, as one person brings his or her face to the other's hand, arm, or leg and inhales the scent.

8. He described his homesickness in detail, saying that he often went to sit alone on the beach. He also did not eat much, in part because he was afraid (*metagu*) when people called him to eat with them (see chap. 7). Realizing, however, that he felt worse when he was alone, he began to spend more time with other people, which is in fact the advice commonly given to those suffering from homesickness.

9. The taboos that obtain in the brother-sister relationship make it difficult for cross-siblings to live in the same house once they reach puberty. At that time, boys often go to sleep in the canoe houses or in some other outbuilding.

10. In his cross-cultural study of child treatment, Rohner (1975) classifies the Ifaluk as "child rejecting." This classification is based primarily on the fact that the Ifaluk give their children to others in adoption but clearly ignores not only the cultural meaning of adoption for the Ifaluk but also the strong positive attitude toward children that Burrows and Spiro (1953) also report.

11. This woman also said she was *song* (justifiably angry) at the brother because he had spoken so harshly and because he had shamed Ilemochang. Declarations of *fago* are often linked with those of *song* when the *fago* is a statement which is intended to identify the needy other as a victim of someone else's wrongdoing; justifiable anger is directed at and defines the victimizer, just as *fago* is directed at and defines the victim.

12. This unusual manner of communicating *fago* was seen as somewhat laughable by others, according to Ilefagomar.

13. See chap. 4 for a discussion of the meaning of *nunuwan*.

14. Married couples will sometimes settle on the land of the husband's mother if it has become depopulated. In order to keep people on the land, such unusual postmarital residence is considered appropriate. Such was not the case in the household in which Yasechaul lived. Yasechaul and his wife, however, did occasionally spend time on her mother's land on Woleai atoll; such travel between the husband's and wife's natal (or adoptive) households is common in interisland marriages.

15. See Myers (1982) for an elegantly presented example of the relation between nurturance and power among the Australian Pintupi.

16. Several people distinguished love by three or four types, including love for family, love for neighbors (identified with religious injunctions to love others), romantic or physical love, and love for God.

17. Davis and Todd (1982) have found that a range of Americans of diverse ages and classes define love in a similar way.

18. In defining love, several people I spoke with made this explicit: "Love is something where you want to do for that individual whatever possible thing you can to make them comfortable and happy."

19. Pity is a concept that also describes the perception of another's misfortune. What pity critically lacks, however, is the emphasis found in both *fago* and compassion on the desire to help the other out of that misfortune. Pity also can be used, as *fago* cannot, to express disdain or disgust for the other.

20. Ifaluk is certainly not unique in either general environmental and social conditions or in its construction of an emotion concept like *fago*. The meaning of the concept of *fago* shows important similarities with related emotion words in other Pacific languages—with the Samoan *alofa* (Gerber 1975), the Hawaiian *aloha,* the Marquesan *ka'oha* (Kirkpatrick 1983), the Maori *aroha* (Smith 1981), and the Tahitian *arofa* (Levy 1973).

21. The island's experience with epidemic disease may have had a similar effect.

22. A high rate of sterility in many Pacific island populations (including Ifaluk) has been hypothesized as being one force behind the popularity of adoption in the region (Goodenough 1970). The prevalence of barrenness, as well as the more general problem of population fluctuations, may have also increased the concern with the nurturance of children who are born. The notion of *fago* is heavily weighted with this focus on feeding and caring for children, including others' offspring.

23. Rubinstein (1979) elegantly discusses the parallel problem of chiefly leaders on Fais and their resultant ambivalence toward their office.

24. On the other hand, a donor parent can be portrayed as somewhat heroic if he or she demonstrates *fago* for a childless or recently bereaved person by giving away a child (either a biological child or one adopted from elsewhere).

Chapter Six

1. The emotion concept of *nguch* (sick and tired/bored/annoyed) may carry an implicit but mild criticism of someone else's behavior, but it does not have the explicit moral weight of *song* (justifiable anger).

2. This name, as well as those used in all references to villages in relating specific events, is a pseudonym.

3. This turn of phrase, as we have seen, is one used to describe the responsibility of all people toward those who are more "needy" than themselves, or, in other words, their subordinates.

4. I may have heard this story more than the average islander. Although I overheard the story at least as often as it was told to me, it could clearly serve as a cautionary tale with special value for a non-native woman.

5. As we have already seen in chap. 5, the emotion of *fago* (compassion/love/sadness) is culturally represented as an equally important motivation for sharing with others.

6. The consumption of sea turtle is surrounded by strict codes of ownership; all turtles caught belong to the chief of Kovalu clan, who may then share them with others. Driftwood and other lumber and certain species of fish are also strictly regulated. Pig, on the other hand, is a more recently introduced item, which is not yet as highly regulated.

7. This was atypical, as the great majority of births occur on Ifaluk. The husband's extensive off-island educational experience, however, led him to see a hospital birth as preferable. Besides its hospital birth, his infant would also be breast-fed on a schedule and fed jars of Gerber baby food that the husband purchased on Yap.

8. I am grateful to Donald Rubinstein for informing me on this point based on his experience in all-male drinking circles on the neighboring island of Fais.

9. While justifiable anger is seen as the basic marker of bad behavior for the child, it is also necessary to follow many assertions of *song* with a later lecture (*folog*). This highly stylized preaching, usually conducted in the evening, involves the polite but prolonged repetition by the parent of local principles of morality and elicitation of the child's acknowledgment of them.

10. See Lutz (1987) for further explication of the reasoning involved in this and other cases of emotional understanding.

11. This threat has not recently been carried out, to my knowledge. To threaten to burn a relative's house or some of his or her belongings is also an expression of extreme grief over that person's death.

12. This pattern of continuous coresidence of the women of a lineage is, of course, a general trend rather than an invariant rule. The out-adoption of young girls to other households often separates some sisters from the rest, who remain in their natal households.

13. As one woman told me, "If a man comes to calm down a woman, she will be afraid and her *song* will leave her."

14. Variation in ethnotheories of anger in diverse sectors of American society has also yet to be described, although Miller (1986) has investigated the assumptions about anger and its socialization that prevail in three underclass Baltimore families, and they are quite different from those described here. What I am here saying about "American" notions of anger is meant to describe only one contemporary model common in the middle class. A recent history of anger in America (Stearns and Stearns 1986) illustrates variation over the past several hundred years as well. The historical trend identified is one of increasing concern with the control or the elimination of anger, first in the family and then at work. As Foucault (1980) has noted of the history of sexuality, increasing efforts at social control over human subjectivity and behavior may not uncommonly be associated with elaborate public discourse rather than silence on the subject (as in this case, anger). It is therefore not in necessary contradiction to the more general thesis that anger has become increasingly subject to social manipulation or construction when Tavris notes a recent shift from a Puritan model of restraint of anger to an emphasis on the necessity for expression of anger. The shift has left both individual uncertainty and social variability over how and whether to get angry: "We are told in one breath not to rock the boat, and in the next that the squeaky wheel gets the grease" (1982:27).

15. In a questionnaire study of the antecedents of anger among large samples of Europeans, Scherer, Walbott, and Summerfield (1986) characterize about 20% of the responses as related to "injustice," 10% to "inconvenience," and 20% to "interactions with strangers," whereas 38% occur in the context of relationships with others. This too indicates that at least the psychological investigators (and perhaps also their subjects) see justifiability or value as a relatively secondary or muted aspect of anger. Lakoff and Kövecses (1987) also note that righteous indignation is a nonprototypic or peripheral sense of anger, at least in American English.

16. The activist nature of our individualism—the assumption, as Tavris notes, "that nature and other people are to be conquered, indeed must be conquered, and that individual striving is essential to survival" (1982:65)— is a necessary component of this cultural logic. Pressing against limitations creates frustration, by definition, and a sense of individual entitlement translates that frustration into righteous indignation. "When we think we deserve it all," Tavris says, "reaping only a portion can enrage" (1982:65). The gender and class differences in the depth or even existence of the sense of entitlement is, however, crucial for understanding not only individual emotional life but also the role of anger in domination in the United States.

17. Averill (1979:45) notes that a number of laboratory and field studies in the United States have found that anger is less likely to be directed toward higher status individuals than it is toward subordinates or peers. This, as was noted, is also true of *song* on Ifaluk.

18. The moral and the ideological need not be treated as synonymous analytic concepts, even as we note that they are clearly two ways of talking about the same kinds of social practices. Links among the political, the moral, and the emotional have been productively forged in several recent anthropological treatments of diverse groups (Abu-Lughod 1986; Bailey 1983; Maher 1984; Myers 1979; Rosaldo 1980). Social convention and power play crucial roles in structuring both the kinds of moral "decisions" people make (i.e., decisions about what is good) and the experience of self, such that moral moves are seen either as the creations of autonomous individuals, the submission of free individuals to a preexisting collective standard, or the multifaceted and shifting and nontranscendent outcome of the demands of a situation or relationship (see chap. 3; Shore 1982). As analytic tools, however, I use "moral" to refer to discourse phrased in terms of value and "ideological" to refer to discourse which, however phrased locally, articulates with power relations to which I wish to draw attention. Agents who oppose prevailing notions of how one ought to behave can be construed, then, as operating in either the domain of morality or that of ideology but more usually will be conceptualized as simultaneously engaged in oppositional practice (Woolard 1985) which is about both good and power.

Chapter Seven

1. The distinction between more and less natural emotions also derives from, or is at least consistent with, that between basic and derived or blended emotions made by many analysts who take an evolutionary and universalist approach (e.g., Ekman 1977; Izard 1977). Basic emotions are generally seen as more important adaptationally, more physiologically organized, and less culturally malleable than derived emotions (lists of which often include such things as guilt, love, or pride).

2. This is a paraphrase of a point made by Averill (1979:11) on the necessity of distinguishing human anger from animal aggression.

3. Several other terms are clustered by the Ifaluk with these last two in formal testing and like them are used to talk about the perception of danger (Lutz 1982). These include *ma* (shame/embarrassment), *lugumet* (discomfort/guilt), *laloileng* (insecurity/worry), and *bobo* (disappointment).

4. This gaze is critical in a way similar to but less dramatic than what LeVine has described in the Gusii (1982b).

5. This generalization may be only strictly true within the confines of one's own race and class. Among white, middle-class Americans, black and lower-class people are often defined as dangerous.

6. The legend is recounted in a shortened, paraphrased translation.

7. Not all dreams are caused by spirits or have spirit themes. Also, not all spirit-induced dreams or omens are negative; in some cases, the message of the dream is one of impending good fortune.

8. There are problems here which may be due to historical change in the period between our respective fieldwork stays. In 1977–78, the hatred for the spirits which Spiro had found central was not apparent, at least in explicit conversation. While the Ifaluk continued to attack the spirits symbolically through such things as spirit medicine, they much more often simply feared and fled the spirits they encountered. Similarly, fear rather than hostility is the predominant meaning people attach to other personifications of danger, such as Koreans or drunks.

9. Writing in the immediate postwar period, Spiro may have had more confidence than many ethnographers in the postcolonial, post-Vietnam era do that Western paradigms, such as the psychodynamic, can substitute for or clearly overarch other local ones.

10. The drunk is further feared for his propensity to say whatever he is thinking, including confronting others with his anger. They are also feared because they make nighttime visits to married women, as well as act boastfully and insult other's abilities.

11. There was apparently some interpersonal violence in the past. The fights sometimes appear to have occurred when two men came to visit the same woman at night. Gasugulibung, a man in his late twenties, told me that he had never observed such physical fights but heard that they had happened in "Japanese times" (between the wars) and "once in a while in American times." These conflicts were said to occur between men of different villages, particularly as a result of its being more difficult for the men of Mai village to enter the more highly ranked Burag village. Sorcery was also said to have been practiced in the past (see Lessa 1961).

12. Although rape appears to be unknown on Ifaluk, men have been known to try to steal sex from sleeping women, retreating when they are detected and chased away.

13. People described their strategies for dealing with *garusrus* people to me by saying that they try to prevent the easily panicked person from encountering the things that frighten her or him. This is done by warning drunk relatives to avoid the house of a *garusrus* person, by not telling him shocking news, or by lying when asked if someone is fighting.

14. Many people do recognize the more general dangers of dependency, as we noted in chap. 2. As one man said, commenting in English on his lack of enthusiasm for American wages and canned food, "Our taro gardens are our bank."

15. A study of the antecedents of fear among Europeans, as measured by questionnaire, showed striking differences with the Ifaluk pattern that reflect these ecological differences (Scherer, Walbott, and Summerfield 1986). Sickness and death figure in under 10% of the antecedents, and supernatural events in under 5%; this in contrast to the Ifaluk objective and subjective

242

confrontation with illness and their very frequent sense of the danger of spirits. "Relationships" figure in 5% of the hundreds of European cases, and interactions with strangers about 15%. Traffic situations account for 20% of the cases, and fears of failure 12%, reflecting the real dangers the residents of industrialized countries are forced to confront.

Chapter Eight

1. After writing this final chapter, I became aware of Obeyesekere's Morgan Lectures (1985), in which he speaks in a very illuminating way of the "three intersubjectivities" that concern anthropologists dealing with other societies. They include first, the intersubjectivity internal to a cultural group; second, the intersubjectivity of the individual anthropologist and his or her informants; and third, the intersubjectivity of the anthropologist and the audiences (and especially the professional ones) for whom he or she writes. The three constructions I outline here are each at least partially the result of the interactions that constitute the basis for those intersubjectivities. Obeyesekere's treatment of the third intersubjectivity emphasizes the idea that anthropologists compose a moral and critical community. While the last perhaps underemphasizes the role of ideology and power in constructing anthropological categories, it can be a useful addition to the view I express here, particularly in suggesting distinctions between the role of ideology in the anthropology of emotions as opposed to the psychology of emotions.

2. Rosaldo notes here that she draws on Geertz's (1973) earlier and similar observation.

3. The first sense in which the experience of emotion may be said to be culturally constructed can be further subdivided on this basis. For heuristic purposes, we may speak of those moments in which practical activity and its demands organize the experience of emotion and those in which reflection on activity is at the forefront. There then may be some difference or even contradiction between the structure of the Ifaluk emotional meaning system as it is evident in everyday, relatively unreflective interaction and that system as it is reshaped in occasional indigenous reflection on the nature of emotional experience.

4. Several sociologists and social psychologists have begun to model emotions along these lines. Averill (1980), for example, characterizes emotions as "transitory social roles" which the individual enacts under the guidance of social expectation about proper performance and the meaning of that performance. Although Hochschild (1979, 1983) defines emotions as primarily private signals that function "as messenger[s] from the self" (1983:x), she explores the ways in which economic and social systems "engineer" or manipulate the individual's emotional experience and expressions. Kemper (1978) examines the discrete emotions as the outcomes of an individual's recognition of power and status differences among people. These three theorists do differ, however, in the extent to which they consider universal

physiological responses to be central to the production and experiential tone of emotion. They have in common a focus on the way emotion is used by an individual to achieve social ends, that is, on the role emotion plays in creating individuals who can properly interact with others in a social world. A number of primarily asocial analyses of emotion (e.g., Plutchik 1962; Izard 1977) have nonetheless laid the groundwork for this approach through their concern with the role of the distinct emotions in motivating and organizing behavior.

5. See Averill (1982) for a useful discussion of the interpersonal transactions involved in emotion.

6. The frequent discontinuity between the individual and the group (as in conflict or mental illness) is also marked by emotion, but this emotion is not precultural as much as it is anticultural (e.g., see Fajans 1985).

7. Rosaldo also notes that such experience is not sufficient for understanding and that his anger and an Ilongot man's anger are *not* the same in other ways.

8. In investigating some American lay notions about mind, D'Andrade (1987:119) finds that emotions are treated by his informants as relatively amorphous entities. This is evident in, among other things, the fact that they are treated as mass nouns rather than count nouns (e.g., we speak of "some anger" rather than "two angers").

9. Others have pointed out that there are also implicit and ideological issues involved in the push toward finding cross-cultural variation. Many of them have to do with the stake anthropology as a paying profession has in bringing back exotic others from the field in order to legitimate its claim to a domain of intellectual control distinct from that of sociology or of psychology.

10. Some elegant and useful analyses of anthropological writing more generally as a product of Western cultural and social systems have been made (e.g., Crapanzano 1977; Dumont 1978; Fabian 1983; Howard 1978; Clifford and Marcus 1986; Wagner 1981) and provide models for what is said here, although only some of them are explicitly concerned with power and its effects on this writing.

11. The relationship between emotion and value or morality may also be reconceptualized more easily when a cultural view of emotions is taken. Solomon, who eloquently presents a philosophical argument for the view that emotions are normative judgments, describes the dilemma this view presents for traditional perspectives on emotion and morality. The view of emotion as normative judgment stands "against those romantics and contemporary bourgeois therapists who would argue that emotions simply *are* and must be accepted without judgment" (1980:258). The romantic shares an implicit and culturally constructed theme with the traditional rationalist, who, in contrast, judges emotion harshly. Both perspectives accept the idea that emotions are natural events whose forms are invariant; both see the central question surrounding emotions as whether or not their control by

the cognitive, executive self is necessary or desirable. When this view is identified as cultural, it becomes possible to imagine another possibility, in which emotion is defined as a form of value-informed choice which is culturally constructed in its terms and often culturally limited in its possibilities. Solomon adds the important point that emotional judgments require our retrospective reflection and assessments to be fully moral ones, that is, judgments about our judgments are required.

References

Abu-Lughod, Lila. 1985. "Honor and the sentiments of loss in a Bedouin society." *American Ethnologist* 12:245–61.

————.1986. *Veiled Sentiments: Honor and Poetry in a Bedouin Society.* Berkeley: University of California Press.

Alkire, William. 1965. *Lamotrek Atoll and Inter-island Socioeconomic Ties.* Urbana: University of Illinois Press.

————.1978. *Coral Islanders.* Arlington Heights, Ill.: AHM.

Arnold, Magda B. 1960. *Emotion and Personality.* New York: Columbia University Press.

Averill, James R. 1974. "An analysis of psychophysiological symbolism and its influence on theories of emotion." *Journal for the Theory of Social Behavior* 4:147–90.

————. 1975. *"A semantic atlas of emotional concepts." JSAS Catalog of Selected Documents in Psychology* (MS. 421) 5:330.

————. 1979. "Anger." In *Nebraska Symposium on Motivation 1978,* vol. 26, ed. H. E. Howe and R. A. Dientsbien. Lincoln: University of Nebraska Press.

————. 1980. "A constructivist view of emotion." In *Emotion: Theory, Research, and Experience,* ed. Robert Plutchik and Henry Kellerman. New York: Academic

————. 1982. *Anger and Aggression: An Essay on Emotion.* New York: Springer-Verlag.

————. 1985. "The social construction of emotion: With special reference to love." In *The Social Construction of the Person,* ed. Kenneth J. Gergen and Keith E. Davis. New York: Springer-Verlag.

Bailey, F. G. 1983. *The Tactical Uses of Passion.* Ithaca, N.Y.: Cornell University Press.

Bates, Marston, and Donald Abbott. 1958. *Coral Island: Portrait of an Atoll.* New York: Charles Scribner's Sons.

Beck, Aaron 1967. *Depression: Clinical, Experimental and Theoretical Aspects.* New York: Harper & Row.

————. 1971. "Cognition, affect and psychopathology." *Archives of General Psychiatry* 24:495–500.

Bellah, Robert N., Norma Haan, Paul Rabinow, and William Sullivan. 1983. "Introduction." In *Social Science as Moral Inquiry,* ed. N. Haan, R. Bellah, P. Rabinow, and W. Sullivan. New York: Columbia University Press.

Benedict, Ruth. 1967. *The Chrysanthemum and the Sword: Patterns of Japanese Culture.* New York: World Publishing (Orig. published 1946.)

Berreman, Gerald D. 1962. *Behind Many Masks: Ethnography and Impression Management in a Himalayan Village.* Ithaca, N.Y.: Society for Applied Anthropology.

Black, Peter. 1978. "Crime and culture: Tobian response to attempted murder." *Midwest Review* 3 (1): 59–69.

————. 1985. "Explaining self-destruction on Tobi." In *Person, Self, and Experience: Exploring Pacific Ethnopsychologies,* ed. Geoffrey White and John Kirkpatrick. Berkeley: University of California Press.

Blum, Lawrence. 1980. "Compassion." In *Explaining Emotions,* ed. Amelie Rorty. Berkeley: University of California Press.

Boehm, Christopher. 1980. "Exposing the moral self in Montenegro: The use of natural definitions to keep ethnography descriptive." *American Ethnologist* 7:1–26.

Bourdieu, Pierre. 1977. *Outline of a Theory of Practice,* trans. Richard Nice. Cambridge: Cambridge University Press.

Briggs, Jean. 1970. *Never in Anger: Portrait of an Eskimo Family.* Cambridge: Harvard University Press.

Broverman, I. K., D. M. Broverman, and F. E. Clarkson. 1970. "Sex role stereotypes and clinical judgments of mental health." *Journal of Consulting and Clinical Psychology* 34: 1–7.

Burgin, Victor. 1986. *The End of Art Theory: Criticism and Post-Modernity.* Houndsmills: Macmillan.

Burrows, Edwin G. 1963. *Flower in My Ear: Arts and Ethos of Ifaluk Atoll.* Seattle: University of Washington Press.

Burrows, Edwin G., and Melford E. Spiro. 1953. *An Atoll Culture: Ethnography of Ifaluk in the Central Carolines.* New Haven: HRAF.

Buss, Allan R. 1979. *Psychology in Social Context.* New York: Irvington.

Campos, Joseph, Susan Hiatt, Douglas Ramsay, Charlotte Henderson, and Marilyn Svejda. 1978. "The emergence of fear on the visual cliff." In *The Development of Affect,* ed. Michael Lewis and L. Rosenblum. New York: Plenum.

Caughey, J. L. 1980. "Personal identity and social organization." *Ethos* 8:173–203.

References

Chance, Michael R. A. 1980. "An ethological assessment of emotion." In *Emotion: Theory, Research, and Experience,* ed. Robert Plutchik and Henry Kellerman. New York: Academic.

Chodorow, Nancy. 1974. "Family structure and feminine personality." In *Woman, Culture and Society,* ed. Michelle Rosaldo and Louise Lamphere. Stanford: Stanford University Press.

————. 1978. *The Reproduction of Mothering: Psychoanalysis and the Sociology of Gender.* Berkeley: University of California Press.

Clifford, James. 1986. "Introduction: Partial Truths." In *Writing Culture: The Poetics and Politics of Ethnography.* Berkeley: University of California Press.

Clifford, James and George Marcus, eds. 1986. *Writing Culture: The Poetics and Politics of Ethnography.* Berkeley: University of California Press.

Comaroff, Jean. 1978. "Medicine and culture: Some anthropological perspectives." *Social Science and Medicine* 15B:115–23.

————. 1983. "The defectiveness of symbols or the symbols of defectiveness? On the cultural analysis of medical systems." *Culture, Medicine, and Psychiatry* 7:47–64.

Corrigan, Philip, and Paul Willis. 1980. "Cultural forms and class mediations." *Media, Culture and Society* 2:297–312.

Crapanzano, Vincent. 1977. "On the writing of ethnography." *Dialectical Anthropology* 2:69–73.

————. 1980. *Tuhami: Portrait of a Moroccan.* Chicago: University of Chicago Press.

————. 1981. "Text, transference, and indexicality." *Ethos* 9:122–48.

Crawford, Robert. 1985. "A cultural account of health: Self-control, release, and the social body." In *Issues in the Political Economy of Health Care,* ed. J. McKinlay. London: Tavistock.

Csikszentmihalyi, M., and E. Rochberg-Halton. 1981. *The Meaning of Things: Domestic Symbols and the Self.* Cambridge: Cambridge University Press.

Dahl, H. 1979. "The appetite hypothesis of emotion: A new psychoanalytic model of motivation." In *Emotions in Personality and Psychopathology,* ed. C. E. Izard. New York: Plenum.

D'Andrade, Roy G. 1981. "The cultural part of cognition." *Cognitive Science* 5:179–95.

————. 1987. "A folk model of the mind." In *Cultural Models in Language and Thought,* ed. D. Holland and N. Quinn. Cambridge: Cambridge University Press.

Darley, J. M., and B. Latané. 1968. "Bystander intervention in emergencies: Diffusion of responsibility." *Journal of Personality and Social Psychology* 8:377–83.

Darwin, Charles. 1872. *The Expression of the Emotions in Man and Animals.* London: Murray.

Davis, Keith E., and M. J. Todd. 1982. "Friendship and love relationships." In *Advances in Descriptive Psychology,* vol. 2, ed. K. E. Davis and T. O. Mitchell. Greenwich, Conn.: JAI.

References

Davitz, Joel R. 1969. *The Language of Emotion*. New York: Academic.

Dentan, Robert Knox. 1978. "Notes on childhood in a non-violent context: The Semai case." In *Learning Non-Aggression: The Experience of Non-Literate Societies*, ed. Ashley Montagu. Oxford: Oxford University Press.

deRivera, Joseph. 1984. "The structure of emotional relationships." In *Review of Personality and Social Psychology*. Vol. 5, *Emotions, Relationships, and Health*, ed. Phillip Shaver. Beverly Hills: Sage.

Devereaux, George. 1967. *From Anxiety to Method in the Behavioral Sciences*. The Hague: Mouton.

Douglas, Mary, and Aaron Wildavsky. 1982. *Risk and Culture*. Berkeley: University of California Press.

Dreyfus, Hubert, and Paul Rabinow. 1983. *Michel Foucault: Beyond Structuralism and Hermeneutics*. 2d ed. Chicago: University of Chicago Press.

Dumont, Jean Paul. 1978. *The Headman and I: Ambiguity and Ambivalence in the Fieldworking Experience*. Austin: University of Texas Press.

Dwyer, Kevin. 1982. *Moroccan Dialogues: Anthropology in Question*. Baltimore: Johns Hopkins University Press.

Eibl-Eibesfeldt, Irenaus. 1980. "Strategies of social interaction." In *Emotion: Theory, Research, and Experience*, ed. R. Plutchik and H. Kellerman. New York: Academic.

Ekman, Paul. 1977. "Biological and cultural differences in facial expressions of emotion." In *The Anthropology of the Body*. ASA Monograph no. 15, ed. J. Blacking. London: Academic.

Ekman, Paul, W. Friesen, and P. Ellsworth. 1972. *Emotion in the Human Face: Guidelines for Research and an Integration of Findings*. New York: Pergamon.

Ellis, Albert. 1962. *Reason and Emotion*. New York: Lyle Stuart.

Ellis, Havelock. 1929. *Man and Woman*. Boston: Houghton-Mifflin.

Emde, Robert N. 1980. "Levels of meaning for infant emotions: A biosocial view." In *Development of Cognition, Affect, and Social Relations*. Minnesota Symposia on Child Psychology, vol. 13, ed. W. A. Collins. Hillsdale, N.J.: Erlbaum.

Errington, Frederick K. 1984. *Manners and Meaning in West Sumatra: The Social Context of Consciousness*. New Haven: Yale University Press.

Etienne, Mona, and Eleanor Leacock, eds. 1980. *Women and Colonization: Anthropological Perspectives*. New York: Praeger.

Fabian, Johannes. 1983. *Time and the Other: How Anthropology Makes Its Object*. New York: Columbia University Press.

Fajans, Jane. 1985. "The ups and downs of Baining personhood: Ethnopsychology among the Baining." In *Person, Self, and Experience: Exploring Pacific Ethnopsychologies*, ed. Geoffrey White and John Kirkpatrick. Berkeley: University of California Press.

Fausto-Sterling, Anne. 1986. *Myths of Gender: Biological Theories about Women and Men*. New York: Basic.

References

Fillmore, Charles J. 1977. "Topics in lexical semantics." In *Current Issues in Linguistic Theory*, ed. R. W. Cole. Bloomington: Indiana University Press.

Fleming, Donald. 1967. "Attitude: The history of a concept." *Perspectives in American History* 1:287–365.

Foucault, Michel. 1980. *The History of Sexuality*. Vol. 1, trans. Robert Hurley. New York: Vintage.

———. 1983. "On the genealogy of ethics: An overview of work in progress." In Dreyfus and Rabinow 1983.

Freeman, Derek. 1983. *Margaret Mead and Samoa: The Making and Unmaking of an Anthropological Myth*. Cambridge: Harvard University Press.

Gaines, Atwood D. 1982. "Cultural definitions, behavior and person in American psychiatry." In *Cultural Conceptions of Mental Health and Therapy*, ed. Geoffrey White and Anthony Marsella. Dordrecht: Reidel.

Gale, Roger W. 1979. *The Americanization of Micronesia: A Study of the Consolidation of U.S. Rule in the Pacific*. Washington, D.C.: University Press of America.

Garai, J. 1970. "Sex differences in mental health." *Genetic Psychology Monographs* 81:123–42.

Gardiner, H. M., Ruth Clark Metcalf, and John G. Beebe-Center. (1937) 1970. *Feeling and Emotion: A History of Theories*. Westport, Conn.: Greenwood.

Geertz, Clifford. 1973. "Person, time and conduct in Bali." In *The Interpretation of Culture*. New York: Basic.

———. 1976. " 'From the native's point of view' : On the nature of anthropological understanding." In *Meaning in Anthropology*, ed. Keith Basso and Henry A. Selby. Albuquerque: University of New Mexico Press.

———. 1984. "Anti-anti-relativism." *American Anthropologist* 86:263–78.

Geertz, Hildred. 1959. "The vocabulary of emotion: A study of Javanese socialization processes." *Psychiatry* 22:225–36.

Gerber, Eleanor. 1975. *The Cultural Patterning of Emotions in Samoa*. Ph.D. diss., University of California, San Diego.

Gergen, Kenneth J. 1973. "Social psychology as history." *Journal of Personality and Social Psychology* 36:309–20.

———. 1985. "The social constructionist movement in modern psychology." *American Psychologist* 40:266–75.

Geuss, Raymond. 1981. *The Idea of a Critical Theory: Habermas and the Frankfurt School*. Cambridge: Cambridge University Press.

Gilligan, Carol. 1982. *In a Different Voice*. Cambridge: Harvard University Press.

Goffman, Erving. 1959. *Presentation of Self in Everyday Life*. Garden City, N.Y.: Doubleday.

Golde, Peggy. 1970. *Women in the Field: Anthropological Experiences*. Chicago: Aldine.

Goldschmidt, Walter. 1975. "Absent eyes and idle hands: Socialization for low affect among the Sebei." *Ethos* 3:157–63.

Good, Byron J., and Mary-Jo Delvecchio Good. 1982. "Toward a meaning-centered analysis of popular illness categories: 'Fright illness' and 'heart distress' in Iran." In *Cultural Conceptions of Mental Health and Therapy*, ed. Anthony Marsella and Geoffrey White. Dordrecht: Reidel.

Goodenough, Ruth Gallagher. 1970. "Adoption on Romonum, Truk." In *Adoption in Eastern Oceania*, ed. Vern Carroll. Honolulu: University of Hawaii Press.

Goodenough, Ward H. 1965. "Personal names and modes of address in two Oceanic societies." In *Context and Meaning in Cultural Anthropology*, ed. Melford E. Sprio. New York: Free Press.

Habermas, Jürgen. 1971. *Knowledge and Human Interests*, trans. Jeremy Shapiro. Boston: Beacon Press.

Hallowell, A. Irving. 1955. "The self and its behavioral environment." In *Culture and Experience*. Philadelphia: University of Pennsylvania Press.

————. 1960. "Ojibwa ontology, behavior, and world view." In *Culture in History*, ed. Stanley Diamond. New York: Columbia University Press.

Heelas, Paul, and Andrew Lock, eds. 1981. *Indigenous Psychologies: The Anthropology of the Self*. New York: Academic.

Heller, Agnes. 1979. *A Theory of Feelings*. Assen: Van Gorcum.

Hezel, Francis X., S. J. 1979. *Foreign Ships in Micronesia: A Compendium of Ship Contacts with the Caroline and Marshall Islands 1521–1885*. Saipan: Trust Territory Historic Preservation Office.

————. 1983. *The First Taint of Civilization: A History of the Caroline and Marshall Islands in Pre-Colonial Days*. Honolulu: University of Hawaii Press.

Hillman, James. 1960. *Emotion: A Comprehensive Phenomenology of Theories and Their Meanings for Therapy*. Evanston, Ill.: Northwestern University Press.

Hochschild, Arlie R. 1975. "The sociology of feeling and emotion: Selected possibilities." In *Another Voice*, ed. Marcia Millman and Rosabeth Kanter. New York: Anchor.

————. 1979. "Emotion work, feeling rules, and social structure." *American Journal of Sociology* 85:551–75.

————. 1983. *The Managed Heart: Commercialization of Human Feeling*. Berkeley: University of California Press.

Holland, Dorothy, and Naomi Quinn. 1987. *Cultural Models in Language and Thought*. Cambridge: Cambridge University Press.

Howard, Alan. 1978. "An arsenal of words: Social science and its victims." *Comparative Studies in Society and History* 20:469–82.

Howell, Signe. 1981. "Rules not words." In Heelas and Lock.

Howells, William. 1973. *The Pacific Islanders*. New York: Scribner's.

Hutchins, Edwin. 1980. *Culture and Inference*. Cambridge: Harvard University Press.

References

Izard, Carroll E. 1977. *Human Emotions*. New York: Plenum.

James, William. 1967. "The emotions." In *The Emotions*, ed. C. Lange and W. James. New York: Hafner.

Jameson, Fredric. 1984. "Postmodernism, or the cultural logic of late capitalism." *New Left Review* 146:53–93.

Jordanova, L. J. 1980. "Natural facts: A historical perspective on science and sexuality." In MacCormack and Strathern.

Joseph, Alice, and Veronica Murray. 1951. *Chamorros and Carolinians of Saipan*. Cambridge, Mass.: Harvard University Press.

Kagan, Jerome. 1978. "On emotion and its development: A working paper." In *The Development of Affect*, ed. M. Lewis and L. Rosenblum. New York: Plenum.

Kemper, Theodore D. 1978. *A Social Interactional Theory of Emotions*. New York: Wiley.

Kirk, L., and M. Burton. 1977. "Meaning and context: A study of contextual shifts in meaning of Maasai personality descriptors." *American Ethnologist* 4:734–61.

Kirkpatrick, John T. 1983. *The Marquesan Notion of the Person*. Ann Arbor, Mich.: UMI.

Kleinman, Arthur. 1980. *Patients and Healers in the Context of Culture: An Exploration of the Borderland between Anthropology, Medicine, and Psychiatry*. Berkeley: University of California Press.

Kohlberg, Larry. 1976. "Moral stages and moralization: The cognitive-developmental approach." In *Moral Development and Behavior: Theory, Research, and Social Issues*, ed. T. Lichona. New York: Holt, Rinehart & Winston.

Lakoff, George. 1987. *Women, Fire, and Dangerous Things*. Chicago: University of Chicago Press.

Lakoff, George, and Mark Johnson. 1980. *Metaphors We Live By*. Chicago: University of Chicago Press.

Lakoff, George, and Zoltan Kövecses. 1987. "The cognitive model of anger inherent in American English." In Holland and Quinn 1987.

Langer, Suzanne. 1967. *Mind: An Essay on Human Feeling*. Baltimore: Johns Hopkins University Press.

Lazarus, R. S. 1977. "Cognitive and coping processes in emotion." In *Stress and Coping*, ed. A. Monat and R. Lazarus. New York: Columbia University Press.

Leacock, Eleanor, and June Nash. 1977. "Ideologies of sex: Archetypes and stereotypes." In *Annals of the New York Academy of Sciences*. Vol. 285, *Issues in Cross-Cultural Research*, ed. Leanore Loeb Adler. New York: New York Academy of Sciences.

Leff, J. 1981. *Psychiatry around the Globe: A Transcultural View*. New York: Dekker.

Lessa, William A. 1961. "Sorcery on Ifaluk." *American Anthropologist* 63:817–20.

———. 1966. *Ulithi: A Micronesian Design for Living*. New York: Holt.

References

LeVine, Robert A. 1980. "Anthropology and child development." In *Anthropological Perspectives on Child Development*, ed. Charles Super and Sara Harkness. New Directions for Child Development, no. 8. San Francisco: Jossey-Bass.
———. 1982*a*. "Gusii funerals: Meanings of life and death in an African community." *Ethos* 10:26–65.
———. 1982*b*. "The self and its development in an African society: A preliminary analysis." In *Psychosocial Theories of the Self*, ed. Benjamin Lee. New York: Plenum.
Lévi-Strauss, Claude. 1963. *Totemism*, trans. Rodney Needham. Boston: Beacon.
Levy, Robert. 1973. *Tahitians: Mind and Experience in the Society Islands*. Chicago: University of Chicago Press.
———. 1984. "Emotion, knowing, and culture." In *Culture Theory*, ed. Richard Shweder and Robert LeVine. Cambridge: Cambridge University Press.
Levy, Robert, and Michelle Z. Rosaldo, eds. 1983. Issue Devoted to Self and Emotion. *Ethos* 11.
Lewis, David. 1972. *We, the Navigators*. Honolulu: University of Hawaii Press.
Lewontin, R. C., Steven Rose, and Leon Kamin. 1984. *Not in Our Genes: Biology, Ideology, and Human Nature*. New York: Pantheon.
Linde, Charlotte. 1987. Explanatory systems in oral life stories. In *Cultural Models in Language and Thought*, ed. D. Holland and N. Quinn. Cambridge: Cambridge University Press.
Lindholm, Charles. 1982. *Generosity and Jealousy: The Swat Pukhtun of Northern Pakistan*. New York: Columbia University Press.
Lingenfelter, Sherwood. 1975. *Yap: Political Leadership and Culture Change in an Island Society*. Honolulu: University of Hawaii Press.
Lutz, Catherine. 1982. "The domain of emotion words on Ifaluk." *American Ethnologist* 9:113–28.
———. 1983. "Parental goals, ethnopsychology, and the development of emotional meaning." *Ethos* 11:246–63.
———. 1984. *Micronesia as Strategic Colony: The Impact of U.S. Policy on Micronesian Health and Society*. Cambridge: Cultural Survival Occasional Papers.
———. 1985. "Cultural patterns and individual differences in the child's emotional meaning system." In *The Socialization of Emotions*, ed. Michael Lewis and Carolyn Saarni. New York: Plenum.
———. 1987. "Goals, events and understanding in Ifaluk emotion theory." In *Cultural Models in Language and Thought*, ed. Dorothy Holland and Naomi Quinn. Cambridge: Cambridge University Press.
Lutz, Catherine, and Robert A. LeVine. 1983. "Culture and intelligence in infancy: An ethnopsychological view." In *Origins of Intelligence*, 2d ed., ed. Michael Lewis. New York: Plenum.

References

MacCormack, Carol, and Marilyn Strathern, eds. 1980. *Nature, Culture, and Gender.* Cambridge: Cambridge University Press.

Maher, Virginia. 1984. "Possession and dispossession: Maternity and mortality in Morocco." In *Interest and Emotion,* ed. H. Medick and D. W. Sabean. Cambridge: Cambridge University Press.

McHenry, Donald F. 1975. *Micronesia: Trust Betrayed.* New York: Carnegie Endowment for International Peace.

Mandler, George. 1975. *Mind and Emotion.* New York: Wiley.

Marsella, Anthony, George DeVos, and Francis Hsu, eds. 1985. *Culture and Self.* London: Tavistock.

Marshall, Mac. 1976. "The effects of Typhoon Pamela on the Mortlock Islands of Truk District." *Micronesian Reporter* 24 (3): 34–39.

———. 1979. "Natural and unnatural disaster in the Mortlock Islands of Micronesia." *Human Organization* 38:265–72.

———. 1981. "Sibling sets as building blocks in Greater Turkese Society." In *Siblingship in Oceania,* ed. Mac Marshall. Ann Arbor: University of Michigan Press.

Marshall, Mac, and Leslie Marshall. 1975. "Opening Pandora's bottle: Reconstructing Micronesians' early contacts with alcoholic beverages." *Journal of the Polynesian Society* 84:441–65.

Mead, George H. 1932. *The Philosophy of the Present.* Chicago: Open Court.

Miller, Peggy J. 1986. "Teasing as language socialization and verbal play in a white working-class community." In *Language Socialization across Cultures,* ed. B. Schieffelin and E. Ochs. Cambridge: Cambridge University Press.

Myers, Fred R. 1979. "Emotions and the self: A theory of personhood and political order among Pintupi Aborigines." *Ethos* 7:343–70.

———. 1982. "Ideology and experience: The cultural basis of politics in Pintupi life." In *Aboriginal Power in Australian Society,* ed. Michael Howard. Honolulu: University of Hawaii Press.

Needham, Rodney. 1981. *Circumstantial Deliveries.* Berkeley: University of California Press.

Obeyesekere, Gananath. 1985. "Depression, Buddhism, and the work of culture in Sri Lanka." In *Culture and Depression: Studies in the Anthropology and Cross-Cultural Psychiatry of Affect and Disorder,* ed. A. Kleinman and B. Good. Berkeley: University of California Press.

Okin, Susan Moller. 1979. *Women in Western Political Thought.* Princeton, N.J.: Princeton University Press.

Ollman, Bertell. 1976. *Alienation: Marx's Conception of Man in Capitalist Society.* 2d ed. Cambridge: Cambridge University Press.

Ortner, Sherry B. 1974. "Is female to male as nature is to culture?" In *Woman, Culture, and Society,* ed. Michelle Z. Rosaldo and Louise Lamphere. Stanford: Stanford University Press.

Osgood, Charles E., W. H. May, and M. S. Miron. 1975. *Cross-cultural Universals of Affective Meaning.* Urbana: University of Illinois Press.

Osherson, Samuel, and Lorna AmaraSingham. 1981. "The machine metaphor in medicine." In *Social Contexts of Health, Illness and Patient Care*, ed. E. Mishler et al. Cambridge: Cambridge University Press.

Panksepp, Jaak. 1982. "Toward a general psychobiological theory of emotions." *Behavioral and Brain Sciences* 5:407–68.

Parkin, David. 1986. "Toward an apprehension of fear." In *Sociophobics: The Anthropology of Fear*, ed. David Scruton. Boulder, Colo.: Westview.

Parsons, Talcott, and Robert F. Bales. 1955. *Family, Socialization, and Interaction Process*. Glencoe, Ill.: Free Press.

Peoples, James G. 1985. *Island in Trust: Culture Change and Dependence in a Micronesian Economy*. Boulder, Colo.: Westview.

Peterson, Glenn T. 1979. "External politics, internal economics, and Ponapean social formation." *American Ethnologist* 6:25–40.

Plutchik, Robert. 1962. *The Emotions: Facts, Theories, and a New Model*. New York: Random House.

————. 1980. *Emotion: A Psychoevolutionary Synthesis*. New York: Harper & Row.

Poole, Fitz John Porter. 1985. "Coming into social being: Cultural images of children in Bimin-Kuskusmin folk psychology." In *Person, Self, and Experience: Exploring Pacific Ethnopsychologies*, ed. Geoffrey White and John Kirkpatrick. Berkeley: University of California Press.

Quinn, Naomi. 1982. " 'Commitment' in American marriage: A cultural analysis." *American Ethnologist* 9:775–98.

————. 1987. "Love and the experiential basis of American marriage." Typescript. (in Quinn's possession).

Rabinow, Paul. 1977. *Reflections on Fieldwork in Morocco*. Berkeley: University of California Press.

————. 1983. "Humanism as nihilism: The bracketing of truth and seriousness in American cultural anthropology." In *Social Science as Moral Inquiry*, ed. Norma Haan, Robert Bellah, Paul Rabinow, and William Sullivan. New York: Columbia University Press.

Riesman, Paul, 1977. *Freedom in Fulani Social Life: An Introspective Ethnography*. Chicago: University of Chicago Press.

Robarchek, Clayton. 1979. "Learning to fear: A case study of emotional conditioning." *American Ethnologist* 6:555–67.

Roff, Sue R., and Roger Clark. 1984. *Micronesia: The Problem of Palau*. Minority Rights Group Report no. 63. New York: Minority Rights Group.

Rohner, Ronald. 1975. *They Love Me, They Love Me Not: A Worldwide Study of the Effects of Parental Acceptance and Rejection*. New Haven: HRAF.

Rorty, A. O. 1976. "A literary postscript: Characters, persons, selves, individuals." In *The Identities of Persons*, ed. A. O. Rorty. Berkeley: University of California Press.

Rosaldo, Michelle Z. 1980. *Knowledge and Passion: Ilongot Notions of Self and Social Life*. Cambridge: Cambridge University Press.

————. 1983. "The shame of headhunters and the autonomy of self." *Ethos* 11:135–51.

References

————. 1984. "Toward an anthropology of self and feeling." In *Culture Theory*, ed. Richard Shweder and Robert LeVine. New York: Cambridge University Press.

Rosaldo, Renato I. 1984. "Grief and a headhunter's rage: On the cultural force of emotions." In *Play, Text, and Story*, ed. Edward Bruner. Proceedings of the 1983 Meeting of the American Ethnological Society. Washington, D.C.

Rosch, Eleanor, and B. B. Lloyd, eds. 1978. *Cognition and Categorization*. Hillsdale, N.J.: Lawrence Erlbaum Associates.

Rubin, J., F. Provenzano, and Z. Luria. 1974. "The eye of the beholder: Parents' view of the sex of newborns." *American Journal of Orthopsychiatry* 44:512–19.

Rubinstein, Donald H. 1979. "An ethnography of Micronesian childhood: Contexts of socialization on Fais Island." Ph.D. diss., Stanford University.

————. 1983. "Epidemic suicide among Micronesian adolescents." *Social Science and Medicine* 17 (10): 657–65.

Ruddick, Sara. 1980. "Maternal thinking." *Feminist Studies* 6:70–96.

Sabini, John, and Maury Silver. 1982. *Moralities of Everyday Life*. Oxford: Oxford University Press.

Said, Edward. 1979. *Orientalism*. New York: Vintage.

Sampson, E. E. 1981. "Cognitive psychology as ideology." *American Psychologist* 36:730–43.

Sartre, Jean-Paul. 1948. *The Emotions: Outline of a Theory*, trans. Bernard Frechtman. New York: Philosophical Library.

Schieffelin, Edward L. 1976. *The Sorrow of the Lonely and the Burning of the Dancers*. New York: St. Martin's.

Scheper-Hughes, Nancy. 1985. "Culture, scarcity and maternal thinking." *Ethos* 13:291–317.

Scheper-Hughes, Nancy, and Margaret Lock. 1987. "The mindful body: A prolegomenon to future work in medical anthropology." *Medical Anthropology Quarterly* 1:1–36.

Scherer, Klaus, H. G. Walbott, and A. B. Summerfield, eds. 1986. *Experiencing Emotions: A Cross-Cultural Study*. Cambridge: Cambridge University Press.

Schudson, Michael. 1978. *Discovering the News: A Social History of American Newspapers*. New York: Basic.

Schwartz, Gary. 1986. "Moral consciousness and ethnocentrism: A comment on Gewertz." *American Anthropologist* 88:175–76.

Scruton, David L. 1986. *Sociophobics: The Anthropology of Fear*. Boulder, Colo.: Westview.

Shafer, Roy. 1984. "The pursuit of failure and the idealization of unhappiness." *American Psychologist* 39:398–405.

Shore, Bradd. 1982. *Sala'ilua: A Samoan Mystery*. New York: Columbia University Press.

Shutler, Richard. 1978. "Radiocarbon dating and oceanic prehistory." *Archaeology and Physical Anthropology in Oceania* 13, nos. 2, 3: 215–28.

Shweder, Richard, and Edmund Bourne. 1982. "Does the concept of the person vary cross-culturally?" In *Cultural Conceptions of Mental Health and Therapy,* ed. Anthony Marsella and Geoffrey White. Dordrecht: Reidel.

Silverman, Martin. 1978. "Maximize your options: A study in symbols, values, and social structure." In *Forms of Symbolic Action,* ed. R. F. Spencer. Seattle: University of Washington Press.

Smith, B. H. 1983. "Contingencies of value." *Critical Inquiry* 10:1–35.

Smith, Jean. 1981. "Self and experience in Maori culture." In Heelas and Lock.

Smith-Rosenberg, Carroll. 1975. "The female world of love and ritual: Relations between women in 19th-century America." *Signs* 1:1–29.

Sohn, H., and A. F. Tawerilmang. 1976. *Woleaian-English Dictionary.* Honolulu: University of Hawaii Press.

Solomon, Robert C. 1977. *The Passions.* New York: Anchor.

———. 1980. "Emotions and choice." In *Explaining Emotions,* ed. Amelie O. Rorty. Berkeley: University of California Press.

Sontag, Susan. 1977. *Illness as Metaphor.* New York: Farrar, Straus & Giroux.

Spiro, Melford E. 1950. "A psychotic personality in the South Seas." *Psychiatry* 13:189–204.

———. 1951. "Some Ifaluk myths and folk tales." *Journal of American Folklore* 64:289–96.

———. 1952. "Ghosts, Ifaluk, and teleological functionalism." *American Anthropologist* 54:497–503.

———. 1953. "Ghosts: An anthropological inquiry into learning and perception." *Journal of Abnormal and Social Psychology* 48:376–82.

Stearns, Carol Z., and Peter N. Stearns. 1986. *Anger: The Struggle for Emotional Control in America's History.* Chicago: University of Chicago Press.

Stenberg, Craig R., Joseph J. Campos, and Robert Emde. 1985. "The facial expression of anger in seven month old infants." In *The Socialization of Emotions,* ed. Michael Lewis and Carolyn Saarni. New York: Plenum.

Strathern, Andrew. 1981. "Noman: Representations of identity in Mount Hagen." In *The Structure of Folk Models.* ASA Monograph no. 20, ed. L. Holy and M. Stuchlik. London: Academic.

Strathern, Marilyn. 1980. "No nature, no culture: The Hagen case." In *Nature, Culture and Gender,* ed. Carol MacCormack and Marilyn Strathern. Cambridge: Cambridge University Press.

Taussig, Michael T. 1980. *The Devil and Commodity Fetishism in South America.* Chapel Hill: University of North Carolina Press.

———. 1984. "Culture of terror—space of death: Roger Casement's Putumayo Report and the explanation of torture." *Comparative Studies in Society and History* 26:467–97.

Tavris, Carol. 1982. *Anger: The Misunderstood Emotion.* New York: Simon & Schuster.

References

Therborn, Göran. 1980. *The Ideology of Power and the Power of Ideology.* London: Verso.

Tomkins, S. S. 1979. "Script theory: Differential magnification of affects." In *Nebraska Symposium on Motivation,* vol. 26, ed. H. E. Howe and R. A. Dientsbier. Lincoln: University of Nebraska Press.

————. 1980. "Affect as amplification: Some modifications in theory." In *Emotion: Theory, Research, and Experience,* ed. R. Plutchik and H. Kellerman. New York: Academic.

Toulmin, Stephen. 1979. "The inwardness of mental life." *Critical Inquiry* 6:1–16.

Tracey, J. I., D. P. Abbott, and Ted Arnow. 1961. *Natural History of Ifaluk Atoll: Physical Environment.* Bulletin 222. Honolulu: Bernice P. Bishop Museum.

Turner, Terence S. 1980. "The social skin." In *Not Work Alone,* ed. J. Cherfas and R. Lewin. Beverly Hills: Sage.

Turner, Victor. 1967. *The Forest of Symbols: Aspects of Ndembu Ritual.* Ithaca, N.Y.: Cornell University Press.

Tyler, Stephen A. 1978. *The Said and the Unsaid: Mind, Meaning, and Culture.* New York: Academic.

Wagner, Roy. 1981. *The Invention of Culture.* 2d ed. Chicago: University of Chicago Press.

Wallace, Anthony F. C. 1970. *Culture and Personality.* 2d ed. New York: Random House.

Wallace, Anthony F. C., and Margaret T. Carson. 1973. "Sharing and diversity in emotion terminology." *Ethos* 1:1–29.

Ward, R. Gerard, ed. 1967. *American Activities in the Central Pacific 1790–1870: A History, Geography, and Ethnography Pertaining to American Involvement and Americans in the Pacific, Taken from Contemporary Newspapers, Etc.* Vol. 2. Ridgewood, N.J.: Gregg.

Weidman, Hazel H. 1970. "On ambivalence and the field." In *Women in the Field,* ed. Peggy Golde. Chicago: Aldine.

White, Geoffrey. 1978. "Ambiguity and ambivalence in A'ara personality descriptors." *American Ethnologist* 5:334–60.

————. 1980. "Conceptual universals in interpersonal language." *American Anthropologist* 82:759–81.

————. 1985. "The interpersonal self in A'ara folk psychology." In White and Kirkpatrick.

White, Geoffrey, and John Kirkpatrick, eds. 1985. *Person, Self, and Experience: Exploring Pacific Ethnopsychologies.* Berkeley: University of California Press.

White, Geoffrey, and Anthony Marsella. 1982. "Introduction: Cultural conceptions in mental health research and practice." In *Cultural Conceptions of Mental Health and Therapy,* ed. Anthony Marsella and Geoffrey White. Dordrecht: Reidel.

Whiting, Beatrice B., and John W. M. Whiting. 1975. *Children of Six Cultures: A Psychocultural Analysis.* Cambridge: Harvard University Press.

References

Wilson, James. (1799) 1966. *A Missionary Voyage to the Southern Pacific Ocean, 1796–1798*. Introduction by Irmgard Moschner. Graz: Akademische Druck. (Repr. of edition pub. London, 1799.)

Wittgenstein, Ludwig. 1966. *Zettel*. Translated by G. Anscombe. London: Blackwell.

Woolard, Kathryn A. 1985. "Language variation and cultural hegemony: Towards an integration of sociolinguistic and social theory." *American Ethnologist* 12:738–48.

Zajonc, Robert B. 1980. "Feeling and thinking: Preferences need no inferences." *American Psychologist* 35:151–75.

Index